D0915615

THE DAMASCUS DOCUMENT
A CENTENNIAL OF DISCOVERY

STUDIES ON THE TEXTS
OF THE DESERT OF JUDAH

EDITED BY

F. GARCÍA MARTÍNEZ
A. S. VAN DER WOUDE

VOLUME XXXIV

THE DAMASCUS DOCUMENT
A CENTENNIAL OF DISCOVERY

Proceedings of the Third International Symposium of the Orion Center
for the Study of the Dead Sea Scrolls and Associated Literature,
4-8 February, 1998

EDITED BY

JOSEPH M. BAUMGARTEN
ESTHER G. CHAZON
AVITAL PINNICK

BRILL
LEIDEN · BOSTON · KÖLN
2000

This book is printed on acid-free paper.

Die Deutsche Bibliothek – CIP-Einheitsaufnahme

The Damascus document: a centennial of discovery : proceedings
of the third international symposium of the Orion Center for the
Study of the Dead Sea Scrolls and Associated Literature, 4 - 8
February, 1998 / ed. by Joseph M. Baumgarten ... – Leiden ; Boston ;
Köln : Brill, 1999
    (Studies on the texts of the desert of Judah ; Vol. 34)
    ISBN 90-04-11462-9

Library of Congress Cataloging-in-Publication Data

Library of Congress Cataloging-in-Publication Data is also available

ISSN   0169-9962
ISBN   90 04 11462 9

PRINTED IN THE NETHERLANDS

CONTENTS

PREFACE

This book is the third volume of symposium proceedings published by the Orion Center for the Study of the Dead Sea Scrolls and Associated Literature. The Orion Center was established in 1995 as part of the Institute of Jewish Studies at the Hebrew University of Jerusalem. Its primary aim is to achieve a better understanding of the history of the Jewish people, its language, literature, thought and religion during the Second Temple period. To this end the Center fosters scholarly discussion and research which integrate the new data from the Dead Sea Scrolls with what is already known about that formative period in the development of Judaism and early Christianity.

The Third International Symposium celebrated the centennial of the Damascus Document's discovery in the Cairo Geniza (CD) and also the final publication of the 4QD manuscripts in the *Discoveries in the Judaean Desert* series. Since its inital discovery, CD has sparked a lively debate particularly about its sectarian origins and halacha, issues with far-reaching implications not only for the development of Jewish law but also for the very nature of Second Temple period Judaism(s) and its continuity into the early medieval period.

With the publication of all the manuscripts, the time was ripe for renewed study and assessment of this important document, its multifaceted content and form, its literary history, its place in the Qumran corpus, the light it sheds on Qumran and other communities, and its contribution to other fields of Judaic studies: history, biblical interpretation, halacha, Jewish thought, Hebrew language, paleography, and codicology. The symposium provided a unique opportunity to bring together scholars working in different disciplines and in different periods, including the medieval Geniza context, and we are pleased to present edited and expanded versions of the symposium papers in this volume.

The preliminary results of the physical reconstruction of 4QD are published by Stegemann in this collection. J. Baumgarten's contribution demonstrates the extent to which the Damascus Document exhibits developments towards early rabbinic law. Specific legal topics are examined by Eshel, Regev, Schremer, Shemesh and Werman. The articles by Hempel, Metso and Schiffman focus on CD's relationship to other legal works in the Qumran corpus (the Community Rule, 4QMMT, and the Temple Scroll); moreover, they underscore the importance of source- and redaction-criticism for understanding the history of the community(ies) behind each work in each stage of its development. Historical perspectives by A. Baumgarten, Davies, Fassberg and Reif round out this volume.

We are deeply indebted to the Orion Foundation and to the Hebrew University of Jerusalem for their ongoing support of our activities and publications. We would also like to thank our colleagues in Jerusalem and throughout the world for their constant encouragement and interest in the Center's projects.

PROF. JOSEPH M. BAUMGARTEN
Dr. ESTHER G. CHAZON
Dr. AVITAL PINNICK

March 1999 – Nissan 5759

ABBREVIATIONS

AB	Anchor Bible
ASOR	American Schools of Oriental Research
BA	*Biblical Archaeologist*
BASOR	*Bulletin of the American Schools of Oriental Research*
BJS	Brown Judaic Studies
BZAW	Beihefte zur Zeitschrift für die alttestamentliche Wissenschaft
CRINT	Compendium Rerum Iudaicarum ad Novum Testamentum
CSCO	Corpus Scriptorum Christianorum Orientalium
DJD	Discoveries in the Judaean Desert
DJDJ	Discoveries in the Judaean Desert of Jordan
DSD	*Dead Sea Discoveries*
HSS	Harvard Semitic Studies
ICC	International Christian Commentary
HTR	*Harvard Theological Review*
JAOS	*Journal of the American Oriental Society*
JBL	*Journal of Biblical Literature*
JCP	Jewish and Christian Perspective Series
JJS	*Journal of Jewish Studies*
JPS	Jewish Publication Society of America
JQR	*Jewish Quarterly Review*
JQR MS	Jewish Quarterly Review Monograph Series
JSJ	*Journal for the Study of Judaism*
JSJSup	Journal for the Study of Judaism Supplement Series
JSOT/ASOR MS	Journal for the Study of the Old Testament/American Schools of Oriental Research Monograph Series
JSOTSup	Journal for the Study of the Old Testament Supplement Series
JSPSup	Journal for the Study of the Pseudepigrapha Supplement Series
JSS	*Jewish Social Studies*
JTS	Jewish Theological Seminary of America
MGWJ	*Monatsschrift für Geschichte und Wissenschaft des Judentums*
NTOA	Novum Testamentum et Orbis Antiquus
RB	*Revue Biblique*
REJ	*Revue des Études Juives*
RevQ	*Revue de Qumrân*
SJLA	Studies in Judaism in Late Antiquity
STDJ	Studies in the Texts of the Desert of Judah
SBLMS	Society of Biblical Literature Monograph Series
SBLSym	Society of Biblical Literature Symposium Series
SBT	Studies in Biblical Theology
VT	*Vetus Testamentum*
VTSup	Vetus Testamentum Supplement Series
WUNT	Wissenschaftliche Untersuchungen zum Neuen Testament
ZAW	*Zeitschrift für die alttestamentliche Wissenschaft*

THE PERCEPTION OF THE PAST IN THE
DAMASCUS DOCUMENT

ALBERT I. BAUMGARTEN

Bar-Ilan University

As Vico observed more than two centuries ago, people accept only the ideas for which their previous development has prepared their minds, and which, let us add, appear to be useful to them.

> E. J. Bickerman, *The Jews in the Greek Age* (Cambridge: Harvard University Press, 1988) 305.

I

My late teacher, Elias Bickerman, argued that ideas only moved people when they seemed useful, and that utility was determined by many aspects of life at any one time and place, in addition to the idea itself. For that reason, the same idea might seem useless or utterly foolish at one moment, while causing mass social action at another. Living in an ideological age, we tend to see ideology otherwise, as a vital cause of many results. We might therefore be tempted to grant ideology a very significant role in our explanations of the past. Bickerman, however, did not assign ideology the same weight. For Bickerman, studying the idea itself was of relatively minor significance, while studying the circumstances which made that idea either effective or irrelevant was far more important.

But what makes an idea useful or effective? Implicit in this question is an appreciation of ideology which makes it more than a reflex of socio-economic status. Ideology is effective because it makes sense of the experience of those who accept it. It does not merely reflect social life but contributes to experience at a particular time and place by giving it meaning; hence, ideology is capable of inspiring action.

Very much the same conclusion concerning the place of ideology has been proposed by another historian, albeit of another period and place, whose personal experience and commitments differed widely from those of Bickerman.[1] I refer to Christopher Hill, who writes:

---

[1] Bickerman was a refugee from Russian communism, active in expatriate circles in Europe in the years following the revolution. He helped his father found the anti-Bolshevik "Patriotic Union of Russian Jews Abroad," which worked for the

> Ideas do not advance merely by their own logic... The logical implications of Luther's doctrine could not be realized in practice in England until political circumstances—the collapse of the hierarchy and the central government—were propitious. Ideas were all important for the individuals whom they impelled into action; but the historian must attach equal importance to the circumstances which gave these ideas their chance.[2]

Hill has recently returned to this theme, comparing ideas and ideology to the steam in an old locomotive. Obviously, without the steam the locomotive could not move, but the locomotive itself, its destination and speed are far more important than mere motion, and they are not controlled by the steam. The layout of the tracks, the way switches are thrown at key intersections and the intentions of the engineer control that aspect of the results.[3] Hill thus concurs that crucial questions on which a historian should focus are: What circumstances made certain ideas either effective and meaningful or irrelevant and trivial at precise times and places?[4] How and why did a specific ideology give meaning to life at a particular moment?

A movement's view of the past, whether its own past or that of some larger group, is part of its general ideological construction, and hence subject to much the same constraints as other elements of its ideology: a view of the past must be useful and circumstances must

restoration of the Czarist monarchy. See further A. I. Baumgarten, "Elias Bickerman," *Abingdon Dictionary of Biblical Interpretation* (forthcoming). See now also M. Himmelfarb, "Elias Bickerman and Judaism and Hellenism," *The Jewish Past Revisited: Reflections on Modern Jewish Historians* (ed. D. N. Myers and D. B. Ruderman; New Haven/London: Yale University Press, 1998) 199-211.

  Hill comes from the Marxist camp and has been criticized for being a doctrinaire Marxist. See, for example, M. G. Finlayson, *Historians, Puritanism and the English Revolution: The Religious Factor in English Politics before and after the Interregnum* (Toronto: University of Toronto Press, 1983) 27-31; J. M. Hexter, "The Burden of Proof," *Times Literary Supplement* (October 24, 1975) 1250-52. For a discussion of the rationale behind the comments of Bickerman and Hill from the perspective of cultural theory, as the "principle of compatibility" between cultural bias and social relations, see M. Thompson, R. Ellis and A. Wildavsky, *Cultural Theory* (Boulder/San Francisco/Oxford: Westview, 1990) 1-5.

  [2] C. Hill, *The Intellectual Origins of the English Revolution* (Oxford: Oxford University Press, 1965) 1-3.

  [3] C. Hill, *The English Bible and the Seventeenth Century Revolution* (Harmondsworth: Penguin, 1994) 415.

  [4] One particularly apt example of how a change in climate can alter the way in which a specific idea is viewed is the response to millenarian hopes in seventeenth century Britain. When these hopes were high in the middle of the century, William Sedgwick set a date for the end, which attracted much attention. This daring caused Sedgwick much embarrassment when the end did not come, and earned him the nickname "Doomsday Sedgwick." Fifty years later, however, when John Mason of Water Stratford set a date for the end of the world, he was regarded with disdain, as a medical case. See Hill, *English Bible*, 243.

make it meaningful for it to prevail. While many modern groups tend to see themselves as obliged to act one way or another as a result of some event(s) in the past, what makes the past seem mandatory, in fact, are commitments in the present, without which the past would not have such normative force. The past is malleable and constantly being revised to suit the needs of the present; pasts which no longer fit new circumstances are regularly discarded, while new pasts are habitually invented to serve changing times.[5]

While few would give up the claim of a connection to the past[6]—the living seem to need the support of the dead—that past, in fact, is often made to order. Thus, it is paradoxical at first, but self-evident on further reflection, to recast a comment of Marx, that the revolutionary is the most avid consumer of precedents.[7] The way to integrate a group's view of the past into a comprehensive understanding of the movement is not to ask how experiences in the past shaped the movement, but to inquire into the correlation between transformations in society and the accompanying variations in views of the past, that is, to investigate what made a certain view of the past effective in a particular context.[8]

This paper is devoted to a study of the ideology of the Damascus Document, specifically of its view of the sectarian and general Jewish past, from the perspective outlined above.[9] The truth or falsity of claims made in the Damascus Document about the past are of little

---

[5] See M. Halbwachs, *On Collective Memory* (Chicago/London: University of Chicago Press, 1992), and the essays collected in *The Invention of Tradition* (ed. E. Hobsbawm and T. Ranger; Cambridge: Cambridge University Press, 1983).

[6] See E. Shils, *Tradition* (Chicago: University of Chicago Press, 1981).

[7] See H. Desroches, *The Sociology of Hope* (London/Boston: Routledge, 1979) 157.

[8] For one such attempt in modern Israeli terms see Y. Zerubavel, *Recovered Roots—Collective Memory and the Making of Israeli National Tradition* (Chicago/London: University of Chicago Press, 1995).

[9] This essay should be compared with S. Walker-Ramisch, "Graeco-Roman Voluntary Associations and the Damascus Document," *Voluntary Associations in the Graeco-Roman World* (ed. J. S. Kloppenborg and S. G. Wilson; London: Routledge, 1996) 128-45. In spite of the promise of methodological sophistication, Walker-Ramisch's results are meager, with much effort yielding little light. Her inquiry leads her to the conclusion that unlike Graeco-Roman *collegia*, whose members were integrated in the life of the *polis*, the Damascus Document emphasized separation from the "sons of the pit," the "turners of the way," and other evildoers (141). Compare further A. I. Baumgarten, "Graeco-Roman Voluntary Associations and Ancient Jewish Sects," *Jews in a Graeco-Roman World* (ed. M. Goodman; Oxford: Oxford University Press, 1998) 93-111.

For a wide ranging comparison of the different sorts of connections ancient Jewish groups claimed with the past, see M. D. Herr, "Continuum in the Chain of Torah Transmission," *Zion* 44 (5739/1979) 43-56 (Hebrew). See also A. I. Baumgarten, "The Pharisaic *Paradosis*," *HTR* 80 (1987) 63-77.

concern to me. Furthermore, I have no theory of Qumran origins
based on the Damascus Document—old or new—to present or defend. My principal interest is in the finely tuned balance between the
realities of sectarian life and the ideological constructions which
made sense of them—the reciprocal relationship between ideology
and experience—and of the role of the view of the past expressed in
the Damascus Document in that process.[10]

                                    II

In order to facilitate the analysis which is the principal objective of
this paper, some general remarks about the nature of the sectarian
way of life advocated by the Damascus Document are necessary. The
contribution of the Cave 4 fragments of the Damascus Document to
understanding this way of life is substantial. Ancient authors regularly situated comments, intended to guide the reader, at the beginning
or at the end of works, indicating what sort of work they had produced and how they wanted it to be read.[11] Ideological statements
therefore were concentrated in passages at the beginning or end of
works. Information about the beginning and end of the Damascus
Document was lacking in the Cairo Geniza manuscripts, but our
knowledge is now much more complete thanks to the Cave 4 texts.

---

[10] For the purposes of this paper I will restrict the principal focus to the
Damascus Document. This should not be taken as agreement with the atomistic
reading of rabbinic sources advocated by J. Neusner. See, in particular, the criticisms of E. P. Sanders, *Jewish Law from Jesus to the Mishnah* (London/Philadelphia:
SCM/Trinity, 1990) 309-31.
    Nevertheless, in order to highlight aspects of the Damascus Document, some
comparisons will be made with what is known of other Jewish movements of the
era, such as the Essenes and Pauline Christianity. Concerning the comparison of
the Damascus Document to the Essenes, I have argued elsewhere that Qumran
texts (including the Damascus Document) should not be given a privileged place in
understanding Greek and Latin authors on the Essenes, and vice versa.
    The analysis will be based on another conclusion which I have argued elsewhere:
the Damascus Document must have a close relationship to other sources also found
at Qumran, even if I remain uncertain concerning the exact nature of that connection. See further A. I. Baumgarten, *The Flourishing of Jewish Sects in the Maccabean Era:
An Interpretation* (JSJSup 55; Leiden: Brill, 1997) 21-22, n. 62.
    Finally, given the discovery of at least eight copies of the Damascus Document at
Qumran, and the ferocious criticism of others throughout the work, I believe the
burden of proof lies on a scholar who would argue that there never was a community that lived in accordance with the Damascus Document, or at the very least, believed that one should. I grant that the connection between a literary work and a
social grouping may be uncertain, and positing a group behind every work, hazardous, but I would consider the rejection of that conclusion, in a case such as this,
hypercritical.
[11] From this perspective, the loss of the beginning of the Temple Scroll is particularly lamentable. Compare the beginning of the Book of Jubilees.

Thus, the Cave 4 fragments confirm the voluntary nature of the movement which lived by the Damascus Document. The righteous were compared to Nazirites: 4Q266 1 1. י לבנ]י אור להנזר מדר[כי רשעה. The wicked were denounced for not having taken similar steps: 4Q266 3 iv 6 // 8:8 [ולא נזרו מעם]. The Nazirite was the chief biblical institution by which someone could voluntarily raise the level of holiness in his or her life. This was done by accepting the obligations of those higher on the scale of sanctity, by behaving in some ways as if one were a priest (never drinking wine, as priests were forbidden to drink wine while serving, for example, and avoiding contact with the dead, as priests did). The basic pattern followed by a Nazirite is well known in other religions: one raises the level of one's holiness by imitating the patterns of observance of those higher on the ladder in India as well.[12]

The evidence of the Cave 4 fragments of the Damascus Document on the voluntary nature of the group coheres well with Philo's comments that membership in the Essene order was voluntary: the Essenes were a *proairesis* based on choice, not birth (Hyp. 11.2).[13] The voluntary nature of sectarianism has also been a prominent feature of social scientific analyses of the phenomenon since Weber and Troeltsch. For those who choose to employ the social scientific category of sectarianism to understand ancient Jewish groups, the explicit utilization of the analogy of the Nazirite in the Damascus Document provides important textual support.

The voluntary acts typical of a group such as one that lived according to the Damascus Document are boundary creation. All cultures employ boundary practices to distinguish insiders from outsiders, however these may be defined in each case. These may include practices concerning food, dress, marriage, commerce and

---

[12] See L. Dumont, *Homo Hierarchicus—The Caste System and Its Implications* (Chicago/London: University of Chicago Press, 1980³) 192. For a recent discussion of the Nazirite see E. Diamond, "An Israelite Self-Offering in the Priestly Code: A New Perspective on the Nazirite," *JQR* 88 (1997) 1-18. Compare A. I. Baumgarten, "Hatta't Sacrifices," *RB* 103 (1996) 337-92.

Perhaps one could argue that the institution of the Nazirite was the established religion's alternative outlet for those forces which would lead Jews of the post-biblical era to find themselves in fringe groups, far from the center of Jewish life, such as at Qumran. I wonder whether this was the reason that "Simon the Righteous," according to rabbinic texts, was reluctant to participate in the rite by which the Nazirite ended the period of abstention. Compare D. Weiss Halivni, "On the Supposed Anti-Asceticism or Anti-Nazarism of Simon the Just," *JQR* 58 (1967-68) 243-52.

[13] Josephus may also have intended to allude to this aspect of all Jewish groups when he employed *proairesis* for the Pharisees (Ant. 13.293) and for the Essenes (Ant. 15.373). Josephus used *hairesis* for the Essenes (War 2.137), and the Sadducees (Ant. 13.293). In Ant. 13.171, the Pharisees, Sadducees and Essenes were called *haireseis*.

worship, to name some of the most common examples. The voluntary boundaries contained in the Damascus Document conform to
this general rule, but the designated stranger, with whom connections were regulated and sometimes forbidden, was of a new sort.
Full contact was permitted only with one's fellow sectarians. Contact
with all others, even those who would normally be considered fellow
insiders (i.e., other Jews), was rigorously restricted.

Here, too, the language of the Damascus Document provides at
least partial confirmation for the conclusions above. The wicked de-
spised and disregarded God's boundaries להסיע גבול אשר גבלו
4Q266 2 i 19-20 // 1:16; in a similar vein, in an- רישו]נים בנחלתם
other place, cf. וכל] אשר [פרצו את גבול התורה מבאי הברית 4Q267
31-2 // 20:25. The dilemma of the age was clearly expressed in this
phrase. To find those who disregarded the bounds of the Torah outside the covenant community would not have been surprising. For
these villains to be *members* of the covenant community presented an
especially difficult situation, requiring the drawing of new boundaries and the establishment of new refuges of purity. The truly righteous, by way of contrast, respected these ancient boundaries
וגבולות הגבותה לנו 4Q266 11 12-13. In the extraordinary times in
which they lived, confronting the apostasy of fellow covenant community members, they had offered the proper response: ובשלום קץ השני]ם
הא]ל[ה] [אין עוד להשתפח לבית יהודה כי אם לעמוד איש על] מצ[ודו]
נבנתה הגדר רחק החוק ...] (4Q266 3 i 4-6 // 4:10-12).

As a result of these commitments, those who lived according to
the Damascus Document gave up a good deal of their personal
identity. To employ terms proposed by Lewis Coser, the sectarian
sacrificed his or her personal identity to a "greedy institution."[14] The
extent of this sacrifice was not the same for all Jewish groups of the
Second Temple period; hence each must be evaluated as precisely
as possible. As opposed to those who lived בתמים קדש (4Q266 3 iii 6
// 7:6-7), whatever that may be,[15] the Damascus Document pre-

---

[14] See L. Coser, *Greedy Institutions: Patterns of Undivided Commitment* (New York: The
Free Press, 1974), esp. 103-16.

[15] The unspecified nature of this state has opened the door for much speculation.
It is one of the pegs on which the conclusion that Qumran was a celibate commu-
nity has been hung. See, for example, E. Qimron, "Celibacy in the Dead Sea
Scrolls and the Two Kinds of Sectarians," *The Madrid Qumran Congress: Proceedings of
the International Congress on the Dead Sea Scrolls, Madrid, 18-21 March 1991* (ed. J.
Trebolle Barrera and L. Vegas Montaner; STDJ 11; Leiden: E. J. Brill, 1992)
1.287-94. See also J. M. Baumgarten, "The Qumran-Essene Restraints on
Marriage," *Archaeology and History in the Dead Sea Scrolls. The New York University
Conference in Memory of Yigael Yadin* (ed. L. H. Schiffman; JSPSup 8; JSOT/ASOR
MS 2; Sheffield: JSOT, 1990) 13-24.

scribed a way of life for people who married and had children. The children needed to be educated and eventually would be married. Normally, these were the parents' tasks, but in the Damascus Document these responsibilities were assigned to the sectarian leader, the *mevaqqer*. He educated the children וה[ואה] ייסר את בניהם [ובנותם(?)] ((?)[ובנותם] וטפם ב[רו]ח ע[נ]וה ובא[הבת חסד] (4Q266 9 iii 6-7) and approved marriages and divorces וכן לכול לוק[ח אשה] והואה בעצה וכן יבן ל[מגרש] (4Q266 9 iii 4-5 // 13:17).

This is an intermediate level of sacrifice of identity. Once reproduction was permitted, even if subject to the rule of the *mevaqqer*, some degree of loyalty beyond that to the movement was inevitable. As Philo noted concerning the Essenes:

> They eschew marriage because they clearly discern it to be the sole or principal danger to the maintenance of the communal life... For he who is either fast bound in the love lures of his wife or under the stress of nature makes his children his first care, ceases to be the same to others and unconsciously has become a different man and has passed from freedom into slavery (Hyp. 11.14 and 11.17).[16]

Accordingly, it is not surprising to discover that the Damascus Document permitted members' concern for biological relatives and criticized other movements that did not. A righteous member cared for his kin [ולוא ימעל איש בשאר בשרו] (4Q266 3 iii 2-3) // איש בשא[ר] בשר[ו] (4Q269 4 ii 4-5 // 7:1). The wicked did not behave likewise [ויתעלמו איש בשאר בשר]ו (4Q266 3 iv 4) // בשא[ר בשרו] (4Q269 6 2 // 8:6). It is instructive to compare one of the reasons for which Hananiah Notos was rebuked—unacceptable devotion to his relatives (4Q477 2 11 8)—as well as Josephus' comments on the Essenes:

> Members may of their own motion help the deserving, when in need, and supply food to the destitute; but presents to relatives are prohibited, without leave from the managers (War 2.134).[17]

The severity of this Essene restriction should be noted. The same destitute person who was not fit to join the Essenes at a meal if he were not a member of their order (War 2.129) could be helped with food freely but assisting one's biological kin was forbidden. The

---

[16] Compare Paul's remarks on the same subject (1 Cor. 7:32-35).

[17] The possible connection between the rebuke of Hananiah Notos and Josephus' remarks on the Essenes was already noted by E. Eshel, "4Q477: The Rebukes of the Overseer," *JJS* 45 (1994) 118. For an alternate understanding of this text, see J. M. Baumgarten, "Zab Impurity in Qumran and Rabbinic Judaism," *JJS* 45 (1994) 277; see also S. A. Reed, "Genre, Setting and Title of 4Q447," *JJS* 47 (1996) 146-47.

Damascus Document thus differed from the Qumran regulations reflected in 4Q477 and from the practice of the Essenes, according to
Josephus, by permitting concern for biological relatives and criticiz-
ing those who neglected their duty.

At the same time as the Damascus Document acknowledged the
legitimacy of those who lived בתמים קדש (as discussed above), it also
indulged in ferocious criticism of others. The identity of those criticized is obscure, as they were called by code names which we cannot always decipher. The tendency of modern scholars is to assume
that they were being chastised for being insufficiently stringent in
their observance of the commandments of the Torah. The example
discussed above indicates that this scholarly tendency may need cor-
rection. Sometimes, the criticism was for being too stringent, and
was grounded in the perspective of an intermediate position between
stringency and leniency (marriage was permitted, subject to the control of the sectarian master; hence some regulated level of concern
with biological relatives was allowed) adopted by the community of
the Damascus Document.

To summarize this part of the discussion, scholars have already
noted that a person who lived according to the Damascus
Document was in an intermediate stage of purity by the standards of
a source such as 1QS.[18] This moderate position on one scale of sectarian extremism is now confirmed by the analysis of the degree to
which connection to one's biological kin was sacrificed. The
Damascus Document emerges as a source whose attitude towards
the surrounding world was more nuanced than scholars may have
realized.[19]

III

I would stress the suitability of the perception of the past, in our text,
for a movement that staked out its position between the extremes
outlined above. Thus, the summary of the history of the movement
at the beginning of text, as known from the Cairo Geniza, has received much attention. I would insist that this passage displays a remarkably benign attitude towards the predecessors of the movement
in the phase represented by the Damascus Document. There was a

---

[18] See L. H. Schiffman, *Law, Custom and Messianism in the Dead Sea Sect* (Jerusalem:
Shazar Center, 1993) 23 (Hebrew).

[19] It bears noting that the moderation of the Damascus Document may not strike
modern readers as remarkable. We might be inclined to place it very close to the
end of the spectrum of separatism, even if not at the extreme end.

twenty year period in which those predecessors knew they were not fulfilling the commandments properly and were like blind men, groping for the way. This situation lasted until the Teacher finally revealed the divine truth (4Q266 2 i 12-15 // 1:8-11). All this is remarkably kind, if patronizing, to these predecessors. One may wonder whether people so described would have agreed with this view of themselves. Because of our modern preconceptions, we may be puzzled by this relatively sympathetic assessment of the predecessors, expecting the harshest denunciation to be reserved for them. Considering the stance between extremes adopted in the Damascus Document, this view of the predecessors may be comprehensible, albeit somewhat condescending.

On the basis of the discussion in the preceding paragraph, one should not conclude that the Damascus Document did not know how to hate: it outlined a cosmic "March of Folly" which began in the ante-diluvian era, with the Watchers of heaven, and continued through the sons of Jacob, the Israelites in Egypt, and the kings of Judah (e.g. David, 5:2-6). These villains had contemporary representatives in those who defiled the sanctuary, entered marriages considered illicit, and denounced the party of truth by denying the validity of its teachings (5:6-12). The Damascus Document knew a whole rogues, gallery of such miscreants: איש/אנשי הלצון, דורשי חלקות, באי הברית הראשונים, שרי יהודה, בוני החיץ וטחי התפל, איש הכזב, בית פלג.

This view of the past had consequences for the present: the contemporary opponents of the truth were the last link in the substantial tradition of error. Parallel to the list of villains, however, was a much smaller number of heroes (there are always exceptions to a rule), such as Abraham, Isaac and Jacob (4Q266 2 ii 21-23 // 3:1-3). This second list also had consequences for the present: the community of the Damascus Document saw itself as one link (possibly, the last link?) in that very thin and much interrupted chain (4Q266 3 ii 12 and 25 // 6:5 and 19). Its members were the true diggers of the well of the Law. Hence, they observed the Sabbath properly, followed the correct calendar and celebrated the Fast Day at its proper time, to cite but a few of the praises showered on the faithful. I suggest that at least part of the purpose of the Damascus Document was to reassure its group of faithful that their minority situation was not unique; although truth had been trampled down from time immemorial, its ultimate victory was inevitable. History thus had a key role in supporting the commitment of those loyal to this way of life, and a view of the past was a crucial component of its ideological foundations.

IV

In my view, the Damascus Document is not the only ancient Jewish sectarian source which displays a mixture of moderation (a condescending attitude towards predecessors combined with harsh criticism of rivals) and a nuanced view of the Jewish past. Was there ever a movement whose position was so self-evidently distinctive that it did not need to distinguish itself carefully from rivals (real, potential or imagined) and articulate a well-considered understanding of the past to support that stance?

I believe the comparison of the Damascus Document with the letters of Paul to be instructive. The comparison is especially apt as Paul and the Damascus Document conceived their movements in terms of the "new covenant" predicted in Jer. 31:31 (compare 1 Cor. 11:25 and CD 6:19 // 4Q269 4 ii 1). Nevertheless, these covenants, different as they may be, did not abandon their connection to the old covenants and heroes.

Paul can be remarkably tolerant in staking out his position between those on either side. In Rome there were those for whom all foods were the same, as well as those who only ate vegetables. There were those for whom all days were the same, and those who considered specific days holy (Rom. 14:1-5). Paul did not belong wholly to either camp: he knew, for example, that nothing was unclean in itself but was unclean for one who thought it unclean, and he respected that stand (Rom. 14:14). He had to find a way for people who disagreed so profoundly with each other to live together in one community, without passing judgement or despising each other (Rom. 14:10). Mutual accommodation should prevail, and those who were strong (i.e., those for whom all foods and days were equal) should bear with the failings of the weak (Rom. 15:1). In a similar mode he informed his Corinthian correspondents that his rule in all the churches was that each member should lead the life assigned to him: circumcised Christians should not remove the marks of circumcision, nor should the uncircumcised seek circumcision (1 Cor. 7:17-20).

We might respond that the tolerance for which Paul called was fragile, naive at best, and conflict inevitable. Paul, however, believed that he was living at the very dawn of the final redemption (see his advice on marriage, 1 Cor. 7:1-16, 25-31, for example), with the decisive events in the process having already taken place. He did not need long-term solutions; hence, Paul may not have been troubled by the instability inherent in his views.

Nevertheless, Paul was uncompromisingly hostile towards those who did not accept the tolerance which he preached. Convenient examples are found in the Galatian correspondence. Paul's harshest remarks came when the status of his Christian converts of Gentile background was challenged. In exasperation Paul expressed the hope that those who troubled his flock concerning circumcision carry their supposed love for that commandment to its logical conclusion and castrate themselves (Gal. 5:12). When he heard that some of his Galatian flock were observing days, months, seasons and years, he feared that he had labored in vain (Gal. 4:10).

In the realm of history, Paul's views were consistent with the intermediate position just outlined.[20] Abandoning all connection to the Hebrew Bible and the Jewish past was out of the question. Paul went to great exegetical effort to claim that Christians were the true seed of Abraham, the sons of the free wife (Rom. 4). They were the genuine heirs of the promises of the covenant. Nevertheless, the ultimate status of the descendants of Abraham by the flesh had not been abrogated (Rom. 11). For the moment, a hardness had come over Israel, and this created an opportunity on which non-Jews should capitalize, both for their own sakes and for that of the Jews, until the end of days when all Israel would be saved (Rom. 11:26). On what terms will all Israel be saved at that time? Paul did not make this explicit, but it seems that he believed the end of days would see the triumph of the message he preached.

For my purposes, the benefit of this analysis of Paul is the resulting understanding of the legitimacy of his predecessors (mixed with a significant degree of condescension) and of interpretations which assigned all the promises of the covenant to the new community headed by Paul. All this concurred with Paul's stance *vis à vis* groups of Christians to either side of his followers. The readings of the Damascus Document and of Paul reinforce each other, emphasizing the need for the careful observation of a movement's relative stance on the spectrum of extremism of its time, and the expression of its position in its perceptions of the past.

V

To return to the Damascus Document, the mandate that history be taught therefore conforms to our expectations. One of the tasks of the sectarian master was to instruct members: [ויספר להם נהיות] עולם [בפ]תריהם (4Q267 9 iv 5) [ויספר להם נהיות עולם ב]פ[ן]תריהם //

---

[20] As in the case of the Damascus Document (see n. 19), a modern reader might not consider Paul's stance so moderate, and would prefer to place it close to one of the extremes of his time and place.

(4Q266 9 ii 19//13:8). Just what were the נהיות עולם? The phrase is
sufficiently broad that it includes any and all of what we would classi-
fy as history, physics and metaphysics. It may even emphasize the
ability to predict the future, as suggested by the use of נהיות in Sir.
48:25 עד עולם הגיד נהיות ונסתרות לפני בואן. This meaning of נהיות
may be reinforced by another passage from the Damascus Document, which describes the results of the process of instruction:
[ויגל עיניהם בנסתרות וא]זנם פתחו וישמעו עמוקות ויבינו [בכול נהיות עד מה
יבוא בם] (4Q266 2 i 5-6 // 268 1 7-8, underlined). In sum, the educa-
tion of members in נהיות עולם included history, among other subjects;
this conclusion is likely in view of the emphasis placed on knowledge
of the past in the Damascus Document. Nevertheless, the aspect of
נהיות עולם which seemed of greatest interest had to do with understanding what was yet to come.

The results of this analysis of the meaning of נהיות עולם confirm
the role of the past according to other passages in the Damascus
Document. What was important about the past for a sectarian was
not some antiquarian interest, but the relevance of the past for present and future, establishing that sectarian's link with previous and
future generations. Accordingly, the multiple meanings of עולם
נהיות, with the emphasis on the future, were at the heart of what a
sectarian should know, and central to what should be taught to children by their master.

Although antiquarianism was far from the concern of a sectarian,
the role assigned to history has one further consequence which may
lead to a convergence of interest between a sectarian and an antiquarian. Curiosity about the past in antiquity was not great. Most
events beyond the traditional memory span of about forty years
were forgotten. Knowledge of the past required effort, only rarely
invested.[21]

There are, however, few forces which impel people to inquire about
the past as powerful as the belief that the end of days is at hand, and
that past, present and future are coming together for their glorious
finale. One Qumran example is provided by 4QMMT C11. The
addressee was invited to study scripture, as well as "[events] of past
ages," as part of the effort to convince him that now was the end of
days. Another example from Jewish antiquity, even more precise in
its extent, is Dan. 11-12, whose author had detailed knowledge of
the history of the hellenistic kingdoms, equal to that of the best pro-

---

[21] See in particular E. J. Bickerman, "La chaîne de la tradition pharisienne,"
Studies in Jewish and Christian History (Leiden: E. J. Brill, 1980) 2.256-59.

fessional historians.[22] These particulars were only of interest to him because he believed that he had cracked the code of history, and was convinced that its culmination was at hand.[23] He sought confirmation for that conclusion from the analysis of history.

The Damascus Document fits this pattern, with its calculation of the history of redemption based on the count of 390 years since the Babylonian Exile. While the number 390 is obviously typological and eschatological, based on Ezek. 4:5, whoever proposed this time reckoning did a good enough job to leave scholars guessing, creating substantial modern discussion.[24] The term of 390 years is thus not merely typological. Considering difficulties of calculation, in the absence of eras and years of fixed length,[25] this shows remarkable interest in and knowledge of history.

On the other hand, the eschatological hopes have been disappointed, and the movement was showing some sense of strain (19:33-20:34). This circumstance also shaped the perception of the past. I suggest that it may help explain the generous use of code

---

[22] See E. J. Bickerman, *Four Strange Books of the Bible* (New York: Schocken, 1967) 115-16. Note, also, that this inquiry into the past may contain the seeds of its own unmaking. As the past is searched more and more thoroughly for signs of the end, the gap between reality and expectation may also be revealed. In short, faith may be overturned or may ultimately seem irrelevant as a result. See J. Fried, "Awaiting the Last Days...Myth and Disenchantment" (forthcoming). See further Hill, *English Bible*, 413-35, and Hill's summary comment, 441: "it was the radical godly whose passionate desire to make sense of the Bible led them into the critical activity which ultimately dethroned it." The closest parallel in ancient Jewish texts is b. San. 97b: "R. Samuel b. Nahmani said in the name of R. Jonathan: Blasted be the bones of those who calculate the end. For they would say (i.e., their predictions make people say), since the predetermined time has arrived and yet it has not come, it will never come."

[23] For the Greek fashion of re-telling the present as if it were prophecy from the past, to which Daniel conforms, see Bickerman, *Four Strange Books*, 116-19. In that sense, it is no accident that the secret of Daniel was uncovered by Porphyry, familiar with Greek literary genres and author of a work on chronology. See further Bickerman, *Four Strange Books*, 130-31.

[24] For one recent attempt see A. Laato, "The Chronology of the Damascus Document of Qumran," *RevQ* 15 (1992) 605-7. The 390 year period of sin following the return from the exile is an excellent example of the pattern of compression of time typical of extreme millenarian movements, in which the recent past is perceived as wholly evil, and one must jump to some more distant point in the past in order to find better days. For a social scientific analysis of this matter, see S. Rayner, "The Perception of Time and Space in Egalitarian Sects: A Millenarian Cosmology," *Essays in the Sociology of Perception* (ed. M. Douglas; London: Routledge & Kegan Paul, 1982) 258. For a discussion of ancient Jewish sources from this perspective see M. Kister, "On the History of the Essene Sect," *Tarbiz* 56 (5747/1987) 3, n. 6 (Hebrew), and A. Rofé, "The Beginning of Sects in Post-Exilic Judaism," *Cathedra* 49 (1988) 12-21 (Hebrew).

[25] See E. J. Bickerman, "The Jewish Historian Demetrius," *Studies in Jewish and Christian History*, 2.358.

names to identify others. The long list of miscreants, summarized above, אנשי/איש הלצון, דורשי חלקות, הראשונים באי הברית, שרי יהודה בוני החיץ, וטחי התפל, איש הכזב, בית פלג. is notable for the fact that every group was called by a sobriquet, thus creating an abundant scholarly literature and a real quandary to determine their identity.[26] I suggest that use of these code names can glorify heroes (in particular when expectations of the end of days are on the upswing) and obscure the message so as to minimize the sense of failure, in the aftermath of disappointment. Whether before or after disappointment, code names can give an aura of eternity to an interpretation of past and present, while making that interpretation flexible enough to be mythologized as needed in the future.[27] They thus find a useful place in several phases of the life of a millenarian movement. [28]

VI

The study offered above is intended to be an example of how a movement's account of its past should be analyzed: it sheds light on the situation at a particular time and place, as those historical circumstances illuminate the specific details of the past remembered and transmitted. Working back and forth, the dialectic can be exploited in order to understand a moment in the life of a group as fully as possible. Then we may comprehend both how its members lived and why they found that way of life meaningful, with ideology and way of life reinforcing each other. To return to Bickerman's terms with which this paper began, the utility of the view of the past as a component in the ideology will then be clear. Alternately, to return to the analogy of the locomotive suggested at the outset, as a re-

---

[26] For a discussion of some of these code names see B. Nitzan, *Pesher Habakkuk— A Scroll from the Wilderness of Judaea (1QpHab)* (Jerusalem: Bialik Institute, 1986) 132-48.

[27] See I. Gruenwald, "From Sunrise to Sunset—On the Nature of Eschatology and Messianism in Judaism," *The Messianic Idea in Jewish Thought. A Study Conference in Honour of the Eightieth Birthday of Gershom Scholem Held 4-5 December 1977* (Jerusalem: Israel Academy of Sciences and Humanities, 1982) 18-36.

[28] The conclusion I am suggesting is based on analogies, in particular that of the Jehovah's Witnesses; see M. J. Penton, *Apocalypse Delayed: The Story of Jehovah's Witnesses* (Toronto: University of Toronto Press, 1985). Their literature seems a meaningless collection of phrases to someone not able to decode it. The code, however, helps conceal the fact that the end for which the Witnesses set several dates (from 1914 to 1975) has not yet arrived. As a result Witnesses are less subject to ridicule. There are reports of Witnesses stealing copies of their older works, which are based on interpretations popular during earlier stages of their movement, from libraries.

sult of the reinforcement offered by ideology and way of life for each other, in which conceptions of the past had an important role, the destination at which the personal train of such a committed member arrived was not only the final one, it was also the only conceivable one and, hence, thoroughly convincing. That committed member's steam had powered him or her to the absolutely true and unique destination at which past, present and eternal future all converged in their ultimate cosmic meaning.

THE LAWS OF THE DAMASCUS DOCUMENT—
BETWEEN BIBLE AND MISHNAH

JOSEPH M. BAUMGARTEN

Baltimore Hebrew College

In this Jubilee year, when there have been multiple events marking fifty years since the discovery of the Dead Sea Scrolls, the initiative of the Orion Center serves as a reminder that it is nearly a centennial since Solomon Schechter prepared his publication of the central foundational document of the Dead Sea Scrolls community, *The Zadokite Fragments*. It is true that for half a century the antiquity of the work in these Genizah manuscripts was still the subject of scholarly debate, but this fact only enhances the good judgment and courage of the editor, who held to his conviction that these were copies of a sectarian text stemming from the period of the Second Temple. Today this judgment is almost universally accepted, although with regard to the code of laws there has, until recently, been some reluctance among biblical scholars to recognize it as an integral part of what is now commonly called the Damascus Document. With the publication of the Cave 4 fragments this can be expected to change.

I concluded the introduction to the Cave 4 D fragments with a paragraph entitled "The Relevance of Rabbinic Sources,"[1] where I took issue with those scholars who consider the late editing of the rabbinic texts as sufficient justification for ignoring them in their portrayal of Second Temple religious history. Since the publication of Megillat Ha-Miqdaš and Miqṣat Maʿaśe Ha-Torah it is well-known that Qumran religious law included rulings which the Mishnah ascribes to the צדוקים (whatever sectarian entities this name might designate) in their debates with the פרושים. Moreover, the polemics in Qumran writings against the Pharisees (דורשי חלקות) have, as their target, practices considered normative in rabbinic sources. The Mishnah, as historians in Israel have recognized, is indispensable for understanding what the Qumran legists were teaching and with whom they were contending. Among the new laws of the Damascus Document are further illustrations of rulings directed against practices sanctioned in Tannaitic sources.

---

[1] *Qumran Cave 4.XIII. The Damascus Document (4Q266-273)* (DJD 18; Oxford: Clarendon, 1996) 21-22.

In the present paper I should like to offer a few observations about the distinctive Qumran approach to the laws of the Sabbath and to appraise some nomenclature common to Qumran and to early rabbinic halakha. Before I do so, however, it behooves me to justify the balanced description of this paper, "—Between Bible and Mishnah." I propose to do so by essaying to identify the biblical source of one of the more intriguing supplements to the Damascus Document, extant only in 4Q270, the so-called Catalogue of Transgressors.

The Catalogue of Transgressors

The list of about fourteen transgressors, with the repeated formula או אשר and a verb in the imperfect, is not fully extant and its place-ment before the corpus of laws is not certain. At the end of the list, the transgressors are collectively denounced for provoking divine wrath. In DJD 18 I tentatively remarked that the genre of the list may be compared with the list of curses (ארור) directed against vari-ous sinners in Deuteronomy 27. However, the curse formula, reflect-ed in 1QS 2:11, is not found in the D catalogue, and the nature of the transgressions is entirely different.

More recently I considered the hypothesis that the או אשר formula with the imperfect verb may derive from the איש אשר formulation with the imperfect which is used repeatedly to describe profanations of holiness in Leviticus 17-22. Closer examination of the contents of the Catalogue of Transgressors does indeed indicate a marked de-pendence upon sins listed in this biblical pericope, although a num-ber of the transgressions in the D catalogue are clearly of a sectarian nature. The following tabulation may serve to provide an overview of the dependence:

The Catalogue of Transgressors

4Q270 2 i-ii	Lev. 17-22
1 שע]ירים או ידרוש באוב ובידעונים	17:7 (שעירים); 19:31, 20:6, 27 (ידעוני,אוב)
2 או אשר יחלל את השם	20:3, 21:6, 22:2, 22:15
3 שם רע ב]בתוליה בבית [אביה	21:14 (אשה בבתוליה)
4 אלמנה אשר] ישכב אחר עמה	
5 או יק]רב אל אשתו ביום	
6 אשר י]מחא להרים [את הקודשים ?	22:1-16 קדשים offered (ירימו) to priests
7 [ ] בשמותם לטמא את רוח קודשו	

8 או ינוגע בנגע צרעת או זוב טמ]אה   22:4 (והוא צרוע או זב)

9 לא תלך רכיל בעמיך 19:16 אשר יגלה את רז עמו לגואים או יקלל א]ת עמו

10 ידבר] סרה על משיחי רוח הקדש

11 או ישחט בהמה וחיה עבר]ה   22:28 אתו ואת בנו לא תשחטו ביום אחד

12 אשר ישכב עם] אשה הרה מקין דם

13 או יקרב א]ל בת [אחיו

14 או ישכב עם זכר] משכבי אשה   18:22 ואת זכר לא תשכב משכבי אשה

Comments

line 2 The fact that participants in the Moloch cult are said to profane the divine name (20:3) raises the possibility that this pagan abomination was mentioned in the missing context, but this cannot be proven.

lines 3-4 Lev. 21:14 refers to the restricted marriages sanctioned for the High Priest. The sinner here alluded to is apparently any layman who marries a maiden or widow of ill repute; cf. 4Q271 3 12 12-13.

line 5 The identification of the day on which marital relations were banned is missing. Jub. 50:8 suggests that it may have been the Sabbath.

line 6 The priestly emoluments listed here include: (a) the fruits of trees in the fourth year after their planting; (b) the tithe of cattle; (c) the redemption of the first-born of unclean animals and of humans; (d) the first shearing of sheep; (e) the assessment for the redemption of persons; (f) a guilt restitution which cannot be returned to its rightful owner. The assignment to the priests of (a), (b), (e) and (f) follows sectarian opinion (MMT B62-64, 11QT 60, CD 9:13-14). Terumah, the sacred portion of the harvest offered exclusively to the priests (Numbers 18), is not listed here. The requirement of ritual purity for its consumption is the major subject of Leviticus 22.

line 7 The extant text does not specify whose names, those of angels or perhaps those of communal authorities, were abused by the offender.

line 8 Lev. 20:4-7 lists scale disease and gonorrhea among defilements which disqualify a priest from eating sacred food. The mention of these physical afflictions in this catalogue of transgressors may perhaps reflect the view that they were symptomatic of sin.

line 9 "One who reveals a secret of his people to the Gentiles, or curses [his people]." 11QTemple 64 likewise describes two kinds of treason: (a) informing against one's people כי יהיה איש רכיל בעמו; (b) cursing one's people by one who goes over to the side of the Gentiles ויברח אל תוך הגואים ויקלל את עמו. The terminology used there for informing is clearly that of Lev. 19:16 לא תלך רכיל בעמיך, which was understood to refer to national betrayal rather than to malicious gossip. The phraseology of our text is markedly close to that found in the En Gedi inscription מן דגלי רזה דקרתה לעממיה.

lines 11-12   The ban on slaughtering pregnant animals in 11QTemple 52:5-7 is juxtaposed with the biblical prohibition against killing the parent and young of oxen and sheep on the same day (Lev. 22:28). Qumran law regarded the fetus as an independent creature.[2] It is possible that the following law forbidding intercourse during pregnancy may also involve concern about harming the fetus.

lines 13-14   The laws of incest in Leviticus 20 are consistently formulated with the איש אשר pattern, from which the או אשר formula of our text presumably derives. However, marriage with one's niece was not biblically prohibited; it was exegetically derived from the ban on marrying one's aunt (CD 5:8-11).

The foregoing survey of biblical sources for the Catalogue of Transgressors shows that it was primarily based on the קדושה laws found in Leviticus 17-22. To these were appended some offenses against sectarian "halakha," which may also have been deemed to be profanations of holiness. The connection with the Leviticus pericope is further supported by the conclusion which follows the enumeration of sinners:

17   [   ] *vac* עוכרי א̇ן̇ת

18   בם חקק אל להעביר בחרון אפו בקץ̇

In the *editio princeps* I followed the suggestion that 6Q15 was a parallel to this text. Hence, I adopted the reading found there, להבעיר "to kindle" as preferable to להעביר with חרון "wrath":

17   [   ] *vac* Those who transgress [   ]

18   Against them God has ordained, to cause his w[rath] to be kindled during the peri[od of iniquity   ]

I now believe that the original reading להעביר "to remove" should not be modified. Lev. 18:24 admonishes Israelites not to defile themselves by imitating the sexual practices of Canaan, "for by all these,

---

[2] J. M. Baumgarten, "A Fragment on Fetal Life and Pregnancy in 4Q270," *Pomegranates and Golden Bells: Studies in Honor of Jacob Milgrom* (ed. D. P. Wright, D. N. Freedman and A. Hurvitz; Winona Lake: Eisenbrauns, 1995) 445-48.

the nations I am casting out before you have defiled themselves." The transgressors of moral limits, designated by the word עוברי in line 17, are subject to a divine curse, as indicated in the expulsion ritual at the end of the Damascus Document: וגבולות הגבלתה לנו אשר את עובריהם ארותה "You have set limits for us and cursed those who transgress them" (4Q266 11 12-13). Non-Israelites, too, were cursed when they transgressed these moral limits, אתה ארותה את עובריהם (11 14), as demonstrated by the fate of the nations who were "vomited out" by the land (Lev. 19:25-28). It is to this law of moral retribution that line 18 most likely alludes: בם חקק אל להעביר בח[רון] אפו "Them did God ordain to remove through the wrath of his anger," with an apparent word play between עוברי and להעביר.

Qumran Law and the Mishnah

Having given due recognition to the fundamental biblical roots of Qumran law, we may now turn our attention to those aspects which link it with early rabbinic halakha. These links were highlighted in the masterful study of Louis Ginzberg that, based only on the Damascus Document and lacking the wealth of other Qumran writings at our disposal, identified the *unbekannte jüdische Sekte* as Pharisaic. Although this conclusion is no longer tenable, there is great heuristic value in reevaluating some of the considerations which led to it.

Laws of the Sabbath

The laws of the Sabbath provide some of the closest approaches between Qumran exegesis and the Oral Law of the Rabbis. Lawrence Schiffman's dissertation contains a detailed discussion of these laws. Here we wish only to make some observations based on Cave 4 halakhic fragments which will, we hope, soon be published.[3]

הוצאה

The biblical injunction, אל יצא איש ממקמו ביום השביעי "Let no man go out of his place on the seventh day" (Exod. 16:29) was rendered in 4Q251 1 4 אל יוצא איש ממקומו כל השבת "Let no man *bring forth*

---

[3] After completing the following survey of the 4Q Sabbath fragments, I found that L. Doering has independently arrived at a number of similar results in his study, "New Aspects of Qumran Sabbath Law from Cave 4 Fragments," *Legal Texts and Legal Issues. Proceedings of the Second Meeting of the International Organization for Qumran Studies, Cambridge, 1995 Published in Honour of Joseph M. Baumgarten* (ed. M. J. Bernstein, F. García Martínez and J. Kampen; STDJ 23; Leiden: Brill, 1997) 251-74.

from his place (during) the entire Sabbath." יוצא is likewise employed in the rules, formulated on the basis of Exod. 16:29, which
prohibit carrying in and out on the Sabbath (CD 11:7 and 4Q265 6
4). Thus, this biblical passage served at Qumran, much as it did in
talmudic halakha (b. ʿErub. 17b, 51a) and in Targum Ps.-Jon. to
Exod. 16:29, both as a source for the limit on walking and the prohibition of carrying in and out of dwellings.

Talmudic halakha, however, analyzed the act of carrying into two
elements: (a) the raising (עקירה) of an object from its place and (b) its
placement (הנחה) in another locus. Only a person who performed
both elements was culpable (m. Shab. 1:1). The severe formulation
in Jub. 50:8 shows no awareness of such conceptualization. "And
whoever lifts up anything that he will carry to take out of his tent or
from his house, let him die." This implies that the very displacement
of an object with the intent to carry it out constitutes a desecration.[4]
Such a view is akin to the practice cited by Josephus as an illustration of Essene stringency with regard to the Sabbath: "Not only do
they prepare their food on the day before, to avoid kindling a fire on
that one [the Sabbath], but they do not venture to remove
(μετακίνησαι) any vessel" (War 2.147). Moving a vessel not prepared for the Sabbath, even without carrying it outside, would for
the Essenes constitute a violation of Exod. 16:5, which required that
the manna for the Sabbath be prepared (והכינו) on the sixth day.

פקוח נפש and מוקצה

Talmudic sources preserve a theory which deemed objects not "prepared" for the Sabbath to be biblically restricted for use (מוקצה).
The prevailing talmudic view, however, attributed the מוקצה restrictions to rabbinic enactments which underwent an evolution from
strict application to virtually all vessels to the later circumscribed
ban of only specific implements.[5]

Qumran law retains the ancient stringency in accordance with
which any implement not designated for Sabbath use could not be
employed, even to save a human life. Thus, certain Jews who fled to
the wilderness in the days of Mattathias did not defend themselves
when attacked on Sabbath. They did not hurl any stone against

---

[4] The theory that the restriction on the moving (טלטול) of objects was derivative
from the prohibition to carry them out (הוצאה) is found in b. Shab. 124b, as noted
by Rabad in his stricture on Rambam, *Yad*, Laws of Shabbat 24.12. Rambam
viewed the טלטול restrictions as independent rabbinic enactments to distinguish the
Sabbath from the workaday routines of the week.
[5] Cf. b. Pes. 47b and Beṣa 2b with the evolutionary relaxation of מוקצה restrictions depicted in t. Shab. 14:1.

their attackers nor block up their hiding places (1 Macc. 2:36). The handling of rocks or soil was apparently forbidden on the Sabbath (cf. CD 11:11), and no allowance was made for the peril to life (פקוח נפש). "Any human being who falls into a place of water ... let no man bring him up with a ladder, a rope, or an implement" (CD 11:16-17).[6] 4Q265 6 confirms the ban on using an implement (כלי), but permits one to cast a garment (בגד) to a drowning man; the latter was permissible because, as an article of attire, it was prepared for use on the Sabbath.[7] It is interesting that this ruling is followed by a reference to a situation involving an army (צבא), which unfortunately is incomplete. We also lack the context of the allusion to war on the Sabbath in 4Q264 1 ii 8 להלחם עמו.[8]

שבות *and Priestly Activities*

The term שבות, which is used in rabbinic sources for rabbinic restrictions intended to preserve the non-secular character of the Sabbath, is not found in Qumran writings. It is, however, apparent that the Sabbath rules found in Jubilees and in the Damascus Document were not limited to those found in the Torah, but also embraced the שבות category of legal "fences" designed to enhance the sanctity of the Sabbath. 4Q264a (Halakha B) now provides a fragmentary collection of such rules: one concerns the one thousand cubit limit on walking outside one's settlement, also found in CD 10:21. This is followed by a regrettably incomplete prohibition beginning with the phrase, "Let no man take," which was extended to the priests and apparently applied also to "the burnt offerings and sacrifices." Interestingly, the operative principle in talmudic halakha was that שבות restrictions did not apply to the Temple, which some opinions extended even to tasks ancillary to sacrifice, such as bringing the paschal offering from beyond the Sabbath limit (m. Pes. 6:1; b. 'Erub. 103a). The next Sabbath restriction in 4Q264a seems to pertain to reading scrolls in order to check their texts, although one

---

[6] The restriction on saving human life is specific and applies strictly to the use of utensils which may not be handled on the Sabbath; cf. L. H. Schiffman, *The Halakha at Qumran* (SJLA 16; Leiden: E. J. Brill, 1975), 126, and L. Doering's dissent in the above-mentioned paper. In normative rabbinic halakha, the primacy of פקוח נפש would override all restrictions.

[7] 4Q265 6 4 has the prohibition [אל יו[צא אי]ש מאהלו כלי ומאכ[ל] "Let no man bring forth from his tent a vessel and food." It is possible that the vessel intended here was a food vessel, taking כלי ומאכ[ל] as hendiadys; otherwise its handling even within the tent would be restricted.

[8] For a historical study of the halakha concerning war on the Sabbath, see M. D. Herr, "The Problem of the Laws of War on the Sabbath in the Second Temple and Mishnaic Periods," *Tarbiz* 30 (1961) 242-56, 341-56 (Hebrew).

is allowed to read them in order to learn. Further, secular talk on the Sabbath was banned in accordance with Isa. 58:13, but conversation about food was legitimate.

M. Ḥag. 1:8 characterizes the laws of the Sabbath as based on little Scripture and much oral halakha, כהררים התלוין בשערה "like mountains suspended by a hair." It is interesting that Qumran exegetes who, as far as we know, had no concept of an authoritative Oral Law, nevertheless attached the observance of precautionary Sabbath restrictions to the scriptural command, שמור את יום השבת לקדשו (CD 10:16-17). This was, according to our restoration of the text of 4Q274 2 i, the passage cited in support of the restriction on sprinkling water for purification on the Sabbath, just as it served in CD 10:16-17 as the basis for requiring the cessation of work on Friday well before sunset. Thus, Qumran law in effect carried out one of the principles attributed to the Men of the Great Assembly, ועשו סיג לתורה "And build a fence about the Torah" (m. 'Abot 1:1). I am therefore inclined to doubt that the sobriquet בוני החיץ, which stems from Ezek. 13:10 and was applied in the Damascus Document to some opponents of the sect (CD 4:19, 8:12), was particularly directed at the proto-rabbinic "fences" which served to protect the Law.[9]

The Topical Nomenclature of Laws

The laws of the Sabbath are set forth in the Damascus Document under the rubric על השבת (10:14). This is one of several such rubrics employed to introduce topical groupings of laws: על הטהר במים "concerning one who purifies himself in water" (10:10), על השבועה "concerning oaths" (9:8), על משפט הנדבות "concerning the law of donations" (16:13).[10] Note also the nomenclature for the class of prohibited sexual unions משפט העריות (5:9), which is paralleled by the topical heading על העריות in 4Q251 12 1. Here we have the first post-biblical evidence for the identification of classes of laws by subject categories.

It is noteworthy that the aforementioned m. Ḥag. 1:8, which characterizes the laws of the Sabbath as lacking scriptural support, lists הטהרות והטמאות ועריות among categories of laws which by con-

[9] Cf. L. H. Schiffman, *Reclaiming the Dead Sea Scrolls. The History of Judaism, the Background of Christianity, the Lost Library of Qumran* (Philadelphia/Jerusalem: JPS, 1994) 250.

[10] We do not include instances where the על formulation introduces single laws, such as על שבועת האשה (CD 16:10) and the repeated use of this formula for particular legal assertions in MMT.

trast have abundant scriptural support. הטהרות והטמאות, counted as one in the Tosefta, corresponds to the rubric על הטהר concerning purification from impurity. עריות, the laws of prohibited marriages, are here designated in plural form just as at Qumran. The Tosefta has supplements to the mishnaic list of halakhot with good scriptural support, among which appear הערכין and ההקדשות. The former also appears at Qumran in plural form in the designation כסף הערכים "valuation money" (4Q159), while ההקדשות corresponds in content to the rules listed in the Damascus Document under the rubric of הנדבות (16:13), which employ the verb קדש for sanctified donations.

In his definitive study of early strata of Tannaitic literature, Yaakov Epstein demonstrated that m. Ḥag. 1:8, which describes the above-mentioned categories of halakhot, stems at the latest from the Herodian period.[11] This is shown by the fact that Abba Yose b. Hanan, a contemporary of the late Second Temple period, already refers to the enumeration of the laws in the Mishnah as "major bodies of halakha" (t. Ḥag. 1:9). Epstein's conclusion is, I believe, in harmony with the similarities in the topical terminology between Qumran and the Mishnah which we have noted. The rudimentary grouping of laws under subject headings at Qumran, although manifested here in a non-Pharisaic context, tends also to add cogency to Epstein's theory concerning the early formation of the nuclei of the tractates of the Mishnah.

Conclusion

Our identification of Leviticus 17-22 as the source of the Catalogue of Transgressors can be taken as an illustration of the pentateuchal roots of Qumran law. As CD 16:2 affirms, "in it (the law of Moses) everything is specified (מדוקדק)." However, this apparently limiting principle has to be appraised in the light of such pentateuchal supplements as the Book of Jubilees, in which chronological things are מדוקדק (CD 16:3), and the Temple Scroll, which contains multiple pentateuchal elaborations. We have further to reckon with the genre of reworked Pentateuch found at Qumran in which, for example, the feasts of oil and wood were inserted into the sequence of festivals of Leviticus 23. Thus, the scriptural basis of Qumran law which, unlike talmudic halakha, also included the Prophets, was to begin with less rigidly defined. Witness the sporadic use of the citation formula

---

[11] J. N. Epstein, *Mebo'ot le-Sifrut ha-Tannaim* (Jerusalem: Magnes; Tel Aviv: Dvir, 1957) 46-47.

אשר אמר for things not found anywhere in Scripture, but in the sectarian interpretation thereof.[12]

One significant Qumran development in the direction of Tannaitic methodology was the rudimentary collection of rules under subject rubrics introduced by the preposition על. Another is the use of nomenclature to identify various areas of halakha similar to that found in the earliest strata of the Mishnah.

The laws of the Sabbath in the Damascus Document, much like those in Jubilees, offer parallels to rules which in talmudic halakha would be classified as שבות, or functionally as fences about the Torah. Yet, they are not distinguished from biblical prohibitions or treated with greater leniency, even when life may be threatened. Moreover, we do not yet find in the Qumran Sabbath laws the kind of conceptual analysis and generalized principles which are familiar from the Mishnah. The foregoing methodological observations seem by and large to be compatible with the chronological placement of the Qumran literature between Bible and Mishnah.

[12] See J. M. Baumgarten, "A 'Scriptural' Citation in 4Q Fragments of Damascus Document," *JJS* 43 (1992) 95-98.

THE JUDAISM(S) OF THE DAMASCUS DOCUMENT[*]

Philip R. Davies

University of Sheffield

A. *The Qumran Scrolls: One Judaism? Whose Judaism?*

Although there have been many descriptions of the "beliefs" of the Qumran community, the attempt to define a "Qumran Judaism" is, I think, a new exercise. It is now at least ten years since I was first invited to undertake such an exercise, and I have resisted the invitation until recently, because I was not convinced it could or even should be done. I am able to accept the basic premise that we have evidence of several Judaic systems at the end of the Second Temple period, including early Christianity, but to add to these either one— or several—"Qumran Judaisms" is a hazardous enterprise.

However, I have now begun to approach the task because I think it is worthwhile to map systematically the profiles of the Qumran texts within the context of Judaic systems generally and to ask the question, What sort of Judaism(s) do their writers espouse? Even if the attempt fails, it may generate useful methodology and important conclusions. The task is given some impetus by the view of Norman Golb that the Qumran texts are no more than the contents of Jewish libraries, by Lawrence Schiffman's contention that they stand firmly within the main lines of what he regards as Judaism, focussed on obedience to the Mosaic law, and by the quite different claims of Eisenman that they reflect a popular messianic-nationalistic movement embracing Maccabees, Zealots and early Christians.[1] Such divergences of opinion suggest the need for a disciplined analysis of the Judaic systems of the Scrolls and, as in the case of Golb, perhaps even cast some doubt on whether there are any such systems to be found here. I am therefore offering some preliminary thoughts, starting with methodological issues and then sketching out provisional conclusions.

---

[*] I would like to thank Prof. Joseph M. Baumgarten for his many helpful comments on this paper, and have tried to address as many of his questions as possible in my final version.

[1] See N. Golb, *Who Wrote the Dead Sea Scrolls? The Search for the Secret of Qumran* (New York: Scribner's, 1994); L. H. Schiffman, *Reclaiming the Dead Sea Scrolls. The History of Judaism, the Background of Christianity, the Lost Library of Qumran* (Philadelphia: JPS, 1994); R. O. Eisenman, *Maccabees, Zadokites, Christians and Qumran* (Studia Postbiblica 34; Leiden: E. J. Brill, 1983).

B. *Method*

The uncomplicated approach of decades ago is not possible. Then, the Community Rule was taken to define a "Qumran Community" and the sum total of the non-biblical manuscripts published at the time (Cave 1 plus Allegro's Cave 4 texts plus CD) was assembled, more or less selectively, into an account of what this sect (widely identified with the Essenes described by Philo, Josephus and Pliny) believed and practised. With further publications and reflections, the diversity of the Scrolls' contents now precludes such an approach. Already, with the publication of the Temple Scroll,[2] Y. Yadin's view that it represented the views of the *yaḥad* was rightly criticized.[3] More recently, the Halakhic Letter, 4QMMT, has underlined the issue of purity laws as a matter of fundamental disagreement, perhaps the basis of a sectarian rift. It is also evident that the calendar and the priestly courses are concerns in some Qumran texts. Again, while the number of formally dualistic texts (once thought to represent the most distinctive Qumran doctrine) represents an extremely small proportion of the whole, the number of wisdom texts (whose "sectarian" character is often difficult to establish) is rather large. Indeed, the recognition that the majority of Qumran texts may not have originated at Qumran itself is becoming widely adopted. Hence, to reduce the contents of the eleven manuscript caves to a "Qumran Judaism" without a rigorous method appears impossible, and perhaps to try to reduce them to a single Judaism at all is imprudent.

Two approaches to the task are possible, nevertheless, and they parallel the two ways in which a biblical theology, for example, might be constructed. One is a canonical, literary, synchronic approach, treating all the texts as of equal status and harmonising them into a system. The result, in the case of the Qumran manuscripts, would be a Judaism of texts, a Judaism that did not necessarily represent the belief system of any one individual, let alone a community. I am interested in the second approach, which addresses itself to real historical systems—Judaisms that at least some people once adhered to—rather than a dogmatic or systematic reading of an entire literary corpus.

Yet, the problems facing a historical analysis are profound. We cannot be certain where these scrolls came from before they were deposited; we cannot agree on the identity of their authors or keep-

---

    [2] Y. Yadin, *Megillat ha-Miqdaš* (Jerusalem: Israel Exploration Society, 1977; ET: *The Temple Scroll*, 1983).
    [3] See B. A. Levine, "The 'Temple Scroll': Aspects of Its Historical Provenance and Literary Character," *BASOR* 232 (1978) 5-23.

ers; we cannot agree on the historical relationship between the writings. There is no good reason, for instance, to give special priority *a priori* to the Community Rule, the Habakkuk pesher, 4QMMT or the Temple Scroll. Each of these texts offers a very different basis for exploring the Judaisms of the Qumran scrolls.

To add to these difficulties, the large number of different hands responsible for the 800 or so manuscripts, the evidence of different recensions of the Community Rule, War Scroll and the Damascus materials, and the proliferation of textual forms of the scriptural scrolls, all complicate to a considerable degree our perception of the nature of this archive. Can we really imagine them to have formed a single communal library? Or were they the possessions of individual members of one or more communities or, indeed, archive copies from different libraries? Can we first establish what significance, if any, attaches to the presence of a text in a cave by the Dead Sea, including Masada? For not every scholar now agrees on the relationship between the Qumran settlement and the Scrolls.

Rather than disqualifying any attempt to define a Judaism or Judaisms of the Qumran Scrolls, these many complications and uncertainties encourage me to believe that the task is worthwhile. If we cannot establish any consensus on historical questions, then perhaps a different approach may be helpful. Perhaps a systematic analysis of the Judaisms of the Scrolls can, in fact, contribute to clarifying historical questions about the coherence of the archive, about the central issues of authorship and ownership, about common and disputed criteria of what Judaism is. It is possible to ask, What categories of thought do these texts share among themselves and with non-Qumran texts? And which do they not share?

It seems to me that such an approach can be successful if it abandons, at least as a starting point, any historical theory and analyzes individual texts or clearly related groups of texts in isolation before attempting a synthesis. We shall be aware from the start that there are links between some of these texts: a solar calendar, the light-darkness dualism, the figure of a Teacher of Righteousness, certain halakhic rulings, the pesher genre. Indeed, these connections invite the scholar to explore systemic connections. But at the level of description, we must begin with discrete texts, not with shared characteristics. It is in individual compositions (whether redacted or not) that we must look for systematic expositions of Judaism, and not in collections of texts whose precise relationship is the goal, not a presupposition, of the analysis.

Not many of the Qumran texts are extensive enough to express a system. We may start with what we call D and S, represented by several manuscripts but chiefly by the Damascus Document and the Community Rule, respectively.[4] Both present a distinct Jewish society, a community or organization and both contain rules, definitions of insiders and outsiders, and doctrines. D also presents a history. I shall start with D because it offers a wider scope, not because I assign to it any particular priority within the Qumran corpus.

C. *The Judaism of the Damascus Sect (D)*

The best preserved manuscripts of D come from the geniza of a mediaeval synagogue in Cairo, and while they overlap with the Qumran manuscripts, unfortunately they do so only partially and their common text is not identical (indeed, even where they overlap, Cairo ms. A is not identical to B). The fragments from Caves 4, 5 and 6 confirm that D texts form a major part of the Qumran archive and that the text of Cairo ms. A is reasonably reliable. It is unwise to "correct" the Cairo manuscripts in order to reconstruct an "original" form of the document, because that implies a theory of a unilinear process of composition and redaction. In addition to D, the S and M materials comprise manuscripts with different arrangements of the same or similar material; let us thus accept that the notion of an "original" S, M or D is just that—a notion. There is for us no definitive version of D, S or M, and we cannot say that the Qumran collection contains *any* definitive edition. I use CD to reconstruct a Judaism on the understanding that nothing I say about that Judaism will be contradicted by the Qumran manuscripts.

The Damascus Document is divided into two sections, customarily known as the Admonition and the Laws; the Cave 4 fragments confirm that they belong together. The Admonition includes a number of statements about the origin of the group or groups to which it testifies, while the Laws contain collections of rulings governing the conduct of the group's "cities" and "camps." Because of space limitations, I shall analyse the Judaism of D under these three headings: Israel, Torah and Temple.

---

[4] Even here, of course, the problem of literary evolution presents an obstacle. There is no one Community Rule but rather a set of manuscripts, probably of different editions of such a composition, and the same is true of a Damascus Document. The possibility that some manuscripts belong to sources, rather than editions, of other compositions (this is probably the case of many texts identified as M[ilḥamah]) is an added difficulty. Perhaps such considerations belong to an investigation of the history of systems.

1. *Israel*

The D group calls itself "Israel," specifically in the sense of the true remnant of Israel and as an Israel, historically speaking, within an Israel (1:4-5, 3:13, 4:4-5, etc.). This is one reason why I regard it as a sect; the other reason is that this particular "Israel" segregated itself spatially and socially from other Judaisms. D speaks of the historical "Israel" that has gone astray in the past and continues to be in error (1:4, 3:14, 4:16, 5:21, 6:1, etc.). The review of that Israel's history (2:16-18) shows it to have come to grief through disobedience, for which it was punished during the exile under Nebuchadnezzar (1:6). The new Israel was reconstituted by a new covenant, a new law and a new lawgiver (3:12-16, 6:2-11). The origins of the "New Covenant" community therefore parallel other accounts that speak of a new start after the Babylonian exile; they effectively dismiss the earlier period as disastrous (e.g., Daniel, Enoch), while paralleling the stories of Ezra and Nehemiah, contained in the canonized narrative of rabbinic Judaism in which a covenant on the basis of divine law is re-affirmed by a repentant community. The claim that D's Israel is the true successor of the scriptural Israel is underlined by extensive quotations and allusions to the books of Moses and the prophets, to an extent that one may, at times, describe CD's text as a tissue or mosaic.[5]

CD regulates dealings not only with non-Jews but also with the Israel that is still in serious error and bound for imminent divine destruction. This other Israel is to be strenuously avoided (although converts are welcome and perhaps even sought), because the fate of the "covenant of the former ones," the pre-exilic Israel, is to be repeated at the end of the present age of wrath which began with the exile. During that long period, historical Israel was led astray by Belial and by its leaders, while the true Israel was preserved. Members of the historical Israel were designated "children of perdition" (בני השחת, 13:14).

The relationship between historical Israel and the Israel of the "Damascus Covenant" is expressed in dualistic and predestinarian terms. In one passage (2:2-13) God is said to have chosen some and rejected others "from eternity," and to foreknow their existence; in each generation a chosen remnant has been left. This unique passage does not, however, introduce the names of heavenly beings. The role of Belial is confined to leading astray the historical Israel

---

[5] The extent of such scriptural allusion has been fully explored by J. G. Campbell, *The Use of Scripture in the Damascus Document 1-8, 19-20* (Berlin: de Gruyter, 1995).

(4:12-13) and trying to lure away members of the New Covenant (cf. 12:2, where "spirits of Belial" are mentioned). Nowhere in this account is there an angelic counterpart to Belial: God is his sole opponent.[6] There is no cosmic or psychological dualism, merely a clear division between those elected and those rejected, with Belial active among both.

CD's Israel is divided into "Israel" and "Aaron" (1:7; 6:2; 19:10-11) and further subdivided into priests, Levites, Israelites and *gerim* (14:3-4). While *gerim* could of course indicate non-Jews, it seems more likely that the term has already acquired its rabbinic meaning, "proselyte." Just as in Ezekiel (e.g., 47:22) a non-Israelite resident of the land is to be reckoned among the tribes of Israel, so from the perspective of CD, other Jews may be admitted to the community, perhaps initially with the lowly status of *gerim*. Thus, members of historical Israel are still distinguished, at least for certain purposes, from non-Jews, and even the slaves of the "Damascus sect" must belong to the "covenant of Abraham."

CD's Israel is organized according to the Book of Numbers, dwelling in "camps"[7] and ordered into thousands, hundreds, fifties and tens (13:1-2). This structure may imply a recapitulation of the origins of historical Israel, with the wilderness period between the reception of the covenant and the entry into the promised land. Israel in the wilderness also had the holy Ark and Sanctuary in its midst; there was no Temple. That the D sect thought itself to be geographically as well as typologically living "in the wilderness" (as has long been argued by S. Talmon[8]) is very probable; thus it believes itself to be the real Israel and models itself accordingly.

---

[6] There is a reference to a "Prince of Lights" (CD 5:18), who raised up Moses and Aaron, while Belial raised up Jannes and Jambres. This should imply a belief in a formally dualistic theology, but nowhere else in the document where the present or future is described do we find any reference to the role of such a character, only to the malignant activity of Belial (see also 16:4-6). It would thus not be correct to say that D is unaware of an assisting angel whose work can be contrasted to Belial. Yet, such a figure is not included in D's account of the contemporary situation and does not play a role in the sect's self-definition.

[7] There is also legislation in D for "cities"; the relationship between the two kinds of settlements is, however, very unclear. In 4QMMT 60, Jerusalem is called the "head of the [c]amps of Israel"; in 30-31 we find, even more confusingly, "camp of their cit[i]es".

[8] S. Talmon, "The Desert Motif in the Bible and in Qumran Literature," *Biblical Motifs, Origins and Transformations* (ed. A. Altman; Cambridge: Harvard University Press, 1966) 31-63; idem, "Between the Bible and the Mishna," *The World of Qumran from Within* (Jerusalem: Magnes, 1989) 11-52 (esp. 41-51).

2. *Torah*

The Israel of CD is constituted by scrupulous obedience to the *torah* as revealed in its own covenant. This new *torah* is created by exegetical development of the scriptural *torah* rather than by a new text, though the new *torah* may be expressed in texts such as CD itself, or even in the Book of Jubilees (mentioned in 16:3-4). Thus the collections of laws in CD which govern communal life are, in nearly every case, clearly derived directly or by exegesis from the laws of Moses.[9] They cover matters of holiness, discipline, Sabbath observance and commerce. The members of the "New Covenant" swear to "return to the *torah* of Moses," the details of which must be learnt by every member before being examined by the *mevaqqer* (15:10-11).

The laws governing the life of this group, then, are regarded as Mosaic *torah*, and a distinction is made between the written scriptural text which the New Covenanters share with historical Israel and its fuller explication in the laws of the group, which are called פרוש (6:14). The scriptural *torah* is also called נגלה ("revealed") while the *torah* of the D sect is נסתר ("hidden").[10] There are of course similarities to rabbinic Judaism's written and oral Torahs, especially in the presentation of the results of exegesis as revealed, but there are also differences. The distinction between "written" and "oral" is absent: the law is not regarded as "dual." CD also legislates for a real but sectarian community, and the Torah is not discussed by learned authorities (Rabbis) but presented as if divinely commanded, *verbatim*. The use of scriptural formulae in D's laws (על ואיש ... לא; על + imperative; -כל ה etc.) reinforces the lack of any distinction between Scripture and the sectarian law as equally and fully binding Torah.

---

[9] Thus I have argued in "Halakhah at Qumran," *A Tribute to Geza Vermes. Essays on Jewish and Christian Literature and History* (ed. P. R. Davies and R. T. White; JSOTSup 100; Sheffield: JSOT, 1990) 37-50. But there are traces of community discipline (the פרוש המשפטים) in the 4QD texts, which have been analyzed by Baumgarten in "The Cave 4 Version of the Qumran Penal Code," *JJS* 43 (1992) 268-76. See also *Qumran Cave 4.XIII. The Damascus Document (4Q266-273)* (DJD 18; Oxford: Clarendon, 1996) and C. Hempel, "The Penal Code Reconsidered," *Legal Texts and Legal Issues. Proceedings of the Second Meeting of the International Organization for Qumran Studies, Cambridge, 1995 Published in Honour of Joseph M. Baumgarten* (ed. M. J. Bernstein, F. García Martínez and J. Kampen; STDJ 23; Leiden: Brill, 1997) 337-48. Hempel suggests that these have been influenced by S terminology (as I also think probable), but agrees that the D community had a penal code. This may indeed be so, and yet the two disciplinary laws that Hempel assigns to D, fornication and "murmuring" against fathers and mothers, have a clear scriptural basis. I cannot therefore concede that D displays a body of sectarian law that is not conceived as scripturally derived.

[10] For full discussion of these distinctions and terminology, see L. H. Schiffman, *The Halakhah at Qumran* (SJLA 16; Leiden: E. J. Brill, 1975).

The calendar (3:13) is undoubtedly a major concern of D's Judaism, and it is something to which historical Israel is "blind." Another major difference between D's Israel and the "historical" Israel lies in attitudes concerning sexual relations (4:19-5:11), specifically intercourse during the menstrual period, divorce/polygamy, and marriage between uncle and niece. In all these cases, CD invokes the scriptures common to it and other Judaisms but interprets according to its own exegesis.

D's *torah* seems to view sexual relations as purely for procreation. Sexual activity apart from the legitimate bounds of a single lawful marriage is denounced as "lust" זנות. Sexual intercourse is intrinsically unclean and may not take place in the "city of the sanctuary" (12:1-2). Its members may marry and raise children (7:6-8) but the implication is that some, perhaps the majority, do not. The hint of a celibate lifestyle among this group is apparently the product of a concern for holiness and it seems to follow that if a D settlement existed within Jerusalem, its members were necessarily celibate.

Another important feature of the *torah* of D is that it is valid only for a specific period of time, from the exile and subsequent revelation of true law to the appearance of an eschatological teacher (6:10-11, 15:6-7). The clear implication is that the validity of this law will be affected by the arrival of this messianic "teacher" (12:23-13:1). There is some evidence of a calculation of this "period of wickedness/wrath" and thus of the appearance of the messiah-teacher (4:8-9). The 390 years of 1:5 probably also reflects such a calculation.

3. *Temple*

Several laws in CD reveal the extent of participation in the Temple cult by members of the "Damascus community" (6:17-18, 9:14, 11:18-19, 12:1-2, 16:13). From these laws it emerges that:

1. offerings were made at the altar, or could be sent. Several different kinds of offerings are mentioned: burnt-offerings (עולות, מנחות, incense, wood, sin-offering), while the performance of the daily תמיד is assumed.

2. Participation in the major festivals may be included, if 12:1-2 applies to visitors to Jerusalem.

3. Vows extend participation in the Temple cult to private and even voluntary acts.

4. The use of Prov. 15:8 in CD 11:18-19 suggests that offerings on the altar may be replaced by righteousness and prayer. But the text is cited to defend the *sanctity* of the altar, running in fact counter to both the spirit and the letter of the biblical text.

The key to the place of the Jerusalem Temple in the Judaism of CD occurs in 6:11-14:

> And all who have entered the covenant are not to enter the sanctuary "to light my altar in vain" unless they follow the observances of the law prescribed for the period of wickedness.

If this translation is correct (the reading is awkward and the passage may have been emended), there is a link between participation in the Temple cult and the "law for the period of wickedness." The Temple lies at the centre of the "wickedness," for 20:22-23 speaks of the time when "Israel sinned and made the sanctuary unclean." Historical Israel inevitably and habitually defiled the Temple but those who possess the (true) law need not abandon it. Israel, specifically its priests, might "light the altar in vain," but it could still be lit in some way by those who observed the law exactly.

D's Judaism partially (but not totally) replaces the function of the Temple with its own institutions. CD 7:14-19, quoting and interpreting Amos 5:25-27 (the prophecy of the exile beyond Damascus) speaks of the exile of the books of the Law and the Prophets. Amos' "tent" is the divine sanctuary; the Temple and the "booth of the king" are "the books of the Law"; the "king" is the "assembly." Hence, the sect's own places of worship are the sites to which the law has been "exiled," from the previous place of worship, the Temple. The Temple is no longer the site of law, though it remains the site of whatever cultic observance is still permissible. The Temple thus remains central to D's Judaism, but must be coupled with observance of the true Torah and cannot, of course, be used validly by those outside the sect.

D. *The Judaism of the Yaḥad (S)*

1. *S as a transformation of D*

The Judaism of the *yaḥad* is represented most obviously in the S texts. Although the Community Rule has certainly played the dominant role in Qumran scholarship, it is not an easy text to unravel.[11] It is obviously an amalgam of genres with little discernible structure. Both on internal grounds and on the basis of comparison with the Cave 4 fragments, it may be seen as either one of a number of pos-

---

[11] Strictly speaking it is only part of a manuscript. The manuscript contains material regarded as separate and dubbed 1QSa and 1QSb. Whether we should really speak of three texts rather than one manuscript is an interesting point; but for the sake of simplicity, let us adhere to the convention.

sible scribal assemblages of material, or as a text that has evolved by
a redactional process that can more or less be reconstructed.[12] It
does not display a coherent sequence or structure and it contains no
historical statements (whether reliable or not). It is not the ideal text
with which to reconstruct the Qumran family of Judaisms.

But the *yaḥad* is also represented in CD and, indeed, CD itself
has, strictly speaking, also to be regarded as a *yaḥad* text; by many
scholars it continues to be regarded as such and is hardly differenti-
ated from the S texts. Yet, it represents a redaction by one group of
a document that substantially comprises the ideology of another.
The reasons for this conclusion I have given elsewhere, and I cannot
review them here.[13] I shall merely cite some of the evidence. Cairo
ms. A (containing the Admonition) is itself the product of an S revi-
sion, because the expected messianic "teacher" appears as a *past* figure in 1:12, while his death is referred to in 20:14-15. At the end of
the Admonition, it is his voice that, along with the sectarian law,
constitutes supreme authority (20:27-28), again corresponding to his
expected function in 6:11. The word *yaḥad* appears in connection
with the contents of ms. B but nowhere in ms. A.

I have argued that it is significant that D has been revised and not
replaced or abandoned. The Judaism of S is a *transformation* of the
Judaism of D or, in its own terms, its proper fulfilment, its final ma-
turity. Simply put, S represents the Judaism of D in which an inter-
im devotion, valid for the "period of wrath," to the correctly interpreted Mosaic law shares authority with a charismatic leader
believed to be a/the messiah forecast in CD. A parallel between the
Judaism of Christianity and other Judaisms is attractive: it should
not be overemphasised or ignored, because the function of the common stock of scriptures in emerging Christianity, which added its
own scriptures, provides a helpful analogy to the continued use of D
texts by the S community or *yaḥad*.

Thus, I regard the Judaism of the *yaḥad* as a development of that
of the "Damascus" group and, because I have argued this case elsewhere, it serves in this instance not as a presupposition but as a part
of my analysis of Qumran Judaisms that has been accomplished already. In what follows, I shall confine myself substantially to the S
material proper.

---

[12] J. Murphy-O'Connor, "La génèse littéraire de la 'Règle de la Communauté',"
RB 76 (1969) 528-49; J. Pouilly, *La Règle de la communauté de Qumrân: son évolution lit-
téraire* (Paris: Gabalda, 1976). See also S. Metso, *The Textual Development of the Qumran
Community Rule* (STDJ 21; Leiden: E. J. Brill, 1997).
[13] P. R. Davies, *The Damascus Covenant. An Interpretation of the Damascus Document*
(JSOTSup 25; Sheffield: JSOT, 1983).

2. *Israel*

In defining the term "Israel," the strong dualism of S is most notable; 1QS calls its members "children of light" (1QS 1:8, 3:24) or
"children of truth" (4:5), apparently regarding the remainder of the
human race, whether Jew or non-Jew, as children of darkness or
falsehood. This dualism, explicated in 1QS 3-4, nevertheless com-
bines not only several sets of terminology (light/dark, truth/false;
righteousness/wickedness) but also offers simultaneously a cosmic
and a psychological version of its dualism, in which the two "spirits"
now appear as subordinate deities to the "god of knowledge," and
also as internalized dispositions similar to the rabbinic good and evil
yetzer (the term *yetzer* does occur elsewhere in 1QS). Thus, the *category* "Israel," maintained and intensified in D, has much less of a role
in this Judaism: historical Israel is not the focus of opposition and
there is no opposition between Israel and the nations. The perspective is universalized both cosmically and psychologically. On an eth-
ical level, the same transformation is evident in the final chapter of
Daniel, where the nationalistic perspective of chs. 2 and 7 is replaced by a righteous/wicked dichotomy. The predestination that
plays on the fringes of CD here occupies a central place. The inter-
im "period of wrath" of CD, between the revelation of true law and
the revelation of true teaching, has its counterpart here in a period
of "dominion of Belial" (1QS 1:23-24), between the creation of two
spirits at the very beginning of time and the final destruction of
Belial and his heavenly and earthly followers.[14]

It has long been taken for granted that the *yaḥad* was a celibate
group. Conceived as a sanctuary (rather than, as in D, a place where
the true law lives and right worship must be practiced), the *yaḥad*
operated under the regime of priestly purity, in which women would
necessarily have been excluded. But this orientation was not entirely
unparalleled, for the attitude of D towards sex as intrinsically unholy
and the evidence that some of its settlements consisted of celibate
males mean that the custom was known, although interpreted differently (much as Paul's Christianity inherited bathing as a rite of en-
trance into Judaism but transformed its imagery into rebirth after
Christ). But the possibility that women were in some way associated
with the *yaḥad* nevertheless continues to be entertained, largely be-

---

[14] In 9:9-11a messianic hope remains: a prophet and the two messiahs (of Aaron
and Israel) are awaited; the members must still be ruled by the "former ordinances"
(i.e., those of D). Such texts warn against assuming 1QS to be a homogenous text.
It is clearly a repository of several stages in the transition from D to S Judaism in
the *yaḥad*; whether these stages can be reconstructed in detail remains dubious.

cause of the discovery of female skeletons, as well as those of children, in a cemetery on the outskirts of Qumran and from the references to marriage in CD and in 1QSa and to women in other documents associated with the *yaḥad*. Such opinions to some degree
reflect a failure (or a refusal) to distinguish between the portrait of
CD and of 1QS, and thus between possibly different Qumran Judaisms.[15]

3. *Torah*

The importance of the "Torah of Moses" is retained, and with it the
importance of correct observation of set times which implies, no
doubt, the 364-day calendar (1:14-15). In S's covenant, however,
less importance is attached to obedience to the covenant *torah* and
more to possession of "knowledge." In D, "Torah" connotes a single
body of revealed law as the basis for communal living. In S's
Judaism, although the will of God and the law of Moses are invoked,
the language is overwhelmingly of esoteric "knowledge" (1:1, 1-2,
etc.), "insight" (2:3, etc.), "counsel" (3:6, etc.) and "truth" (3:7, 4:6,
etc.). The large number of wisdom texts now recovered from Cave 4
appear to strengthen the impression that the owners of these texts
succumbed to a "wisdom" worldview, which might explain their at-
tachment to dualism. But the wisdom of 1QS resembles a form of
gnosticism, a term that needs to be used with caution, although it
may be justified. The Judaism of S, to be sure, does not separate the
god of creation from the god of salvation but it does appear to regard esoteric *knowledge* as a *sine qua non* of salvation. This represents a
decisive movement beyond CD's notion of a specially revealed *torah*.
The esoteric body of knowledge is imparted to each member by a
maskil (not a *mevaqqer*, as in D); the term itself has roots in wisdom
terminology (and also in Daniel 12).

Evidence that the *yaḥad* was a more rigorously regimented society
than that/those of D is apparent in the emphasis on the allotted status of each member (2:20-23), repetition of the word "authority" (of

---

[15] See, for example, J. M. Baumgarten, "The Qumran-Essene Restraints on
Marriage," *Archaeology and History in the Dead Sea Scrolls: The New York University
Conference in Memory of Yigael Yadin* (ed. L. H. Schiffman; JSPSup 8; JSOT/ASOR
MS 2; Sheffield: JSOT, 1990) 13-24, specifically 20: "...celibacy at Qumran was
never made into a universal norm. It was confined to those who emulated a 'perfection of holiness' requiring uninterrupted purity, and even for them perhaps only
in the later stages of their lives. This would account for the fact that the *Messianic
Rule*, in describing the practices of Israel at large, assumes that marriage would continue to be the 'order of the land'" (Baumgarten is quoting from CD 7:6).

Zadokites and others) and the practice of sharing goods in common (not found in CD). This is commensurate with a small group founded on the teachings of a charismatic leader, especially one threatened by a larger parent movement which was still regarded as hostile having, in the view of the members of the *yaḥad*, "rejected" the Teacher.

4. *Temple*

The hostile attitude of CD towards the defiled Temple cult, which was a product of high reverence for the sanctuary, is replaced in 1QS by an apparent rejection of its efficacy. A group of men constituting a "council of the community" are described in terms that present them as a human sanctuary:

> ... the community council shall be built on truth, like an eternal plantation, a holy house for Israel and the foundation of the Holy of Holies for Aaron ... to atone for the world ... the tested rampart, the prized cornerstone ... the most holy dwelling for Aaron ... a house of perfection and truth (8:5-9).

Similarly, the Temple cult will be superseded:

> ... in order to atone for guilt of rebellion and for sin of unfaithfulness so as to win [divine] favour for the land without the flesh of burnt offerings and the fat of sacrifices ... rightly-offered prayer shall be the fragrance of righteousness and perfection of way a delightful freewill offering ... the men of the *yaḥad* shall set apart a house of holiness for Aaron ... (9:4-6).

In an even more radical manner, we might add, the function of water as a cleansing agent is downplayed: "it is by the holy spirit of the *yaḥad* in [God's] truth that [a man] can be cleansed from all his iniquities" (3:7-8). Also, circumcision is downplayed, for "he shall rather circumcise in the *yaḥad* the foreskin of his *yetzer* ..." (5:5).

The conclusion to be drawn about the Judaism of S is that common institutions of all Judaisms were not abandoned, but their efficacy was confined to the *yaḥad*. Every Jewish symbol is strictly disciplined into a single ideological and social construction: the *yaḥad*. A much tighter structure is evident here than among the D groups, who do not even give a name to their communities, regarding themselves rather as members of the new, true covenant of Israel and of God. Judaism is defined not as the right practice and belief of the true Israel, defined by and loyal to the scriptures as they are read (as in D), but by a radical differentiation in other categories (light/darkness) and greater stress on cultic purity and community discipline (as opposed to a rigid adherence to the law of Moses). It represents, I think, quite a different sort of Judaism, in which continuity in space and time with other Judaisms is relatively unacknowledged.

E. *Other Qumran Judaisms?*

What we can identify clearly as "D" and "S" materials do not constitute the entirety, or even the bulk, of the Qumran literature. Are either of these Judaisms reflected also in other texts? The Rule of the Congregation (1QSa), for example, appears to describe a restored Israel and the majority of scholars[16] regard this "congregation" as an eschatological one. The term "last days" (1:1), however, could apply, from the perspective of the authors, to their own time or a future one. Equally, the closing words, "according to this ruling they shall proceed at every meal where ten men are gathered together," could designate a continuing practice in the present or the future. Stegemann has proposed that this text is in fact the earliest rule of the *yaḥad*, predating the rules of both CD and 1QS, which he regards as applying to the same communities,[17] while Hempel has argued that in its original form this was a non-eschatological rule of the D group (which she identifies as the "parent Essene movement"), revised from the perspective of the *yaḥad*.[18]

The case of "M" (= *Milḥamah*, מלחמה "war") material illustrates a further range of difficulties, for "M" does not stand for a system, a Judaism, or a particular social organization, but merely for a topic.[19] Indeed, 1QM is a specific recension of materials that are found in other recensions in Cave 4. Further, it displays a combination of fragments of two or more ideological systems. The dualistic framework in which cols. 15-19 are cast must be compared with that of 1QS, where "children of light" and "children of darkness" (in 1QM the terminology is more consistent) constitute the opposing forces, although the "Kittim" are also on the side of "darkness." However, cols. 2-9 and most of col. 14 exhibit, by contrast, a nationalistic ideology in which Israel and the nations oppose each other. The vari-

---

[16] L. H. Schiffman, "The Temple Scroll and the Systems of Jewish Law of the Second Temple Period," *Temple Scroll Studies* (ed. G. J. Brooke; JSPSup 7; Sheffield: JSOT, 1989) 239-55.

[17] H. Stegemann, *Die Essener, Qumran, Johannes der Täufer und Jesus* (Freiburg: Herder, 1993).

[18] C. Hempel, "The Earthly Essene Nucleus of 1QSa," *DSD* 3 (1996) 253-69.

[19] Again the search for a definitive edition of this "document" is fruitless. Instead, it is necessary to focus on an actual text. The conclusions assumed here are those argued in my *1QM, The War Scroll from Qumran* (Rome: Biblical Institute Press, 1977).

ous elements have probably been fused (with limited success) in col. 1, where a dualistic battle precedes world-wide conquest.

Finally, I shall consider briefly two texts that are frequently claimed to be central to "Qumran Judaism," 4QMMT and 11QT. Although 4QMMT, if it is a single text,[20] cannot deliver sufficient evidence of a system, several current commentators have taken the view that it reveals that the origins of "Qumran Judaism" lie in a dispute between Temple authorities and a dissident group over issues of cultic (specifically purity) law. The fragments plausibly convey the impression of differing traditions, expressed with some force but without outright hostility. 4QMMT may imply that some formal separation has already taken place, however (C7: "we have separated ourselves [פרשנו] from the multitude [רוב] of the people"). Some support for a formal separation may be found in the description of Jerusalem as the "camp of holiness" and "head of the camps of Israel" (cf. B60-62, 29-30). Settlements called "camps" are distinctive of the organization of the D sect which, as has been seen, also venerated the holiness of Jerusalem and the Temple. Further, a concern for what the writers regard as illicit sexual union is also expressed more than once (B48, B75, B82), consistent with a major source of opposition between the writers of CD and their opponents. It is therefore entirely permissible to include 4QMMT as a text consistent with the Judaism of D, though not with that of S. Nevertheless, if the writers had not yet constituted themselves as a sectarian Israel, developing a distinct self-understanding as a true Israel within Israel, it is uncertain whether they had yet sufficiently articulated a system that we could identify as a distinct "Judaism."

The Temple Scroll has also been taken from time to time as a central text of "Qumran Judaism," although, as mentioned earlier, its publication sparked a dispute about whether it was "sectarian," predicated on its similarities to the contents of 1QS. It can probably be concluded that these two texts have no marked affinities.

Some affinity with the Judaism of D, on the other hand, seems likely.[21] For instance, in both 11QT 45:11 and CD 12:1, the phrase "city of the sanctuary" occurs, and no sexual activity is permitted therein, according to both texts. But the range of material available for comparison is not extensive, given the different subject matter of the two texts. The issue of precise legal correspondences between

---

[20] See Strugnell in *Qumran Cave 4.V. Miqṣat Maʿaśeh Ha-Torah* (ed. E. Qimron and J. Strugnell; DJD 10; Oxford: Clarendon, 1994) 203-6.

[21] See P. R. Davies, "The Temple Scroll and the Damascus Document," *Temple Scroll Studies*, 201-10.

11QT, CD and 4QMMT has been taken up by Schiffman,[22] though not definitively because, like so many Qumran scholars, he is concerned with aspects of Jewish systems in Qumran documents rather than with systems themselves.

F. *Further Problems*

1QM includes a dualistic system very close to that of 1QS, as well as fragments of a description of an Israel similar to that of 1QSa, while in col. 2 a restored Temple service is depicted and both priestly and lay leadership are defined (11QT?). The range of source materials as well as the range of ideological parallels alerts us to an important problem in the agenda of reconstructing Qumran Judaisms. When can we be certain that the Judaism of a text represents the Judaism of real Jews rather than of a compiler of a document? And if even one single text can reflect the views of an author/editor, how far is this person creating a Judaism? 1QM is a text composed from a number of sources, influenced by the dualism of S but also by other fragments from other Judaisms; that is really all. The relationship between it and any particular group to whom we might assign a Judaism is by no means clear. We may be dealing here (as we are, of course, with 1QS) with the product of a scribal recension that represents an individual effort at harmonizing varied texts into a coherent account of the final victory of light, Israel and God and the defeat of darkness, Rome and non-Jewish nations. The horrible suspicion that such a possibility raises is that in the Qumran archive we do not always (if at all) directly confront the ideological products of Jewish societies, but archival texts which represent copied, edited or even amalgamated versions of older texts.

The temptation to force as many texts as possible into the mold or molds just created (or discovered) for "D" and "S" Judaisms must be resisted. It is clear that not all Qumran texts represent a single Judaism and that several texts do not imply, or allow us to infer from them, a systematic Judaism; some texts may even be eclectic in this respect. The reason for the composition (or preservation) of texts in the Qumran archive may in each separate case have much, little or nothing to do with the articulation of a specific Judaism.

It is necessary to resist the temptation to incorporate common denominators of Qumran texts into the reconstruction of a "Qumran

---

[22] Schiffman, "The Temple Scroll and the Systems of Jewish Law of the Second Temple Period."

Judaism," for example, the existence of a calendar following a 364-day year of twelve 30-day months (plus four intercalated days). Several earlier studies have assumed the use (or even invention) of this calendar to be a definitive mark of the "Qumran community," but the dominance of this calendar in the Qumran archive does not prove that all such texts represent a "Qumran Judaism." A calendar alone does not make a Judaism, and it has not yet been demonstrated that 1 Enoch and Jubilees, where the same (or a similar) calendar is embraced, articulate a "Qumran Judaism." The same is true of the Song of the Sabbath Sacrifice collection. The heavenly liturgy to which they attest is *consistent* with a feature of S's Judaism in which a human community constitutes itself as a "Holy of Holies" but the tradition of a heavenly Temple cult to which humans may have access is itself widely attested outside this form of Judaism. The essential point is that we may well expect to find at Qumran texts *consistent* with a certain Judaism, but this does not entail that these texts actually express that Judaism. The number of texts amenable to fruitful comparison is, in fact, very small.

G. *Conclusions*

The definition of the Judaism(s) of the Dead Sea Scrolls poses a challenge that has so far not been very rigorously defined or addressed. The challenge is, above all, a methodological one. If, however, despite the many difficulties presented by the nature of the evidence, it is possible to identify and articulate its Judaic system(s), then the approach outlined above seems the most promising. With an initial identification of two such systems (D and S) and a hypothesis about the relationship between the two, there exists a critical foundation for the enterprise. On this basis, using the range of Qumran texts, other Qumran Judaisms can be sought and the evolution of these two Judaisms can also be investigated. However, it will be impossible to bring the entire archive within the scope of such a programme, and the realisation that several of these texts do not describe a Judaism and perhaps do not intend to describe a Judaism, means that the results will always be limited, and perhaps always provisional. This being said, the task is valuable not only for our understanding of the Qumran texts and their history but also for our growing but still very incomplete appreciation of the religious systems of late Second Temple Judah, a time and place which Jews and Christians especially, but also all many others, find of inescapable interest and importance.

CD 12:15-17 AND THE STONE VESSELS
FOUND AT QUMRAN[*]

Hanan Eshel

Bar-Ilan University

Introduction

The first man-made tools and vessels were of stone. These were later replaced by pottery and metal vessels and, from that time on, the use of stone vessels was limited to grinding and crushing, a practice which continues to the present. In the late Second Temple period, from the first century BCE to the second century CE, there was a stone vessel industry in the Jerusalem region whose products were used for storage and measurement.[1] These stone vessels were made for observant Jews who observed the laws of purity strictly since, according to rabbinic halakha, stone vessels remain pure.[2]

Stone vessels used for storage and measurement were found at Qumran and related sites—about two hundred pieces at Qumran; seventy fragments at Ein Feshka; and a few pieces at Ein el-Guwehr.[3] I found this archeological evidence puzzling. If, as some scholars claim, the sect held that stone vessels, like other vessels, are susceptible to impurity, how can we explain the presence of so many stone vessels at Qumran? This led me to re-examine two related sectarian halakhot.

[*] Thanks are due to Prof. M. Kister for his useful comments.

[1] For the archeological data regarding stone vessels used for measurement and storage in the late Second Temple period, see I. Magen, *The Stone Vessel Industry in Jerusalem during the Second Temple Period* (Jerusalem: Society for the Preservation of Nature, 1988) (Hebrew); J. M. Cahill, "The Chalk Assemblages of the Persian/Hellenistic and Early Roman Periods," *Excavations at the City of David, 1978-1985* (ed. A. De Groot and D. T. Ariel; Qedem 33; Jerusalem: Institute of Archaeology, Hebrew University of Jerusalem, 1992) 3.190-274; R. Deines, *Jüdische Steingefäße und pharisäische Frömmigkeit. Ein archaologisch-historischer Beitrag zum Verstandnis von Joh 2,6 und der judischen Reinheitshalacha zur Zeit Jesu* (WUNT 2; Tübingen: Mohr, 1993).

[2] M. Kel. 10:1; m. Oh. 5:5, 6:1; m. Par. 5:5; m. Miq. 4:1; m. Yad. 1:2.

[3] R. Donceel and P. Donceel-Voute, "The Archeology of Khirbet Qumran," *Methods of Investigation of the Dead Sea Scrolls and the Khirbet Qumran Site: Present Realities and Future Prospects* (ed. M. O. Wise et al.; New York: New York Academy of Sciences, 1994); P. Bar-Adon, "Another Settlement of the Judean Desert Sect at 'En el-Ghuweir on the Shores of the Dead Sea," *BASOR* 227 (1977) 15-18.

11QTemple 49:11-16

The first halakha is found in the Temple Scroll. From it we learn that, according to the sectarian halakhic system, millstones (רחיים) and mortars (מדוכה) can become impure:

וביום אשר יוציאו ממנו את המת יכבדו את הבית מכול
תגאולת שמן ויין ולחת מים. קרקעו וקרותיו ודלתותיו יגרודו
ומנעוליו ומזוזותיו ואספיו ומשקופיו יכבסו במים.
ביום אשר יצא המת ממנו יטהרו את הבית ואת כול כליו
וכול כלי עץ ברזל ונחושת, וכול כלים אשר יש להמה

טהרה ובגדים ושקים ועורות יתכבסו

> And on the day on which they will take the dead body out of it, they shall sweep the house of any defiling smirch of oil and wine and moisture of water; they shall scrape its floor and its walls and its doors, and they shall wash with water its locks and its doorposts and its thresholds and its lintels. On the day on which the dead body will leave it, they shall purify the house and all its vessels, (including) mills and mortars, and all vessels made of wood, iron and bronze, and all vessels that may be purified. And (all) clothing and sacks and skins shall be washed (col. 49:11-16).

The use of the phrase תגאולת שמן ויין ולחת מים "defiling smirch of oil and wine and moisture of water" evinces a resemblance between the halakha of the Temple Scroll and rabbinic halakha, according to which liquids make objects susceptible to impurity. Both systems are based on Lev. 11:34, 38, which states that food becomes impure only after it touches liquid. Therefore, if harvested crops which are no longer connected to the soil touch liquids, they are susceptible to impurity. These halakhot are discussed in m. Makshirin.

Yadin noted that the author of the Temple Scroll based himself here on Numbers 19, which he edited and expanded according to other laws in the book of Numbers.[4] Concerning the uncleanness of vessels Num. 19:14-15 states:

זאת התורה אדם כי ימות באהל כל הבא אל האהל וכל
אשר באהל יטמא שבעת ימים. וכל כלי פתוח אשר אין צמיד
פתיל עליו טמא הוא

> This is the procedure: When a person dies in a tent, whoever enters the tent and whoever is in the tent shall be unclean seven days; and every open vessel, with no lid fastened down, shall be unclean.

---

[4] Y. Yadin, ed., *The Temple Scroll* (Jerusalem: Israel Exploration Society, The Institute of Archaeology of the Hebrew University of Jerusalem and The Shrine of the Book, 1983) 2.212-16. See also M. O. Wise, *A Critical Study of the Temple Scroll from Qumran Cave 11* (Studies in Ancient Oriental Civilization 49; Chicago: Oriental Institute of the University of Chicago) 225.

The law from the Temple Scroll mentioned above fails to distinguish between open vessels and those which are closed with a lid. This distinction is found in 4Q274 frg. 3 col. ii:

וכול אשר יש לו חותם [וטמא]ן לטהור יותר

and any (vessel) which has a seal...[shall be unclean] for a more pure person.[5]

The author of the Temple Scroll integrated the description of the booty which fell into the hands of the Israelites as a result of the war with the Midianites (Num. 31:19-23) into the law of impure vessels which are in a dead person's house.

The description of the instructions to the Israelites follows:

ואתם חנו מחוץ למחנה שבעת ימים. כל הרג נפש וכל נוגע בחלל
תתחטאו, ביום השלישי וביום השביעי אתם ושביכם. וכל בגד
וכל כלי עור וכל מעשה עזים וכל כלי עץ תתחטאו. ואמר
אלעזר הכהן אל אנשי הצבא הבאים למלחמה, זאת חקת
התורה אשר ציוה ה׳ את משה: אך את הזהב ואת הכסף את
הנחושת את הברזל את הבדיל ואת העפרת, כל דבר אשר
יבא באש תעבירו באש וטהר, אך במי נידה יתחטא, וכל אשר
לא יבא באש תעבירו במים[6]

You shall then stay outside the camp seven days; everyone among you or among your captives who has slain a person or touched a corpse shall cleanse himself on the third and seventh days. You shall also cleanse every cloth, every article of skin, everything made of goats' hair, and every object of wood. Eleazar the priest said to the troops who had taken part in the fighting, "This is the ritual law that the Lord has enjoined upon Moses: Gold and silver, copper, iron, tin, and lead—any article that can withstand fire—these you shall pass through fire and they shall be clean, except that they must be cleansed with water of lustration; and anything that cannot withstand fire you must pass through water..." (Num. 31:19-23).

In the Temple Scroll three types of liquids—oil, wine, and water—are mentioned as susceptible to defilement. Nevertheless, the phrase מכול תגאולת שמן seems to imply that oil is more susceptible to defilement than wine and water. Accordingly, we may be more precise in our reading of the Temple Scroll: while the author of this halakha made global mention of "wood, iron, and copper vessels" (כלי עץ ברזל ונחושת), he did not include stone vessels among the other ones. Therefore it seems that the composition of the Temple Scroll antedated the development of the Jewish stone vessel industry.

---

[5] J. M. Baumgarten, "Liquids and Susceptibility to Defilement in New 4Q Texts," *JQR* 85 (1994) 96-100.

[6] The author of the Temple Scroll probably identified "everything made of

CD 12:15-17

The second law that concerns stone vessels is found in the Damascus Document:

וכל <u>העצים האבנים והעפר</u> אשר יגואלו בטמאת האדם <u>לגאולי</u>
<u>שמן</u> בהם כפי טמאתם יטמא הנ[ו]גע בם

> And all the wood, stones, and dust which are defiled by human impurity while having oil stains on them, according to their impurity shall he who t[o]uches them become impure (12:15-17).

The readings of the early editions of this text were corrected in an important article J. Baumgarten devoted to this halakha.[7] Based on his article, the readings שמן (oil) rather then שמו (his name), as well as בהם instead of כהם, were accepted. In the same article Baumgarten singled out the term, גאולי שמן ("while having oil stains on them"), as the crucial phrase in this halakha. According to his interpretation, it should be emphasized that the presence of oil stains on wood, stone, and dust serves to transmit impurity.[8] Louis Ginzberg has suggested that the halakha under consideration suffered from homoioteleuton, and originally read: וכל <כלי> והאבנים והעפר "And all the wood, stones, and dust **vessel**"; alternately, a *yod* was dropped, and the text should read וכל<י> "And vessels of wood, stones, and dust."[9]

I find this proposal acceptable for three reasons; the first is technical:

1. This halakha is followed by another law which reads: ...וכל כלי מסמר, "and any vessel, nail...." Therefore we may argue that the beginning of our halakha was formulated in the same manner.

2. In rabbinic halakha stone vessels and dust vessels are mentioned together as not being susceptible to impurity.[10]

---

goats' hair" (Num. 31:20) with the "sack" mentioned in Lev. 11:32. At Qumran, Masada, and other caves in the Judean desert, articles made of wool, cotton, and goats' hair were discovered; the latter was usually used for sacks. See A. Sheffer and H. Granger-Taylor, "Textiles from Masada," *Masada 4: The Yigael Yadin Excavations 1963-1965, Final Reports* (Jerusalem: Israel Exploration Society, Hebrew University of Jerusalem, 1994) 173.

[7] J. M. Baumgarten, "The Essene Avoidance of Oil and the Laws of Purity," *RevQ* 6/22 (1967) 183-92. For an opposing view, see S. B. Hoenig, "Qumran Rules of Impurities," *RevQ* 6/24 (1969) 559-67. Nevertheless, the halakhot of the Temple Scroll discussed above as well as 4Q513, to be discussed below, prove that Baumgarten was correct. The prohibition is based on purity laws and not on pagan defilement as Hoenig suggests elsewhere ("Oil and Pagan Defilement," *JQR* 61 [1970] 63-75).

[8] See J. M. Baumgarten and D. R. Schwartz, "Damascus Document (CD)," *The Dead Sea Scrolls: Hebrew, Aramaic, and Greek Texts with English Translations* (ed. J. H. Charlesworth; Tübingen: Mohr-Siebeck, 1995) 2.53.

[9] L. Ginzberg, *An Unknown Jewish Sect* (New York: JTS, 1976) 81-82, 115.

[10] In all the halakhot cited in n. 2 above, dust vessels are mentioned together with stone vessels.

3. Without the suggested reconstruction, according to the Damascus Document dust is susceptible to the corpse impurity. If so, then all the dust of the world is impure because of graves.[11]

Therefore, in light of Ginzberg's rendering I explain this halakha as dealing with wood, stone, and dust vessels.[12] Thus, it seems probable that the sectarian halakha was formulated in opposition to rabbinic halakha, which held that stone vessels or unfired clay vessels remain pure.[13] The author of the Damascus Document started with wood, most probably because Lev. 11:32 explicitly states that wooden vessels are susceptible to uncleanness: "And anything on which one of them falls when dead shall be unclean: be it any article of wood, or a cloth, or a skin, or a sack...."

As opposed to rabbinic halakha, the author of the Damascus Document believed that stone and unfired clay vessels can become impure after being exposed to oil. They are similar, in this respect, to wooden vessels, which according to Leviticus are susceptible to uncleanness.[14] Therefore it seems that according to the halakhic system represented in the Damascus Document, oil makes stone vessels susceptible to uncleanness. This halakha might be based on the fact that, according to Genesis, Jacob twice poured oil on stones in order to make them holy:

וישכם יעקב בבקר ויקח את האבן אשר שם מראשתיו
ושם אותה מצבה ויצק שמן על ראשה

Early in the morning, Jacob took the stone that he had put under his head and set it up as a pillar and poured oil on the top of it (Gen. 28:18)

---

[11] It is difficult to interpret CD 12:15-17 on the basis of 11QTemple 49:11-16 as a reference to floors for the following reasons: (a) the house is not mentioned at all in CD; (b) if CD speaks of floors, why is oil alone mentioned in CD and neither wine nor water, as in the Temple Scroll? For these reasons, it seems preferable to accept Ginzberg's reading. (4Q513 frg. 13 is very fragmentary. Although Baillet read ומערות in line 1, this reading is questionable.)

[12] Baumgarten and Yadin do not accept Ginzberg's rendering. See Baumgarten, "Essene Avoidance of Oil," 190-91; Yadin, *Temple Scroll*, 1.329. Baumgarten accepts S. Schechter's view that this halakha deals with raw materials (*Fragments of a Zadokite Work* [Cambridge: Cambridge University Press, 1910; reprinted, New York: Ktav, 1970] li). In Baumgarten's opinion, this halakha testifies to a dispute between the author of CD, who believed that raw materials are susceptible to impurity, and the Rabbis, who held that unfinished vessels (גולמין) are not susceptible to impurity. Against that one might argue that, according to m. Kel. 12:8, unfinished wooden vessels are susceptible to uncleanness. Note also that the status of unfinished metal vessels was a disputed point between R. Gamliel and the Rabbis (see m. 'Ed. 3:9, m. Kel. 12:6). As metal vessels are not mentioned in CD's halakha, it is difficult to argue that this is the disputed point between its author and the Rabbis. Yadin does not explain on what basis he rejects Ginzberg's restoration.

[13] M. Oh. 5:5.

and again in Gen. 35:14:

והצב יעקב מצבה במקום אשר דבר איתו מצבת אבן ויסך
עליה נסך ויצק עליה שמן

> and Jacob set up a pillar at the site where He had spoken to him, a
> pillar of stone, and he offered a libation on it and poured oil upon it.

We may assume that the Qumranites believed that oil had some effect on stone; perhaps that oil primed it to become a pillar (מצבה).
Support for this assumption comes from a halakha in 1QM, which
reads[15]:

ובנפול החללים יהיו הכו[וה]נים מריעים מרחוק ולוא יבואו
אל תוך החללים להתגאל בדם טמאתם כיא קושים
המה ו[לו]א יחלו שמן משיחת כהונתם בדם גוי הבל

> When the slain fall down, the pri[est]s shall keep blowing from afar.
> They shall not come to the midst of the slain (so as) to become defiled in
> their unclean blood, for they are holy. They shall [no]t profane the oil of
> their priestly anointing through the blood of nations of vanity (9:7-9)

while 4QMᶜ 5:4-5 reads[16]:

והכוהנים יצאו מבין החללים ועמדו מזה ... <u>ולא יחללו</u>
<u>שמן כהונתם</u>

> The priest shall get away from the slain...they shall not profane the oil
> of their priesthood.

The formulation of these halakhot is interesting for two reasons.
First, it is clear that the priests must preserve their purity by avoiding any contact with the dead, which has nothing to do with oil; second, one can become impure even without touching liquids. If this is
the case, we may ask why the author of the War Scroll linked the
prohibition against priestly contact with the dead to "the oil of their
priesthood." It is possible that his formulation of these laws was influenced by the sectarian halakhic concept that anointing an object
with oil makes it more susceptible to uncleanness than other liquids.
The phrase גאולי שמן found in the Damascus Document, as well as
the phrase תגאולת שמן found in the Temple Scroll, imply that oil is
more susceptible to defilement than other liquids.[17] The term

---

[14] It should be noted that both wood and stone mortars are mentioned in m. Beṣ.
1:7. We may therefore assume that the author of the Temple Scroll wanted to show
that wood and stone are the same.

[15] Y. Yadin, ed., *The Scroll of the War of the Sons of Light against the Sons of Darkness*
(London: Oxford University Press, 1962) 300-1.

[16] M. Baillet, ed., *Qumrân grotte 4.III (4Q482-4Q520)* (DJD 7; Oxford: Clarendon,
1982) 50.

מגואלים בשמן is also mentioned in a fragmentary context (4Q513 frg. 13), together with liquids and defilement.[18]

It remains to see how the author of the Damascus Document understood the Temple Scroll. As Yadin noted, the phrase רחים ומדוכה found in the Temple Scroll is borrowed from Num. 11:7-8[19]:

> והמן כזרע גד הוא ועינו כעין הבדלח. שטו העם ולקטו
> וטחנו ברחים או דכו במדוכה ובשלו בפרור ועשו
> אתו עגות והיה טעמו כטעם לשד השמן

> Now the manna was like coriander seed, and in color it was like bdellium. The people would go about and gather it, grind it between millstones or pound it in a mortar, boil it in a pot, and make it into cakes. It tasted like rich cream [lit. "cream of oil"].

In Yadin's opinion the millstone (רחיים) and the mortar (מדוכה) were mentioned in the Temple Scroll because they are the most common stone vessels.[20]

If my understanding is correct, evidently when the Temple Scroll was composed, stone vessels were used only for grinding and crushing, and therefore stone vessels as such are not mentioned in the Temple Scroll. It seems that the author of the Damascus Document was aware that the millstone and the mortar mentioned in the Temple Scroll were regularly in contact with oil. That can be adduced from rabbinic literature where we find the phrase רחיים של זיתים (millstones of olives; m. Zab. 4:2), and from m. Ṭevul Yom which states:

> ... השום והשמן של צולין שנגע טבול יום במקצתן פסל את כולם ...

> השום והשמן של תרומה שנגע טבול יום במקצתן לא פסל אלא
> מקום מגעו.

> ואם היה השום מרובה הולכים אחר הרוב ...

> אבל אם היה מפוזר במדוכה טהור מפני שהוא רוצה בפיזורו

> ... the garlic and the oil of unconsecrated food part of which a Ṭebul Yom touched—he has rendered the whole unfit ... the garlic and the oil of heave-offering which a Ṭebul Yom touched—he has rendered unfit only the place which he touched.

---

[17] On the meaning of גאולי שמן in CD, להתגאל in 1QM, and תגאולת שמן, see C. Rabin, *The Zadokite Documents* (Oxford: Clarendon, 1958) 62-63; Baumgarten, "Essene Avoidance of Oil," 184-86; Yadin, *Temple Scroll*, 1.329.

[18] J. M. Baumgarten, "Halakhic Polemics in New Fragments from Qumran Cave 4," *Biblical Archaeology Today: Proceedings of the International Congress on Biblical Archaeology* (Jerusalem: Israel Exploration Society, Israel Academy of Sciences and Humanities, 1985) 390-99.

[19] Yadin, *Temple Scroll*, 2.216.

[20] Yadin, *Temple Scroll*, 1.330.

But if the garlic was more, they follow the greater part ... But if it was chopped up in a mortar (מדוכה), it is clean, because he [the owner] wants to scatter it (2:3).

We may therefore conclude that millstones were used in order to crush olives and that garlic was crushed in a mortar together with oil.[21] The author of the Damascus Document assumes that the millstones (רחיים) and mortars (מדוכה) mentioned in the Temple Scroll were both regularly in contact with oil.

According to sectarian halakha, oil is more susceptible to defilement than other liquids. This concept can be compared with Josephus' statement concerning the Essenes: "Oil they consider defiling, and anyone who accidentally comes in contact with it scours his person; for they make a point of keeping a dry skin..." (War 2.123).[22] This statement may also reflect the view that oil is more susceptible to defilement than other liquids.[23]

Conclusion

Based on the halakhot from the Temple Scroll and the Damascus Document discussed above, other scholars maintain that stone vessels had no special status at Qumran, and were susceptible to defilement like any other vessel.[24] I have tried to show that, according to sectarian law, stone vessels were not susceptible to defilement as long as they were not in contact with oil. Namely, according to this view, liquids other than oil do not make the stone vessel susceptible to defilement. Thus it seems that the Qumranites, like other Jews of the Second Temple period who strictly observed the laws of clean and unclean vessels, used stone vessels to store all kinds of dry and liquid foodstuffs, but not oil. The difference between sectarian and rabbinic law lies in the distinction that according to the Sages stone vessels are never susceptible to defilement, while according to the Damascus Document 12:15-17 they are susceptible to defilement after coming in contact with oil.

---

[21] See C. Albeck's exegesis of this Mishnah in *Seder Tohoroth* (Jerusalem and Tel Aviv: Mossad Bialik and Dvir, 1959) 462 (Hebrew).

[22] See Baumgarten, "Essene Avoidance of Oil," 183-84.

[23] Baumgarten, "Essene Avoidance of Oil," 191, argues that rabbinic dicta echo the view that oil is more susceptible to defilement than other liquids. M. Toh. 3:2 states in the name of R. Meir: השמן תחילה לעולם; namely, if oil has congealed it is still regarded as a liquid and is susceptible to first-degree defilement.

[24] Ginzberg, *Unknown Jewish Sect*, 81; Yadin, *Temple Scroll*, 1.330, 2.216; E. Regev, "The Use of Stone Vessels at the End of the Second Temple Period," *Judea and Samaria Research Studies: Proceedings of the Sixth Annual Meeting–1996* (ed. Y. Eshel; Kedumim-Ariel: The Research Institute, The College of Judea and Samaria, 1997) 79-95 (Hebrew).

THE LINGUISTIC STUDY OF THE DAMASCUS DOCUMENT: A HISTORICAL PERSPECTIVE

Steven E. Fassberg

Hebrew University of Jerusalem

The analysis of the language of the Damascus Document, in particular the vocabulary and phraseology of the text, has served as the basis for the differing views on the identity, customs, and beliefs of the sectarian community mentioned in the Cairo Geniza manuscripts of the work (CD). Consequently, today, a century since the discovery of the document, it is only fitting that attention be given to the history of linguistic research into the Damascus Document. There have been several surveys of the scientific literature, such as J. A. Fitzmyer's prolegomenon to the 1970 reprint of S. Schechter's *editio princeps*[1] or P. R. Davies' book, *The Damascus Covenant*.[2]

This paper will trace the study of the language of the Damascus Document from the initial publication of the manuscripts by Schechter in 1910 through the publication of the first of the Dead Sea Scrolls in 1950-51, the publication of the Damascus Document fragments from Qumran Caves 5 and 6 in 1962 by J. T. Milik, to the recent publication of the Cave 4 Qumran fragments in 1996 by J. M. Baumgarten. I shall concentrate on grammatical studies, since vocabulary and phraseology have been treated in almost every study that deals with the Damascus Document, whereas the grammar has been, to a large extent, neglected. I shall conclude with some observations on the language of the recently published Qumran Cave 4 fragments and remarks on certain features of the Cairo Geniza manuscripts in the light of the orthography and language of the 4QD fragments and other Dead Sea Scrolls.

1. *The Years 1910–1949*

The first stage in the history of linguistic research into the Damascus Document began with the *editio princeps* of Schechter in 1910. In the

---

[1] S. Schechter, *Documents of Jewish Sectaries* (New York: Ktav, 1970) 19-37.

[2] P. R. Davies, *The Damascus Covenant: An Interpretation of the "Damascus Document"* (JSOT Supp. 25; Sheffield: JSOT, 1982) 3-47.

introduction to his *Documents of Jewish Sectaries*, Schechter succinctly summarized the language of MS A:

> The language of the MS. is for the most part pure Biblical Hebrew. The first three pages rise even to the dignity of Scriptural poetry, though a good deal of it is obscured by the unfortunate condition in which the text is at present. But there are in it terms and expressions which occur only in the Mishna or even only in the Rabbinic literature dating from the first centuries of the Middle Ages....[3]

He went on to list the following lexical items and expressions: וּפרוש, גלגל השמש, זכו לשוב, הרואה את דם זובה, העריות, ויסוד הבריאה, חבו, במובה, המוכן, למשכים and גוים (with the meaning "Gentiles"), סרך, בית השתחות, מדרש התורה, מדוקדק, בממון, חבור ישראל, להרשותו, the introductory formulae for citing a biblical passage כאשר אמר, ככתוב, כאשר כתוב, ואשר א', and כתוב ביד, the absence of the Tetragrammaton and the use of אל "God." On the difference between the biblical citations and their appearance in the Damascus Document, he wrote: "deviations from the Masoretic text are mere textual corruptions of a careless scribe and not to be explained by the variae lectiones suggested by any known version, or quotation by any ancient authority."[4] Elsewhere in the introduction Schechter noted the unusual terms ספר ההגו, מבקר (which today is taken as הגי),[5] מעמד, and ספר מחלקות העתים (Book of Jubilees). In the notes accompanying the text, he compared the Hebrew of the documents to the Hebrew of biblical, rabbinic, and Karaite writings, and also to expressions in intertestamental literature. Schechter's linguistic comments consist of comparison to biblical and rabbinic passages and numerous emendations in the text, which made better linguistic sense. The importance he assigned to rabbinic Hebrew can be seen in his terse and frequent remark: "see Rab. dict."

Reaction to Schechter's publication of CD was swift. Of the many articles and comments which immediately appeared, one should note especially I. Lévi's "Un écrit sadducéen antérieur à la destruction du Temple," which consisted of different readings of the text with translation and notes.[6] In his introduction to the text, he included a section on the language of the manuscripts in which he compared the Hebrew of the document to that of Ben Sira with its borrowing and

---

[3] S. Schechter, *Documents of Jewish Sectaries* (Cambridge: Cambridge University Press, 1910) 1.xi.

[4] Schechter, *Documents of Jewish Sectaries*, 1.xii.

[5] See below.

[6] I. Lévi, "Un écrit sadducéen antérieur à la destruction du Temple," *REJ* 61 (1911) 161-205; 63 (1912) 1-19.

reworking of biblical elements and presence of Aramaic.[7] Surprisingly, Lévi did not find evidence of rabbinic Hebrew in the document:

> La langue est déja par elle-même un témoin instructif d'une époque ancienne. C'est de l'hébreu pur, enrichi d'éléments araméens, comme c'est le cas pour l'Ecclésiastique; en outre, et comme en cet ouvrage, certains termes ou locutions nouvelles qui se retrouvent dans la littérature postbiblique y ont une acception différente. Il est surtout digne de remarque qu'on n'y sent pas l'influence ni de l'hébreu de la Mischna et du Midrasch, ni de l'araméen scolastique ou populaire du Talmud... La langue de Ben Sira est bourrée de centons bibliques. Il semble que telle était alors la mode.

Neither Schechter nor Lévi, however, attempted to describe aspects of the language apart from certain lexical items. The first to comment on the grammar, in addition to the lexicon, was M. H. Segal in notes on Schechter's publication in *JQR* in 1911-12,[8] which he expanded upon in a lengthy Hebrew article published in 1912 in *Haschiloah*.[9] Segal, like Lévi, also presented the text and offered many emendations (both scholars did so without actually seeing the manuscripts and on the basis of Schechter's transcription and the two photographs in his book). Segal pointed out several salient grammatical phenomena found in the documents[10]: the use of the *waw conversive* (the imperfect consecutive and the perfect consecutive), noting that in MS A the imperfect consecutive occurs where the simple perfect is used in MS B; the common use of the infinitive construct which, among other things, expresses obligation (e.g., אין עוד להשתפח, 4:10); the *pi'el* verbal nouns נקום וניטור (8:5); the genitive expressed by the construct chain as well as by *lamedh* (e.g., המקבר למחנה, 13:7); the relative pronoun אשר, only once -ש; iterative action expressed by the use of שוב as an auxiliary verb (e.g., ושב והודיע, 9:19); the pronominally suffixed forms אחיהו and פיהו, as opposed to אחיו and פיו; and numerals placed after the counted noun (e.g., שנים עשרים, 1:10). He also presented what he considered to be a complete list of lexemes and expressions which are either unattested in the Old Testament or are

---

[7] It is ironic that Schechter, who first published the Hebrew version of Ben Sira from the Geniza in 1899, did not notice this, though he does cite a passage in Ben Sira in the notes (xxxiii at 2.10, n. 16).

[8] M. H. Segal, "Notes on 'Fragments of a Zadokite Work'," *JQR* N.S. 2 (1911-12) 133-41, especially 139-40; idem, "Additional Notes on 'Fragments of a Zadokite Work'," *JQR* N.S. 3 (1912-13) 301-11.

[9] M. H. Segal, "ספר ברית-דמשק עם מבוא והערות," *Haschiloah. Litterarisch-wissenschaftliche Monatsschrift* 26 (Januar-Juni, 1912) 390-406, 481-506.

[10] Segal, "ספר ברית-דמשק עם מבוא והערות," 391-93; idem, "Notes," 139-41.

[11] Segal, "Notes," 140-41.

rarely attested in the Old Testament but occur in the Mishnah and midrashim. In his English article he summarized:

> The Mishnic [*sic*] usages found in this document may, however, be very old. They are certainly anterior to the Christian era. The general purity of the author's style and grammar, the facility with which he writes in flowing Biblical Hebrew, and his adroitness in twisting round biblical phrases and adapting them for his purpose, all prove him to have belonged to a whole circle of writers who cultivated the composition of books in an early and archaic style in imitation of the earlier canonical literature. In other words, the author belonged to the school of writers from which emanated the Palestinian apocalyptic and pseudepigraphical literature which was certainly composed in a tolerably pure Biblical Hebrew, with a more or less large admixture of Mishnic expressions and forms. The language of the present work affords us, therefore, an excellent illustration of the character and style of the Hebrew originals of such works as the Book of Jubilees, the Testaments of the Twelve Patriarchs, and even of the Apocalypses of Baruch and Ezra.[11]

He added later: "Our text is then entirely free from all *direct* Aramaic influence."[12]

In 1913, R. H. Charles added his voice in general agreement as to the character of the language of the Damascus Document in his edition of the Apocrypha and Pseudepigrapha:

> It is good Hebrew enriched by a few Aramaisms like the Book of Daniel and Sirach, though in a less degree. It contains also a few Mishnaic and Talmudic expressions, but in certain cases the phrases in question bear a different meaning in post-Biblical Jewish literature. The language, as has been generally recognized, is not that of the Mishnah, the Midrashim, or the Talmud. Like Sirach, our author makes constant use of O. T. diction, but, unlike him, he quotes its text frequently in the name of the writer....[13]

Note that he, too like Lévi, stressed the similarity to Ben Sira.

An important and comprehensive linguistic treatment of the vocabulary and orthography (but not grammar) of the Damascus Document was presented by L. Ginzberg in a series of articles in *Monatsschrift für Geschichte und Wissenschaft des Judentums* 55-58 (1911-14), later published as *Eine Unbekannte jüdische Sekte* in 1922. Ginzberg was the first to describe the orthography of the Damascus Document[14] and he did so since, as he stated, some of his suggested emendations presupposed the special orthography of the

---

[12] Segal, "Additional Notes," 311, n. 10.
[13] R. H. Charles, *The Apocrypha and Pseudepigrapha of the Old Testament in English* (Oxford: Clarendon, 1913) 2.786.
[14] L. Ginzberg, *Eine unbekannte jüdische Sekte* (New York, 1922) 3-4.

document.[15] He commented on the considerable use of *scriptio plena* in marking the vowels *o* and *i*, and the *scriptio defectiva* of ימו "his days" (10:9) and חפצו "his desires" (= "his work," 11:2). In a lengthy chapter entitled "Zur Textkritik, Sprach- und Sach-erklärung," Ginzberg analyzed in detail many lexical items and expressions.

Ginzberg also devoted a special chapter to the language of CD which, according to his son, was completed before the outbreak of World War I, but was only published posthumously in 1976 in an expanded English version of the German original.[16] In this chapter Ginzberg presented a list of 144 lexical items, which he divided into "new words and idioms which occur neither in biblical nor in Talmudic-midrashic literature" (23 items), "rabbinisms" (31 items), and "biblical purisms" (15 items). He limited himself to one grammatical comment: "A prominent feature of our document's style is the employment of the imperfect with the WAW consecutivum."[17] Like Lévi and Charles, he stressed the linguistic parallels in lexicon between Ben Sira and CD. He noted the mosaic patchwork of the document, and yet at the same time believed that the document reflected a linguistically unified composition: "Though our document is amorphous, featuring excerpts from various sources which are arranged without system and relationship, yet one can detect a certain uniformity with regard to diction and grammar."[18] He concluded the chapter with: "Our investigations of the language of the document have *thus completely confirmed the conclusions reached in the previous chapters: our document presents a work of the first century B.C.E.*"[19]

Most scholars concurred with the view of the Hebrew as expressed by Schechter, Segal, and Ginzberg. Some, however, disagreed. Note, for example, the dissenting voice of A. Büchler:

> The most striking feature of the language, however, is the continuous employment of whole phrases and sentences of the Bible the like of which we find in none of the literary productions of the pre-Christian, pre-Talmudic, and Talmudic times (except the Hebrew Ben-Sira which should not be used as evidence owing to its contentious character)... Besides this, the very hard, clumsy, sometimes almost impossible

---

[15] He described MS A, not MS B, because he felt that the latter agreed on the whole with Masoretic orthography.

[16] L. Ginzberg, *An Unknown Jewish Sect* (tr. R. Marcus et al.; New York: JTS, 1976) 274-303.

[17] Ginzberg, *Unknown Jewish Sect*, 282.

[18] Ginzberg, *Unknown Jewish Sect*, 282.

[19] Emphasis in the original; Ginzberg, *Unknown Jewish Sect*, 303.

Hebrew in the halakic part which is not merely due to the style of the author, strikes one as late.[20]

A concise survey of differing opinions on the Hebrew of CD can be found in H. H. Rowley's *The Zadokite Fragments and the Dead Sea Scrolls*.[21] Of those arguing that the Damascus Document was a late, medieval composition, the name of S. Zeitlin stands out.[22]

The translation and commentary of F. F. Hvidberg[23] and the edition of L. Rost[24] also merit attention. The upper apparatus provided by Rost contains previously suggested scholarly emendations, while the bottom apparatus includes references to biblical, rabbinic, and intertestamental literature. Unlike the editions of Segal and Lévi, the readings of Hvidberg and Rost were based on an examination of photographs.

2. *The Years 1950—Present*

The discovery of the Dead Sea Scrolls in 1948 and the publication of the first scrolls from Cave 1 in 1950-51 (1QIsa[a], 1QpHab, and 1QS) marked a dramatic turning point in the study of the Damascus Document. The similarity in language and phraseology between the Qumran material and the Cairo Geniza manuscripts removed all doubt that the Damascus Document was indeed composed during the Second Temple period, notwithstanding the vociferous protests of Zeitlin, who continued to maintain that CD was late, as was the Qumran material.[25] From this point on, most works dealing with the Hebrew of the Dead Sea Scrolls refer also to the Geniza manuscripts of the Damascus Document, and all subsequent works on the Damascus Document relate the language of the document to the finds from Qumran. Mention should also be made of A. M.

---

[20] A. Büchler, review of S. Schechter, *Documents of Jewish Sectaries*, *JQR* N.S. 3 (1910-13) 467-69.

[21] H. H. Rowley, *The Zadokite Fragments and the Dead Sea Scrolls* (Oxford: Blackwell, 1952) 1-3.

[22] S. Zeitlin, review of R. T. Herford, *The Pharisees*, *JQR* N.S. 16 (1925-26) 385-86.

[23] F. F. Hvidberg, *Menigheden af den nye Pagt i Damascus* (København, 1928).

[24] L. Rost, *Die Damaskusschrift* (Berlin: de Gruyter, 1933).

[25] He did so repeatedly. See "'A Commentary on the Book of Habakkuk' Important Discovery or Hoax?," *JQR* 39 (1948-49) 235-47; idem, "The Hebrew Scrolls: Once More and Finally," *JQR* N.S. 41 (1950-51) 35-53; idem, "The Hebrew Scrolls: A Challenge to Scholarship," *JQR* N.S. 41 (1950-51) 255-64; idem, *The Zadokite Fragments: Facsimile of the Manuscripts in the Cairo Genizah Collection in the Possession of the University Library, Cambridge, England* (JQR MS 1; Philadelphia: Dropsie College, 1952) 1-32. Zeitlin was not alone, however. See also P. R. Weis, "The Date of the Habakkuk Scroll," *JQR* N.S. 41 (1950-51) 125-54.

Habermann's 1952 edition containing 1QS, 1QpHab, and CD, not only because of the concordance he supplies for these three works, but rather for his complete vocalization of the documents and the linguistic interpretation that the vocalized text reflects.[26]

C. Rabin's 1954 edition of CD,[27] based on an examination of the manuscripts and new photographs, was an important step forward in the study of the language of the document. Rabin's new readings, his erudition in Hebrew, Semitics, and biblical studies, and his references to the Dead Sea Scrolls provided students of the Damascus Document with a firm basis for study. The edition is replete with linguistic and philological notes and references to the Hebrew of the Scrolls, biblical, mishnaic and medieval Hebrew, as well as other languages and sources.

In addition to new readings, Rabin's greatest contribution is his attention to grammatical forms and syntactic uses, not only lexical items. He related phenomena to parallel features of classical biblical, late biblical and mishnaic Hebrew; he also noted the many instances of linguistic hypercorrections. See, for example, his remarks on the periphrastic genitive with anticipatory pronoun, which is representative of late biblical Hebrew, in קציהם לכל הוי עולמים "their ages of all those who exist" (2:9); the late biblical Hebrew usage of עמד "arise" as attested in בעמוד איש (1:14) vs. the use of classical biblical Hebrew קום; the verb קוץ governing with the preposition מ- as in mishnaic Hebrew ויקוץ מעשות (20:2) vs. biblical Hebrew קץ ב-; the mishnaic Hebrew infinitive לירוש (1:7) vs. biblical Hebrew לרשת; בעול (14:9) as qal passive participle with active sense as is common in mishnaic Hebrew; the inverted word order for emphasis in בדבר מות ענה בו "it was in a capital matter that he testified against him" (9:6-7); the Aramaic form with preserved nun in להנצילם "so as to save them" (14:2), which according to Rabin "throws light on the scribe's mother tongue."

---

[26] A. M. Habermann, ʿEdah we-ʿEduth. Three Scrolls from the Judaean Desert. The Legacy of a Community Edited with Vocalization, Notes and Indices (Jerusalem: Machbarot le-sifrut, 1982) (Hebrew). He published an expanded version in 1959, incorporating newly published manuscripts: Megilloth Midbar Yehuda: The Scrolls from the Judean Desert Edited with Vocalization, Introduction, Notes and Concordance (Jerusalem: Machbarot le-sifrut, 1959) (Hebrew). Similarly, the vocalization presented in E. Lohse, Die Texte aus Qumran. Hebräisch und Deutsch mit masoretischer Punktation. Übersetzung, Einführung und Anmerkungen (Darmstadt: Wissenschaftliche Buchgesellschaft, 1964), is interesting for the linguistic and philological analysis underlying the vocalization. A fourth edition of Lohse's book was published in 1986. See also the inclusion of the vocabulary of CD in K. G. Kuhn, Konkordanz zu den Qumrantexten (Göttingen: Vandenhoeck & Ruprecht, 1960).

[27] C. Rabin, The Zadokite Fragments (Oxford: Clarendon, 1954).

Rabin was fully abreast of the state of research into the Hebrew of the Dead Sea Scrolls, as evidenced by his frequent comparisons to grammatical features and lexical items in the Scrolls. His references to and comments on late biblical and mishnaic Hebrew also reveal his knowledge of recent advances in both areas, as can be seen, for example, in his mention of mishnaic manuscripts, whose importance for the study of Hebrew had been demonstrated by J. N. Epstein, H. Yalon, and S. Lieberman.[28]

In 1956, two years after the appearance of Rabin's edition, M. Baillet published the fragments of the Damascus Document from Qumran Cave 6 (6QD)[29] and, among other things, compared the orthography of the Geniza passages to the parallel passages in 6QD. The publication of Qumran fragments of the Damascus Document conclusively proved that the CD was a medieval copy of an older work. In 1957 A. Rubinstein[30] contributed a discussion of irregular uses of tenses in MS B of CD. The same year Rabin touched on the language of CD, among other topics, in his *Qumran Studies*.[31] In 1958 Rabin revised his edition, *The Zadokite Documents*, and also had occasion to discuss further the language of CD in an influential article on the historical background of Qumran Hebrew, in which he argued that "in the period preceding the formation of the Qumran sect there was in common use in Palestine a literary language in which BH and MH elements coexisted upon a mainly MH grammatical foundation"[32]; in this important study he presented involuntary mishnaisms in the lexicon and grammar of the Damascus Document as well as biblical hypercorrections of mishnaic expressions.

In 1962, Qumran fragments of the Damascus Document from Cave 5 (5QD) were published by J. T. Milik in DJDJ 3,[33] and M.

---

[28] See in the *Zadokite Fragments*, 43, note to l. 28 on אֻנ with *qameṣ* in pointed mishnaic manuscripts vs. אֻנ in printed editions; 68, note to l. 2 on the consistent assimilation of *nun* verbs I-n in mishnaic manuscripts. E. Y. Kutscher's ground-breaking article on the importance of reliable manuscripts to the study of mishnaic Hebrew, "Lashon Ḥazal," *Henoch Yalon Jubilee Volume* (ed. S. Lieberman; Jerusalem: Kiryat Sefer, 1963), had not yet appeared at the time Rabin's edition was published.

[29] M. Baillet, "Fragments du Document de Damas. Qumrân, Grotte 6," *RB* 63 (1956) 513-23.

[30] A. Rubinstein, "Notes on Some Syntactical Irregularities in Text B of the Zadokite Documents," *VT* 7 (1957) 356-61.

[31] C. Rabin, *Qumran Studies* (Oxford: Oxford University Press, 1957).

[32] C. Rabin, "The Historical Background of Qumran Hebrew," *Aspects of the Dead Sea Scrolls* (ed. C. Rabin and Y. Yadin; Scripta Hierosolymitana 4; Jerusalem: Magnes, 1958), 156.

[33] M. Baillet, J. T. Milik, and R. de Vaux, eds., *Les "Petites Grottes" de Qumrân* (DJDJ 3; Oxford: Clarendon, 1962).

Baillet presented the official publication of the fragments from Cave 6 (6QD) in the same volume.[34] Four years later a fragment from Cave 4 (4QDᵃ) appeared[35] followed by another in 1972.[36]

The most important contributions to the linguistic study of the Qumran documents in the 1970's and 1980's were two grammars and one dictionary. The 1976 doctorate on the Hebrew of the Dead Sea Scrolls by E. Qimron[37] constituted the first comprehensive grammar (orthography, phonology, and morphology) of the Qumran material; in 1986 Qimron published an English version of his doctorate, which updated and supplemented the 1976 thesis with chapters on syntax and on vocabulary.[38] In both versions of the grammar Qimron excluded the Geniza manuscripts of the Damascus Document, but included the 5QD and 6QD fragments. All of the Hebrew from the Geniza manuscripts, on the other hand, together with the 5QD and 6QD material, was included in the *Historical Dictionary of the Hebrew Language 200 B.C.E.—300 C.E.*, which appeared in microfiche form in 1988.[39] Perusal of the Damascus Document material in the dictionary demonstrates its organic linguistic link to other documents from the same period.

In addition, the 1970s and 1980s witnessed the appearance of new grammatical studies devoted to specific linguistic phenomena. In 1973 G. W. Nebe[40] analyzed some problematic uses of את in the Damascus Document. A year later J. Carmignac[41] discussed the

---

[34] A preliminary publication of 6QD appeared in M. Baillet, "Fragments du Document de Damas."

[35] J. T. Milik, "Fragment d'une source Psautier (4QPs89) et fragments des Jubilés, du Document de Damas, d'une phylactère dans la Grotte 4 de Qumrân," *RB* 73 (1966), 104-5.

[36] J. T. Milik, "Milkî-ṣedeq et Milkî-rešaʿ dans les anciens écrits juifs et chrétiens," *JJS* 23 (1972) 135-36

[37] E. Qimron, *A Grammar of the Hebrew Language of the Dead Sea Scrolls* (Ph.D. diss.; Hebrew University of Jerusalem, 1976) (Hebrew).

[38] E. Qimron, *The Hebrew of the Dead Sea Scrolls* (HSS 29; Atlanta, GA: Scholars Press, 1986).

[39] *The Historical Dictionary of the Hebrew Language: Materials for the Dictionary Series I: 200 B.C.E.—300 C.E.* (Jerusalem: ha-Akademiah la-lashon ha-Ivrit, 1988). In 1998 an updated and enlarged CD-ROM version of the microfiche, "Ma'agarim," appeared. The Hebrew of CD is included also in the most recent dictionaries of biblical Hebrew: L. Koehler, W. Baumgartner et al., *Hebräisches und aramäisches Lexikon zum Alten Testament*² (6 vols.; Leiden: E. J. Brill, 1967-96); W. Gesenius, *Hebräisches und aramäisches Handwörterbuch über das Alte Testament*¹⁸ (ed. R. Meyer and H. Donner; Berlin: Springer-Verlag, 1987-); D. J. A. Clines, *The Dictionary of Classical Hebrew* (Sheffield: Sheffield Academic Press, 1993-).

[40] G. W. Nebe, "Der Gebrauch der sogenannten 'Nota accusativi' את in Damaskusschrift XV, 5-9 und 12," *RevQ* 8/30 (1973) 257-63.

[41] J. Carmignac, "L'emploi de la négation אין dans la Bible et a Qumran," *RevQ* 8/31 (1974) 407-13.

morphology and syntax of the negative אֵין in the Old Testament
and Qumran, including the Damascus Document, comparing features to later biblical and mishnaic Hebrew: the syntagm אֵי + infinitive; the lack of pronominal suffix on אֵין as in אֵין הם מבדיל (CD
5:6-7); the distancing of אֵין from the noun it negates with interven-
ing elements as in אֵין בהם בינה (CD 5:17). M. Bar-Asher,[42] in an article in 1981 on misunderstood spellings in Tannaitic manuscripts,
suggested that מוֹעֵט in 1QS and CD was unrelated to the participial
מוּעֵט in Tannaitic sources; the CD and Qumran form developed
from מְעַט > מוּעֵט (assimilation of the *šᵉwa* to the labial *mem*), whereas
the participial מוּעֵט in Tannaitic manuscripts either was the result of
haplography from מְמוּעֵט or possibly an old internal *qal* passive participle. T. Thorion-Vardi[43] discussed at length the use of the tenses
in the Zadokite documents in 1985 and the same year Y. Thorion[44]
presented a comprehensive analysis of the use of the preposition -בְּ
in Qumran documents, among them the Damascus Document. The
next year Carmignac[45] published an investigation of the uses of the
infinitive absolute in Ben Sira and in Qumran documents, including
the Damascus Document.

This decade has witnessed several important publications that
bear directly on the linguistic analysis of the Damascus Document.
In 1990 J. M. Baumgarten published fragments of 4QD[a, d, g, h] on
skin disease.[46] Two years later E. Qimron presented a new transcription of CD with an apparatus containing comments on what should
have been written in the manuscripts (i.e., Qimron corrects the
errors in the manuscripts[47]), variant readings from the Qumran documents, and short philological notes and references; the volume
includes high quality photographs of the two Geniza manuscripts.[48]
This edition is an indispensable aid for further linguistic analysis of
the Damascus Document. In 1995 Baumgarten and D. R. Schwartz
presented, in the Dead Sea Scrolls series edited by J. H. Charles-

[42] M. Bar-Asher, "Misunderstood Spellings," *Leshonenu* 45 (1981) 91-92 (Hebrew).
[43] T. Thorion-Vardi, "The Use of the Tenses in the Zadokite Documents," *RevQ*
12/45 (1985) 65-88.
[44] Y. Thorion, "Die Syntax der Präposition B in der Qumranliteratur," *RevQ*
12/45 (1985) 17-63.
[45] J. Carmignac, "L'infinitif absolu chez Ben Sira et à Qumrân," *RevQ* 12/46
(1986) 252-61.
[46] J. M. Baumgarten, "The 4Q Zadokite Fragments on Skin Disease," *JJS* 41
(1990) 153-65.
[47] E.g., in 3:1 the manuscript clearly shows תעי, and in the apparatus one finds
"Read תעו," which is more grammatical. Many of the corrections involve confusion
of *waw* and *yodh*.
[48] *The Damascus Document Reconsidered* (ed. M. Broshi; Jerusalem: Israel Exploration
Society, Shrine of the Book, Israel Museum, 1992).

worth, an edition of CD with translation and notes[49]; the same volume includes the 4QD fragments on skin disease, 5QD and 6QD. A noteworthy addition to this edition is the appendix by Y. Ofer on the use of the vocalization (Babylonian and Tiberian) and other signs (erasure, the single grapheme sign for אל, also a possible emendation sign) in the Geniza manuscripts.[50] Ofer believes that the concentration of vowel signs in the first pages of the Geniza manuscripts and the mixed use of Babylonian and Tiberian signs indicate that both systems of vowel signs were probably inserted by a single redactor.

The most significant contribution to the study of the Damascus Document, however, is the publication in 1996 of all the 4QD material by Baumgarten based on material provided by Milik.[51] These long awaited fragments provided scholars with the necessary information for the challenge of piecing together all the different material from the Geniza and Qumran toward the goal of reconstructing a single text. On the relationship of the 4QD fragments to the text of the Geniza manuscripts, Baumgarten notes, "The 4Q manuscripts tend to enhance the general reliability of the text extant in the Genizah versions of the Damascus Document. This is a pleasant surprise, in view of Schechter's rather dim view of the scribal quality of his manuscripts....the 4Q manuscript readings turn out to be, by and large, quite compatible with those of Text A."[52]

I should like to complete my survey with a few remarks on some features in the 4QD fragments and related phenomena in the Cairo Geniza manuscripts. The *plene* orthography of the 4QD fragments comes as no surprise, taking into consideration the other Dead Sea Scrolls. In retrospect, however, the extent to which *plene* orthography is still preserved in the Geniza manuscripts is interesting, as Ginzberg noted almost 90 years ago.[53]

One finds, in the 4QD fragments, long forms of pronouns (e.g., הואה, 4Q266 7 iii 7; אוזנמה, 4Q268 1 7) alongside shorter forms (e.g., הוא, 4Q266 6 i 8; מהונם, 4Q267 9 iii 2). Medieval CD preserves two examples of long pronouns: Ginzberg noted that במה in להתהלך במה

[49] J. M. Baumgarten and D. R. Schwartz, "Damascus Document," *The Dead Sea Scrolls: Hebrew, Aramaic, and Greek Texts with English Translations. Vol. 2: Damascus Document, War Scrolls, and Related Documents* (ed. J. H. Charlesworth; Tübingen: Mohr-Siebeck/Louisville: John Knox, 1995) 4-79.
[50] Baumgarten and Schwartz, "Damascus Document," 10-11.
[51] J. M. Baumgarten, *Qumran Cave 4.XIII. The Damascus Document (4Q266-273)* (DJD 18; Oxford: Clarendon, 1996).
[52] Baumgarten, DJD 18.6.
[53] See n. 14 above.

(6:10) is a long pronominal suffix, as in Qumran[54]; another example is אל יטהר במה[55] (10:12; cf. עד מה יבוא במה, 4Q268 1 8). CD also possesses the forms of the long suffixes on אחיהו (14:5) and פיהו (13:4), as attested in 4QD (e.g., אחיהו, 4Q267 9 v 8; פיהו, 266 9 ii 14); these long forms are the rule in the Scrolls.

Ginzberg noted that the orthography of the 3 m.s. suffix on pl. nouns with *waw*, as against Masoretic *waw* and *yodh*, attested in the 4QD fragments, occurs already in the Geniza manuscripts in the words, ימו "his days" (10:9) and חפצו "his desires" (11:2 and 10:20). These similarities are obvious today in the light of the Dead Sea Scrolls,[56] Samaritan Hebrew and Aramaic,[57] although Ginzberg could not have known at the time that the defective orthography reflected a contracted diphthong *o*.

The 4QD fragments exhibit a pausal-looking verbal form in ימשולו (4Q271 5 i 18; ימשלו, CD 12:2); such pausal-looking forms are well known in the Qumran texts. They are also attested in CD: וישמרו (3:3), whose Babylonian vocalization reflects *wayyišmōrū*, ויחפורו (6:3), and possibly ישפוכו (10:18, unless one reads ישפוט along with Rabin and Qimron). According to Qimron's transcription, another example occurs in ויעבורו ברית (CD 1:20), as against those scholars who read the *hifʿil* ויעבירו. It has been argued that the orthography with *waw* demonstrates general penultimate stress, as in Samaritan Hebrew, Western Aramaic dialects, and also mishnaic Hebrew.[58] Others have maintained that the *waw* merely represents a reduced *u/o*-vowel and that stress was on the ultima.[59]

The 4QD fragments do not reveal examples of the syntagm יצר הרע, לשון הרע, i.e., expressions in which only the adjective has the definite article and not the noun that is modified. This syntactic phenomenon, which is attested infrequently in biblical Hebrew, is more common in mishnaic Hebrew.[60] The Geniza material, however,

---

[54] Ginzberg, *Unknown Jewish Sect*, 28, n. 73, and 53, n. 152. Qimron writes in the note to his transcription: בהם, בם =.

[55] Qimron has the same note here as in 6:10.

[56] Qimron, *Hebrew of the Dead Sea Scrolls*, 33.

[57] Z. Ben-Ḥayyim, *Studies in the Traditions of the Hebrew Language* (Madrid/Barcelona: Instituto Arias Montano, 1954) 79; idem, "Traditions in the Hebrew Language with Special Reference to the Dead Sea Scrolls," *Aspects of the Dead Sea Scrolls*, 202.

[58] E.g., Kutscher and Ben-Ḥayyim. For a discussion and bibliography on the subject, see Qimron, *Hebrew of the Dead Sea Scrolls*, 40-41.

[59] Qimron, *Hebrew of the Dead Sea Scrolls*, 40-41. See also I. Yeivin, "The Verbal Forms יקטולו, יקטולנו in DSS in Comparison to the Babylonian Vocalization," *Bible and Jewish History: Studies in Bible and Jewish History Dedicated to the Memory of Jacob Liver* (ed. B. Uffenheimer; Tel-Aviv: Universitat Tel-Aviv, ha-Fakultah le-madaʿe ha-ruaḥ, 1971) 256-76 (Hebrew).

does possess this syntagm: ברית החדשה (20:12),[61] perhaps מורה היחיד "the unique teacher" (20:1, unless emended to מורה היחד "the teacher of the Community") and also יורה היחיד (20:14).[62] Unfortunately, these passages are not preserved in the 4QD fragments.

Two lexical items deserve special mention. The realization of both depends upon the reading of a *waw* or *yodh*. The first is הגו/הגי. The widely cited Geniza form הגו in the expression בספר הגו (10:6, 13:2, 14:8), shows up in 4QD fragments with *yodh*[63]: בספר הגי (266 8 iii 5); ההוגי (267 9 v 12); and בספר ההגי[ן] (270 6 iv 17). The realization *hăgî* now seems certain (see also הגי, 1QSa 1:7, and הגיא, 4Q491 11:21),[64] though the supralinear *waw* in 4Q267 does suggest a reading of *hógî*.[65]

The second lexeme is שפחה, found in 4Q266 12 7 and 4Q270 4 14 and, according to the transcription in DJD 18, שופחה. Qimron has argued that *yodh* "is extremely rare"[66] as a *mater lectionis* for short *i* in closed syllables in the Dead Sea Scrolls[67] and in such cases prefers to read *waw*, e.g., רוקמה instead of ריקמה (1QM 5:6, 9, 14). This interpretation of Qumran orthographic practice may underlie Baumgarten's decision to read *waw* in שופחה. As is well-known, however, it is difficult, sometimes even impossible, in many manuscripts to distinguish between *waw* and *yodh*. If the reading with *waw* is correct, then the *o/u* vowel results from the assimilation to the following labial *pe*. The regressive assimilation of *a* to *o* before labials and *reš* is

---

[60] For a survey, see G. B. Sarfatti, "Definiteness in Noun-Adjective Phrases in Rabbinic Hebrew," *Studies in the Hebrew Language and Talmudic Literature Dedicated to the Memory of Dr. Menaḥem Moreshet* (ed. M. Z. Kaddari and S. Sharvit; Ramat-Gan: Bar-Ilan University, 1989) 153-67 (Hebrew).

[61] Only the *ḥeth* is preserved in 4Q269 4 ii 1. Baumgarten reconstructs ברית ה[ח]דשה.

[62] See Rabin, *Zadokite Documents*, 37, n. 1 to 20:1. Qimron, for example, prefers היחד.

[63] See Baumgarten, DJD 18.67.

[64] See M. Goshen-Gottstein, "'Sefer Hagu,'—The End of a Puzzle," *VT* 8 (1958) 286-88, who believes that ההגו should be read ההגי and was realized as *hahege*. Rabin, *Zadokite Documents*, 50, note to 10:6, suggested that the orthography reflected *hăgî*, a borrowing from Aramaic. Qimron (*Hebrew of the Dead Sea Scrolls*, 21, 66) also interprets the orthography to reflect *hăgî*, but implies that the form reflects the Hebrew ל"ה noun pattern (like בכי, בלי). See also Baumgarten, DJD 18.67.

[65] See Baumgarten, DJD 18.110.

[66] Qimron, *Hebrew of Dead Sea Scrolls*, 19, n. 5. See also idem, "The Distinction between Waw and Yod in the Qumran Scrolls," *Beth Mikra* 18 (1973) 112-22 (Hebrew).

[67] Note, however, that it is attested in CD (Ginzberg, *Eine unbekannte jüdische Sekte*, 3-4) לתיתו (1:6), וניבוריהם (3:9), והניצל (4:18), נתפשים (4:20), נימול (16:6), and it can also be found in reliable manuscripts of mishnaic Hebrew; J. N. Epstein, *Mabo' le-Nusaḥ ha-Mishnah* (Jerusalem, 1948) 2.1241-73.

a phenomenon that is attested in the Scrolls, in mishnaic Hebrew, and frequently in Palestinian Aramaic dialects.[68] It is not found elsewhere in this lexeme in Hebrew, however, whereas the orthography with *yodh* does occur, for example, in reliable manuscripts of mishnaic Hebrew, as demonstrated in *The Historical Dictionary of the Hebrew Language*.[69]

Finally, 4Q266, unlike other 4QD fragments and Qumran fragments in general, contains examples of what appears to be the Aramaic 3 m.s. pronominal suffix *-eh*. One finds אפה "his anger" (2 ii 21; as against אפו in the corresponding passage עד אשר חרה אפו בם, CD 2:21); לחללה טמאתם (5 ii 6) "to profile him with their uncleanness"; בדרשה אותו (8 i 2) "when he examines him" (cf. בדרשו אתו, CD 15:11); ולפי דעתה "according to his knowledge" (8 i 6; cf. ולפי דעתו, CD 15:5); רעה "with his neighbor" (8 ii 6; cf. ע[ם רעהו, 4Q270 6 iii). This apparent Aramaism is not all that surprising since both Hebrew and Aramaic were spoken and written at this period. The use of the Aramaic 3 m.s. pronominal suffix on nouns is possibly attested also in 1QpHab 10:11 כבודה,[70] unless the *he* is the archaic biblical orthography for the Hebrew suffix *o*, which does not seem to be attested elsewhere in the Dead Sea Scrolls.[71] Note that the Aramaic form of the 3 m.s. pronominal suffix on pl. nouns, -והי, appears to be found a number of times at Qumran, unless the examples should be read as the Hebrew pronominal suffix -יהו.[72]

Conclusion

In conclusion, the study of the Hebrew of the Damascus Document has made tremendous strides in the hundred years since the discovery of the Geniza manuscripts. Although many words and expressions aroused immediate interest and were discussed in the light of parallels to biblical, rabbinic, and medieval literature, the study of

---

[68] E. Y. Kutscher, *The Language and Linguistic Background of the Isaiah Scroll (1QIsaᵃ)* (STDJ 6; Leiden: E. J. Brill, 1974) 496-97; Qimron, *Hebrew of the Dead Sea Scrolls*, 39-40, argues that the sound shift occurs not only before labials and *reš* but also liquids.

[69] See MS Kaufmann *Qiddushin* 3:13 and MS Vatican 66 *Sifra ʾAhare* 8:3.

[70] Qimron, *Grammar of the Hebrew Language*, 78-79, 237.

[71] An unusual orthographic practice is found in one Aramaic document, an Aramaic deed of sale from Kefar Baro published by Milik in "Un contrat juif d'an 134 après J.-C.," *RB* 61 (1954) 182-90, in which *he* seems to represent final *ū* in רשה "authority" (l. 9).

[72] See Qimron, "Waw and Yod," 107; idem, *Hebrew of the Dead Sea Scrolls*, 61. -יהו is rare in biblical Hebrew on plural nouns (5x); -והי is attested once in biblical Hebrew (Ps. 116:12).

the grammar, on the whole, lagged behind the study of the vocabulary, with the notable exceptions of the contributions of M. H. Segal before the discovery of the Dead Sea Scrolls, and C. Rabin and E. Qimron since the publication of the Scrolls. The relationship of phenomena in the Damascus Document to features in late biblical Hebrew, mishnaic Hebrew, and the Hebrew of the Dead Sea Scrolls has been proven beyond doubt. Moreover, the Geniza manuscripts of the Damascus Document, once disparaged linguistically, are now recognized as medieval copies that still possess features of an earlier authentic type of Hebrew.[73]

---

[73] As such, they merit linguistic investigation. Research on the grammar of the Dead Sea Scrolls and CD proceeds unabated. For example, see the recent article of M. F. J. Baasten on nominal clauses in which CD is investigated alongside 1QS, 4QS^{a-j}, 1QSa, 1QSb, 1QpHab, 11QT, and 1QM: "Nominal Clauses Containing a Personal Pronoun in Qumran Hebrew," *The Hebrew of the Dead Sea Scrolls and Ben Sira. Proceedings of a Symposium held at Leiden University 11-14, December 1995* (ed. T. Muraoka and J. F. Elwolde; STDJ 26; Leiden: E. J. Brill, 1997) 1-16.

THE LAWS OF THE DAMASCUS DOCUMENT
AND 4QMMT*

Charlotte Hempel

Lucy Cavendish College— University of Cambridge

למשכיל

For Michael Knibb

Introduction

In the light of the recent publication of the Cave 4 manuscripts of
the Damascus Document, the balance of admonitory material *vis-à-
vis* Laws has changed considerably in favour of its legal components.
Whereas the first hundred years or so of research on the Damascus
Document have focused primarily, though not exclusively, on the
Admonition it is foreseeable that the next centenary celebration will
look back on a substantial increase of studies dealing with the legal
part of the document. In this paper I will attempt a preliminary
comparative study of the Laws of the Damascus Document and the
halakhic portion of 4QMMT, a question that has recently been addressed by Lawrence Schiffman in a paper entitled "The Place of
4QMMT in the Corpus of Qumran Manuscripts" and, more briefly,
by Philip Callaway.[1]

Before addressing the particular issues at stake let me briefly outline where I am approaching this question from. In a recent mono-
graph on the Laws of the Damascus Document I have proposed a

* I would like to thank the organizers of this symposium for their kind invitation
and generous hospitality during my visit. I would further like to thank the participants for their comments in the discussion of my paper from which I benefitted
greatly. I am especially grateful to Prof. Joseph M. Baumgarten for a number of
erudite suggestions which he generously shared with me on reading the penultimate
version of this paper.

[1] Cf. L. H. Schiffman, "The Place of 4QMMT in the Corpus of Qumran
Manuscripts," *Reading 4QMMT. New Perspectives on Qumran Law and History* (ed. J.
Kampen and M. J. Bernstein; SBLSym 2; Georgia: Scholars Press, 1996) 81-98,
esp. 90-94, and P. R. Callaway, "4QMMT and Recent Hypotheses on the Origin
of the Qumran Community," *Mogilany 1993. Papers on the Dead Sea Scrolls* (ed. Z. J.
Kapera; Qumranica Mogilanensia 13; Kraków: Enigma, 1996) 15-29, esp. 26. See
also J. Strugnell, "MMT: Second Thoughts on a Forthcoming Edition," *The
Community of the Renewed Covenant. The Notre Dame Symposium on the Dead Sea Scrolls* (ed.
E. Ulrich and J. C. VanderKam; Notre Dame: University of Notre Dame Press,
1994) 57-73, 68.

source- and redaction-critical analysis of this corpus.[2] In the wake of
my source-critical work on the Laws I have undertaken a number of
comparative studies to which this paper may now be added.[3] I have
come to the view that since the Laws of the Damascus Document
comprise a disparate collection of material some of its components
may be fruitfully compared with a collection such as that preserved
in the Community Rule, whereas others have a great deal more in
common with a work such as 4QOrdinances[a] or the halakhic part of
4QMMT.

Apart from a number of miscellaneous traditions and traces of
redactional activity I distinguish two main literary strata in the Laws
of the Damascus Document: a stratum of halakha and a stratum of
community organization. I am well aware that some are uncomfort-
able with the use of the term "halakha" in the context of the Dead
Sea Scrolls.[4] I retain the terminology because it expresses the distinction I am trying to make very well. The alternative of speaking
simply of "laws" with lower case "l" seems unsatisfactory to me because that term is customarily used with upper case "L" to refer to
the part of the Damascus Document that is distinguished from the
Admonition.

4QMMT and Communal Legislation in D

Turning now to the specific question at hand it seems that when it
comes to establishing the relationship between the Laws of D and
4QMMT we can safely exclude the communal legislation stratum.
There is nothing in MMT that refers to matters pertaining to the organization and authority structure of a particular community.[5] By

---

[2] C. Hempel, *The Laws of the Damascus Document. Sources, Traditions and Redaction*
(STDJ 29; Leiden: Brill, 1998).

[3] Cf. C. Hempel, "The Earthly Essene Nucleus of 1QSa," *DSD* 3 (1996) 253-67;
eadem, "The Penal Code Reconsidered," *Legal Texts and Legal Issues. Proceedings of the
Second Meeting of the International Organization for Qumran Studies, Cambridge, 1995
Published in Honour of Joseph M. Baumgarten* (ed. M. J. Bernstein, F. García Martínez
and J. Kampen; STDJ 23; Leiden: Brill, 1997) 337-48; and eadem, "4QOrd[a]
(4Q159) and the Laws of the Damascus Document," *Proceedings of the International
Congress of the Dead Sea Scrolls. Fifty Years after Their Discovery, Jerusalem, July 1997*
(Jerusalem: Israel Exploration Society, forthcoming).

[4] Cf. Strugnell, "Second Thoughts," 65-66; also idem, "More on Wives and
Marriage in the Dead Sea Scrolls: (*4Q416* 2 ii [Cf. *1 Thess* 4:4] and *4QMMT* §B),"
RevQ 17 (1996) 537-47, esp. 541, n. 7. Prof. Shemaryahu Talmon has expressed
similar reservations in a discussion at the Hebrew University's Orion Center in
April 1996.

[5] This has frequently been noted; cf. Y. Sussman, "The History of the Halakhah
and the Dead Sea Scrolls. Preliminary Talmudic Observations on *Miqsat Ma'aśe ha-*

contrast the point of reference seems to be Israel at large, with particular emphasis on the distinctive position of the priesthood *vis-à-vis* the laity.

It is worth noting that the Laws of the Damascus Document are virtually unique among the Qumran documents as well as the wider body of intertestamental literature in combining almost seamlessly communal legislation with halakhic material that lacks reference to a particular organized community. Thus, we have the Community Rule and the Rule of the Congregation[6] as the two main representatives besides the Damascus Document that preserve communal legislation on the one hand, and a host of writings that preserve halakhic traditions on the other hand. Almost uniquely the Laws of the Damascus Document preserve both elements side by side. I say *almost* uniquely because the curious text 4QSerekh Damascus (4Q265), at least according to my understanding, comprises the only further example available to date.[7]

A further feature that deserves to be mentioned here is the shared employment of camp terminology in MMT and in the communal legislation of D.[8] It seems to me that the use and meaning of the terminology is quite distinct in both documents. In the Damascus Document the term camp (מחנה) appears as a unit in the organization of the movement described in the communal legislation. The terminology is used in this sense very unselfconsciously in this text and no need was felt, it seems, to offer a definition. In 4QMMT camp terminology occurs in two passages.[9] In the section dealing with the place of slaughter (4Q394 3-7 ii 14b-19 par.) the references to the camp occur in an exegetical context.[10] The passage in ques-

Torah (4QMMT)," Appendix 1 in E. Qimron and J. Strugnell, *Qumran Cave 4.V. Miqsat Maʿaśe ha-Torah* (DJD 10; Oxford: Clarendon, 1994) 179-200, 186; also Qimron and Strugnell, DJD 10.113 and 121; Strugnell, "Second Thoughts," 68.

[6] For the view that the bulk of 1QSa constitutes communal legislation see my "Earthly Essene Nucleus."

[7] See, however, most recently E. J. C. Tigchelaar's reconstruction and interpretation of 4Q420-421 and 4Q264a in "Sabbath Halakha and Worship in *4QWays of Righteousness: 4Q421* 11 and 13 + 2 + 8 par *4Q264a 1-2*," *RevQ* 18/71 (1998) 359-72.

[8] This feature has been discussed previously by H. Stegemann, "The Qumran Essenes—Local Members of the Main Jewish Union in Late Second Temple Times," *The Madrid Qumran Congress* (ed. J. Trebolle Barrera and L. Vegas Montaner; STDJ 11; Leiden: E. J. Brill, 1992) 1.83-166, esp. 134-37.

[9] Cf. L. H. Schiffman, "The Temple Scroll and the Systems of Jewish Law of the Second Temple Period," *Temple Scroll Studies* (ed. G. J. Brooke; JSPSup 7; Sheffield: JSOT, 1989) 239-55, esp. 248-49.

[10] See L. H. Schiffman, "Sacral and Non-Sacral Slaughter According to the *Temple Scroll*," *Time to Prepare the Way in the Wilderness. Papers on the Qumran Scrolls by Fellows of the Institute for Advanced Studies of the Hebrew University, Jerusalem, 1989-1990*

tion, though fragmentary, constitutes a piece of halakhic exegesis based on Lev. 17:3-4, as noted by Qimron.[11] The scriptural base text includes a reference to the camp which is identified with Jerusalem in the interpretation offered subsequently. The exegetical context of the references to the camp are accentuated by the technical term כָּתוּב,[12] introducing the reference to Leviticus 17 as well as the multiple occurrence of the third person singular pronoun in the technical sense attested frequently in exegetical texts from Qumran. The second section that employs camp terminology is found in 4Q394 8 iv 8b-12a par. and begins with the prohibition of dogs entering Jerusalem.[13] Although the original prohibition is not scriptural the subsequent justification beginning with כִּי is written in the same exegetical style as the previous section on camps. That is, an element of the prohibition, "the camp of holiness" (מחנה הקודש), is identified with Jerusalem, and the third person singular pronoun is used repeatedly. It seems possible that the term "the camp of holiness" and the exegetical leap to identify this with Jerusalem are based on Deut. 23:15 where the notion of the holiness of the camp is developed. Finally, it is worth noting that in both sections in MMT that employ camp terminology Jerusalem is identified as the camp, and that this identification is followed in both cases by an affirmation in deuteronomic style of the election of Jerusalem as "the place which He has chosen from all the tribes of Israel."[14] In sum, the Laws of

---

(ed. D. Dimant and L. H. Schiffman; STDJ 16; Leiden: E. J. Brill, 1995) 69-84. Further, E. Eshel, "4QLev^d: A Possible Source for the Temple Scroll and *Miqṣat Maʿaśe Ha-Torah*," *DSD* 2 (1995) 1-13.

[11] Cf. Qimron and Strugnell, DJD 10.156-57. For a discussion of the scriptural background, see M. J. Bernstein, "The Employment and Interpretation of Scripture in 4QMMT: Preliminary Observations," *Reading 4QMMT*, 29-51, esp. 39-40; G. J. Brooke, "The Explicit Presentation of Scripture in 4QMMT," *Legal Texts and Legal Issues*, 67-88, 72. Brooke shows that on closer inspection Lev. 17:3 has been re-ordered here rather than paraphrased, a term that implies rewording, as was argued previously.

[12] On the use of כתוב in MMT see Brooke, "Explicit Presentation of Scripture in 4QMMT," 71.

[13] E. Qimron has recently identified a fragment of a third copy of the Temple Scroll (11QT^c) that includes a prohibition of rearing chickens in Jerusalem and noted its affinity to the attitude about dogs in Jerusalem in 4QMMT; cf. E. Qimron, "Chickens in the Temple Scroll (11QT^c)," *Tarbiz* 64 (1995) 473-76 (Hebrew), and E. Qimron, *The Temple Scroll. A Critical Edition with Extensive Reconstructions. Bibliography by F. García Martínez* (Beer Sheva: Ben-Gurion University of the Negev Press; Jerusalem: Israel Exploration Society, 1996) 69. See also J. M. Baumgarten, "The 'Halakhah' in *Miqṣat Maʿaśe Ha-Torah* (MMT)," *JAOS* 116 (1996) 514, where he argues that the halakhic concern about dogs articulated in MMT may bear upon the practice of burying animal bones attested at Qumran.

[14] The latter phrase is partly restored in the Composite Text (B32-33) based on 4Q394 3-7 ii 19 par. 4Q397 3:5. Since the opening words of such a statement are

the Damascus Document and MMT employ camp terminology in a distinct manner. In the Laws of D camp terminology is used to refer to what appear to be well-established administrative and organizational units, whereas in MMT camp terminology occurs in two passages in an exegetical/definitional context with a Jerusalem-centric perspective.[15]

4QMMT and Halakha in D

Let me now turn to the halakha stratum of the Damascus Document and its relationship to the halakhic section of MMT. Here correspondences can be observed on a number of levels. I will begin with three observations of a general kind and then turn to a number of specific texts.

General Observations

1 The halakha stratum of the Laws of D shares with the halakhic section of MMT a lack of reference to a particular community that defines itself in distinction from society at large.
2 On a formal level both the halakha stratum of the Laws of D and the halakhic section of MMT frequently employ headings introduced by the preposition על "concerning."[16] This preposition seems to have been the standard way of compiling strings of halakhic statements or expositions in the late Second Temple period. Baumgarten has drawn attention to the historical significance of this phenomenon.[17] Outside of D and MMT it is found also in 4QOrdinances[a] and the still unpublished 4QHalakhah A.[18]

----

clearly preserved in 4Q394 3-7 ii 19 (היא המקום אשר) the editors' restoration seems plausible.

[15] For a discussion see Qimron, DJD 10.143-45.

[16] Prof. J. M. Baumgarten has drawn my attention to the difference in length of the blocks of material introduced by על headings in D and MMT respectively, and to the fact that whereas these headings appear to be rubrics in D they introduce single statements in MMT. It is also noteworthy that great variety in the length of the blocks of material thus introduced exists already within D itself. One need only compare the brief sections on women's oaths (CD 16:10-12) or oaths (CD 9:8b-10a) to the long treatment of the Sabbath (CD 10:14-11:18b).

[17] Cf. J. M. Baumgarten, *Qumran Cave 4.XIII. The Damascus Document (4Q266-273)* (DJD 18; Oxford: Clarendon, 1996) 14-15, as well as his contribution to the present volume (17-26).

[18] For preliminary editions of the text see J. T. Milik in *Les "Petites Grottes" de Qumrân. Exploration de la falaise. Les grottes 2Q, 3Q, 5Q, 6Q, 7Q à 10Q. Le rouleau de cuivre* (ed. M. Baillet, J. T. Milik and R. de Vaux; DJDJ 3; Oxford: Clarendon, 1962) 300, where the text of frg. 5 only is transcribed; *A Preliminary Edition of the Unpublished Dead Sea Scrolls. The Hebrew and Aramaic Texts from Cave Four. Fascicle Three* (ed. B. Z.

3 A particular sub-category of halakha in D deals with matters pertaining to the priesthood. I have chosen the term *torot* to identify
this sub-category, a term derived from Jacob Milgrom's analysis
of Leviticus 1-16 where he defines *torot* as "the special lore of the
priesthood."[19] Moreover, in a paper on the origins of the Temple
Scroll Hartmut Stegemann has applied the term *torot* to the laws
contained in the Temple Scroll.[20] I have assigned the two sizeable
blocks of additional legal material from 4QD that deal with the
disqualification of certain categories of priests[21] and the section
dealing with the diagnosis of skin disease[22] to this category. As I
will argue below, a great deal of the additional legal material in
4QD reflects priestly concerns. However, what seems to set apart
the sections on priestly disqualifications and skin disease is that
whereas much of 4QD gives the impression of having been written *by priests*, these particular sections seem to have been written *by
priests* as well as *for priests* and, one might add, *about priests*. It is of
course well-known that priestly concerns lie at the heart of the halakhot in MMT also.

Specific Texts

1. *The 4QD Material on the Disqualification of Priests*
The material on the disqualification of certain categories of priests
preserved in 4QD[a] 5 ii 1-16; 4QD[b] 5 iii 1-8; 4QD[h] 2:1-2; 4 i 5-11
shares with the halakhic portion of MMT an explicit focus on priestly concerns. This hardly needs spelling out for the disqualification
material and is equally beyond dispute regarding MMT. In the latter case one need only look at the refrain, "For the priests shall take

---

Wacholder and M. G. Abegg; Washington, DC: Biblical Archaeology Society,
1992) 34-40; and most recently *The Dead Sea Scrolls Study Edition. Volume One 1Q1-
4Q273* (ed. F. García Martínez and E. J. C. Tigchelaar; Leiden: Brill, 1997) 496-
501.

[19] J. Milgrom, *Leviticus 1-16. A New Translation with Introduction and Commentary* (AB
3; New York: Doubleday, 1991) 2.

[20] Cf. H. Stegemann, "The Origins of the Temple Scroll," *VTSup* 40 (1988) 235-
56, esp. 255, where he describes the laws of the Temple Scrolls as "old *tôrôt* originating among the priests at the temple in Jerusalem."

[21] Cf. J. M. Baumgarten, "The Disqualifications of Priests in 4Q Fragments of
the 'Damascus Document,' a Specimen of the Recovery of Pre-rabbinic Halakha,"
Madrid Qumran Congress, 2.503-13.

[22] Cf. J. M. Baumgarten, "The 4Q Zadokite Fragments on Skin Disease," *JJS* 41
(1990) 153-65, and E. Qimron, "Notes on the 4Q Zadokite Fragments on Skin
Disease," *JJS* 42 (1991) 256-59.

[23] The textual remains of this phrase are substantially preserved in both the first
and third instance. In 4Q394 3-7 i 19 - ii 1a, remnants of a further occurrence of
this refrain may be preserved.

heed concerning x so as not to cause the people to bear sin," which occurs three times in MMT (4Q394 3-7 i 14-16; 4Q394 3-7 i 19 - ii 1a; 4Q394 3-7 ii 13-14)[23] and is based on Lev. 22:16.[24]

Related to this priestly flavour is the common concern articulated in both texts with the purity of the sanctuary and the offerings. Furthermore, both texts include statements that describe the conduct of some priests as falling short of the expected standard, cf. 4QD[a] 5 ii 10-11 which refers to a priest who has caused his name to fall from the truth and the critique of intermarriage with Israelites (on Qimron's interpretation[25]) or with Gentiles (on Baumgarten's interpretation[26]) practised by some priests, according to 4Q396 1-2 iv 4-11. Whatever interpretation one favours for the latter fragmentary passage it seems clear from 4Q396 1-2 iv 9-11 that some priests are being criticised for their nuptial practices. To be sure, the shortfall in the behaviour of priests criticised in each text is of a different kind, and there is nothing to indicate in 4QD[a] 5 ii that priestly marital practices are an issue in D. It is nevertheless noteworthy that both texts seem to contain material commenting on priestly misconduct of some kind.

This overlap, though general, suggests that both texts reflect inner-priestly disputes. It has already been convincingly suggested by Schiffman that inner-priestly disputes form the background to 4QMMT.[27] I would like to add to this that this particular part of the Laws of D points in a similar direction. I would not want to attach any further labels to these priestly groups since it seems to me that the debates about the names to be given to the Qumran groups, legitimate though they may be, should not dominate the discussion of the issues raised by their writings.[28]

---

[24] Cf. Qimron and Strugnell, DJD 10.48, n. on B13. See also Bernstein, "Employment and Interpretation of Scripture in 4QMMT," 36.

[25] Cf. Qimron and Strugnell, DJD 10.171-75.

[26] Baumgarten's position is spelled out by Qimron, DJD 10.55, n. on B75 and 171, n. 178a, and Baumgarten has argued his case in "The 'Halakhah' in *Miqsat Ma'aśe Ha-Torah*," 515-16. Grabbe has recently expressed his support for Baumgarten's interpretation, cf. L. L. Grabbe, "4QMMT and Second Temple Jewish Society," *Legal Texts and Legal Issues*, 89-108, 103, n. 53. See also R. A. Kugler, "Halakic Interpretative Strategies at Qumran: A Case Study," *Legal Texts and Legal Issues*, 131-40, esp. 135-36, who concludes his analysis, "we are left with an ambiguous passage, at least with respect to precisely whom priests may not marry," 136.

[27] Cf. L. H. Schiffman, "The New Halakhic Letter (4QMMT) and the Origins of the Dead Sea Sect," *BA* 53 (1990) 64-73.

[28] A similar sentiment is expressed by Strugnell, "Second Thoughts," 65. See also J. M. Baumgarten's recent cautious assessment of this issue in "Sadducean Elements in Qumran Law," *The Community of the Renewed Covenant*, 27-36, and the balanced and cautious argumentation by Y. Sussman, "History of the Halakhah," 192-96 and 200. Further, Grabbe, "4QMMT and Second Temple Jewish Society"; L. H.

Finally, the theological rationale given for the disqualification of priests with imperfect pronunciation from reading the Torah in 4QD^a 5 ii 1-3 reflects a broadly equivalent approach to physical defects as is expressed with regard to the blind and the deaf in 4QMMT (4Q394 8 iii 19 - iv 4). According to 4QD priests with defective pronunciation are barred from reading the Torah in case they mislead in a capital matter. 4QMMT seems to criticize the presence of blind and deaf people in the vicinity of the purity of the Temple because the deaf are unable to hear the commandments and the blind may inadvertently fail to act according to the laws on mixtures.[29] Thus, in all three cases the theological concern is obedience to the Torah which may be put in jeopardy by physical imperfections.[30] A rather different rationale for excluding the blind and the deaf from the congregation is expressed in CD 15:15b-17a par. 4QD^a 8 i 6-7 and 1QSa 2:4b-9. Both texts include the blind and the deaf in lists of persons to be excluded from the congregation because of the presence of angels.[31] On my analysis of the Laws of D the exclusion passage in CD 15 par. occurs in the context of a piece of communal legislation on the admission into the covenant community.

Schiffman, "The Sadducean Origins of the Dead Sea Scroll Sect," *Understanding the Dead Sea Scrolls* (ed. H. Shanks; London: SPCK, 1993) 35-49; idem, "New Halakhic Texts from Qumran," *Hebrew Studies* 34 (1993) 21-33; J. C. VanderKam, "The People of the Dead Sea Scrolls: Essenes or Sadducees," *Understanding the Dead Sea Scrolls*, 50-62. See also A. I. Baumgarten, "Rabbinic Literature as a Source for the History of Jewish Sectarianism in the Second Temple Period," *DSD* 2 (1995) 14-57, esp. 22-30.

[29] The Hebrew term used is תערבת; for linguistic comments see Qimron, DJD 10.96.

[30] Cf. Qimron and Strugnell, DJD 10.160, where Qimron observes with reference to the blind and the deaf in 4QMMT "... none of them are able to act in accordance with the laws of purity." See also A. Shemesh, "'The Holy Angels are in Their Council': The Exclusion of Deformed Persons from Holy Places in Qumranic and Rabbinic Literature," *DSD* 4 (1997) 201, n. 60.

[31] See also the material in 4Q396 1-2 i 5-6 par. and 4Q394 8 iii 12b-19a par. which is critical of various categories of people entering the assembly and marrying Israelites. Cf. further 1QM 7:4b-6a, 4QFlor 1:3b-5a and 11QT^a 45:12-14. For scholarly discussions see J. M. Baumgarten, *Studies in Qumran Law* (SJLA 24; Leiden: E. J. Brill, 1977) 75-87; G. J. Brooke, *Exegesis at Qumran. 4QFlorilegium in its Jewish Context* (JSOTSup 29; Sheffield: JSOT, 1985) 178-83; M. J. Davidson, *Angels at Qumran. A Comparative Study of 1 Enoch 1-36, 72-108 and Sectarian Writings from Qumran* (JSPSup 11; Sheffield: Sheffield Academic Press, 1992) 185-86; Qimron and Strugnell, DJD 10.145-47; L. H. Schiffman, "Exclusion from the Sanctuary and the City of the Sanctuary in the Temple Scroll," *Hebrew Annual Review* 9 (1985) 301-20; idem, "Purity and Perfection: Exclusion from the Council of the Community in the *Serekh Ha-'Edah*," *Biblical Archaeology Today* (ed. Janet Amitai; Jerusalem: Israel Exploration Society, 1985) 373-89; idem, *The Eschatological Community of the Dead Sea Scrolls. A Study of the Rule of the Congregation* (SBLMS 38; Atlanta: Scholars Press, 1989) 47-48; Shemesh, "'The Holy Angels are in Their Council'"; Y. Yadin, *The Temple Scroll* (Jerusalem: Israel Exploration Society, 1983) 1.289-91.

It suffices to stress here that the theological emphases reflected in the material on the disqualification of priests and the exclusion of the blind and the deaf in 4QMMT overlap.

2. The 4QD Material on Skin Disease, Flux[32] and Childbirth

A similar relationship exists between the block of material dealing with skin disease, flux and childbirth in 4QD^a 6 i-iii; 4QD^d 7; 4QD^g 1 i-ii; 4QD^h 4 ii and the halakhic portion of MMT. This part of the Laws of D is heavily based on Leviticus 12-15 and, as noted above, particularly the portion dealing with skin disease has a pronounced and explicit priestly character. A concern for the purity of the sanctuary, a dominant theme in MMT, is reflected in 4QD^a 6 ii 4 where women with a discharge are prohibited from entering the sanctuary. As noted by Baumgarten such a prohibition is not scriptural and was probably derived by analogy to the legislation on childbirth in Lev. 12:4.[33] Finally, 4QD^a 6 ii 4 reflects the same halakhic position on the question of purification as it is expressed in MMT, as Schiffman has already noted.[34] Thus, both 4QD^a 6 ii 4 and 4Q396 1-2 iv 1a insist that an impure person (a woman with a discharge in the case of D and a person with leprosy in the case of MMT) remains so until sunset on the eighth day.[35] The same halakhic position comes to the fore in 4QD^d 8 ii 3b-6 par., which deals with the topic of purification after contracting corpse impurity and the passage laying down the requirements for those preparing the red cow in MMT (4Q394 3-7 i 16b - ii 1a par.). Both passages insist on the sprinkler waiting for sundown.[36] Finally, Avi Solomon has recently argued that CD

---

[32] Cf. J. M. Baumgarten, "The Laws about Fluxes in 4QTohora^a (4Q274)," *Time to Prepare the Way in the Wilderness*, 1-8, and idem, "Zab Impurity in Qumran and Rabbinic Law," *JJS* 45 (1994) 273-77. See also J. Milgrom, "4QTohora^a: An Unpublished Qumran Text on Purities," *Time to Prepare the Way in the Wilderness*, 59-68. Whereas Baumgarten argues that 4Q274 1:1-4a deals with *zab* impurity Milgrom is of the opinion that the same lines pertain to skin disease.

[33] Baumgarten, DJD 18.56.

[34] See Schiffman, "Place of 4QMMT," 90.

[35] Cf. J. M. Baumgarten, "Pharisaic-Sadducean Controversies about Purity," *JJS* 31 (1980) 157-70; L. H. Schiffman, "*Miqṣat Maʿaśe Ha-Torah* and the Temple Scroll," *RevQ* 14 (1990) 435-57, esp. 438-42; idem, "Pharisaic and Sadducean Halakhah in the Light of the Dead Sea Scrolls. The Case of the *Ṭebul Yom*," *DSD* 1 (1994) 285-99; and Qimron and Strugnell, DJD 10.166-70.

[36] Cf. Baumgarten, DJD 18.130-32; Qimron and Strugnell, DJD 10.152-54, and the articles by Baumgarten and Schiffman cited in the preceding note. Cf. also M. Broshi, "Anti-Qumranic Polemics in the Talmud," *The Madrid Qumran Congress*, 2.589-600, esp. 591-92. The same halakhic position is expressed also in 4Q277 1:5-6. For a preliminary transcription, translation, and commentary on this text see J. M. Baumgarten, "The Red Cow Purification Rites in Qumran Texts," *JJS* 46 (1995) 112-19.

11:21-12:1 is best understood against the background of the *Ṭevul yom* debate.[37]

3. *4QD Halakha Dealing with Agricultural Matters*

Legal questions relating to the agricultural sphere, particularly the harvest, make up a large proportion of the additional legal material from Cave 4 in D (cf. 4QD^a 6 iii a; 4QD^e 3 i; 4QD^a 6 iii par. 4QD^b 6 and 4QD^e 3 ii[38]; 4QD^a 6 iv; 4QD^f 2:1-5 par. 4QD^e 3 iii 13-15). In an article on 4QOrd^a (4Q159) Francis Weinert suggested some years ago that the agricultural questions dealt with in 4Q159, particularly the material on the rights of the poor to gather grapes and grain in 4Q159 1 ii 2-5, suggest an agricultural milieu. Thus, he argues, "*4Q159* would seem to presume an agricultural situation where poverty lies in the background."[39] Should the same be said about D? I think not. Rather, it seems to me that the agricultural issues raised in D are dealt with from the particular point of view of the priesthood. The key issue is the harvest and the appropriate contributions to the priests and the sanctuary. Thus, on a general level this very substantial portion of 4QD shares the priestly character of the halakhic portion of MMT. Incidentally, I do not agree with Weinert's assessment of the situation behind 4Q159 as indicative of poverty and agriculture, since the topic of gleanings addressed there is based on scripture (cf. Deut. 23:25-26), and the writer's concern is exegetical rather than a social comment.

A specific topic that is addressed both in 4QD^a 6 iv 4 and 4Q396 1-2 iii 2b-3a is the fourth year produce.[40] Although the legislation in 4QMMT does not explicitly refer to the fourth year Qimron has shown that 4QMMT is closely based on Lev. 19:23-24, the biblical text on the produce of the fourth year.[41] According to Lev. 19:23-25 the fourth year produce from the fruit trees is to be offered to the Lord. In addition to 4QD and 4QMMT a host of post-biblical sources interpret this law to mean that the fourth year produce belongs to the priests (cf. Jub. 7:35-37, 11QT^a 60:3-4; 1QapGen

---

[37] See A. Solomon, "The Prohibition Against *Ṭevul Yom* and Defilement of the Daily Whole Offering in the Jerusalem Temple in CD 11:21-12:1: A New Understanding," *DSD* 4 (1997) 1-20.

[38] On this text and its parallels in 4QD^a and b, cf. J. M. Baumgarten, "A Qumran Text with Agrarian Halakhah," *JQR* 86 (1995) 1-8. Note that the numeration of fragments has changed since this article appeared, and I have adopted the numeration as it appears in Baumgarten's *editio princeps* of the 4QD manuscripts.

[39] F. D. Weinert, "*4Q159*: Legislation for an Essene Community Outside of Qumran?," *JSJ* 5 (1974) 179-207, 206.

[40] Cf. Schiffman, "Place of 4QMMT," 90-91.

[41] Cf. Qimron and Strugnell, DJD 10.164-65.

12:13-15).[42] As far as this paper is concerned it is of interest that the position advanced with regard to the fourth year produce is shared by 4QMMT and D.

4. *Texts Expressing Concern about Defilement through Contact with Gentiles*
Concern to avoid defilement through contact with Gentiles, particularly the pagan cult, is voiced in a number of passages in the Laws of D.[43] CD 12:6b-11 provides a series of restrictions on dealings with Gentiles[44] which includes a prohibition of selling clean animals or birds to the Gentiles lest they sacrifice. This is followed in CD 12:9b-10a by a prohibition of selling produce from the threshing floor or wine press to the Gentiles. This prohibition is taken by Ginzberg and Schiffman to refer to the sale of untithed produce.[45] However, the alternative mentioned by Ginzberg, and kindly brought to my attention by Prof. Baumgarten, was to regard m. 'Abod. Zar. 1:1 as the background to this prohibition, in which case this part of the halakhot on relations with Gentiles would share the concern with cultic misuse by Gentiles dominant elsewhere in this series of regulations. In the additional legal material from Cave 4, 4QD[a] 5 ii 5-6 seems to refer to the impurity of priests taken captive by the Gentiles.[46] Finally 4QD[d] 8 ii 1-3 refers to the dangers of defilement through Gentile sacrifices, if we accept Baumgarten's interpretation of the third person masc. pl. suffix in line 1,[47] as well as metals that have been used in pagan cults. As far as 4QMMT is concerned, as restored in the *editio princeps* 4Q394 3-7 i 6b-8a prohibits bringing Gentile wheat into the temple. However, too little text is preserved to allow us even to be certain about the subject matter addressed, and in a review article of DJD 10 Baumgarten has rightly drawn attention to the textual uncertainties of this ruling.[48] We are on slightly firmer ground in 4Q394 3-7 i 11b-12a par. which deals with the

---

[42] For a comprehensive discussion see J. M. Baumgarten, "The Laws of 'Orlah and First Fruits in the Light of Jubilees, the Qumran Writings, and Targum Ps. Jonathan," *JJS* 38 (1987) 195-202; M. Kister, "Some Aspects of Qumranic Halakhah," *The Madrid Qumran Congress*, 2.571-88, esp. 575-88; and Schiffman, "*Miqsat Ma'aśe Ha-Torah* and the Temple Scroll," 452-56.

[43] See Schiffman, "Place of 4QMMT," 92.

[44] Cf. L. H. Schiffman, "Legislation concerning Relations with Non-Jews in the *Zadokite Fragments* and in Tannaitic Literature," *RevQ* 11 (1989) 379-89.

[45] See L. Ginzberg, *An Unknown Jewish Sect* (New York City: JTS, 1976) 77-78, and Schiffman, "Legislation concerning Relations with Non-Jews," 387-88.

[46] Following the interpretation of 4QD[a] 5 ii 6 proposed by Baumgarten, DJD 18.51.

[47] Cf. Baumgarten, DJD 18.131.

[48] Cf. Baumgarten, "The 'Halakhah' in *Miqsat Ma'aśe Ha-Torah*," 512.

sacrifices of Gentiles. Whatever the exact scenario envisaged here, it
is clear that this part of 4QMMT as well as a number of passages in
the Laws of D address the danger of defilement through contact
with Gentiles.

5. *The Catalogue of Transgressions in 4QD*[49]
A fragmentary catalogue of transgressions preserved in 4QD^c 2 i 9 -
ii 21 is particularly instructive for an analysis of the relationship between the Laws of the Damascus Document and the halakhic portion of MMT.[50] It is instructive to distinguish between the body of
the catalogue, the actual list of transgressions, and the conclusion
found at the end of the catalogue. The conclusion to the catalogue is
found in 4QD^c 2 ii 17b-18 in the form of a warning against transgressors of the consequences of provoking divine wrath. Immediately following this conclusion, lines 19-21 begin with a call to
hearken that is reminiscent of similar calls in the Admonition and
read "And now listen to me all who know righteousness"
(ועתה שמעו לי כל יודעי צדק). In particular this call to hearken may be
compared to 4QD^a 1 a-b 5; CD 1:1; 2:2, 14.[51] In his outline of the
contents of the Damascus Document, Baumgarten has placed the
fragments containing this catalogue at the end of the Admonition
rather than taking it as part of the legal portion of D, and I believe
he was following Milik's placement here. It seems likely that the
presence of the call to hearken influenced this editorial decision.

Furthermore, in an outline of the contents of 4QD that appeared
some years before his official edition Baumgarten notes in his description of the catalogue of transgressions, "The author *concludes*
[emphasis mine] with an appeal to the יודעי צדק to choose between
the 'ways of life' and the 'paths of perdition'."[52] Rather than taking
this call to hearken and the subsequent admonition to follow the
ways of life and to avoid the paths of destruction as a conclusion to
the preceding catalogue of transgressions, it seems preferable to un-

---

[49] On this material, see the contribution by J. M. Baumgarten in this volume,
17-26.
[50] Cf. Baumgarten, DJD 18.142-46.
[51] See also 4Q298 which attests similar calls to attention, cf. S. Pfann, "4Q298:
The Maskil's Address to All Sons of Dawn," *JQR* 85 (1994) 203-35 and M. Kister,
"Commentary to 4Q298," *JQR* 85 (1994) 237-49. See also 4Q185, cf. A. Lange,
*Weisheit und Prädestination. Weisheitliche Urordnung und Prädestination in den Textfunden von
Qumran* (STDJ 18; Leiden: E. J. Brill, 1995) 253, n. 83. See also S. Pfann and M.
Kister in *Qumran Cave 4.XV. Sapiential Texts, Part 1* (ed. T. Elgvin et al.; DJD 20;
Oxford: Clarendon, 1997) 1-30.
[52] J. M. Baumgarten, "The Laws of the *Damascus Document* in Current Research,"
The Damascus Document Reconsidered (ed. M. Broshi; Jerusalem: Israel Exploration
Society, Shrine of the Book, Israel Museum, 1992) 51-62, 53.

derstand the call to hearken as an introduction to what follows as is indeed the case in all the other instances where a similar call to attention occurs in the Admonition of the Damascus Document.

I am delighted to learn that Prof. Stegemann concurs and has gone further in his contribution to this volume by thinking through the probable consequences of the presence of admonitory material at this point for the overall structure of D.[53] He is surely right when he argues that we should reckon with a substantial admonitory section to have followed this call. An initial understanding of this call to attention as a conclusion can be accounted for by the fragmentary nature of the material. Because of accidents of preservation virtually everything that followed our call to hearken has been lost, so that as the fragments now stand it looks at first sight as if this call concludes the preceding list of transgressions.

For our present purposes it is most instructive to focus on the fragmentary list of transgressions preserved in 4QD^e 2 i 9-ii 17a. This list includes a number of issues that are developed in more detail elsewhere in the Laws of D, and, what is more, several of the topics addressed in the catalogue are included in the halakhic portion of 4QMMT as well as in 11QT. This overlap between 4QD, 4QMMT, and 11QT has been noted by a number of scholars.[54] It is noteworthy, furthermore, that the catalogue does not raise any topic dealt with in the communal legislation stratum of the Laws and that the overlap is restricted to the halakha stratum. That is to say, there is nothing in the list of transgressions that speaks in terms of a particular organized community. Baumgarten takes the reference to "those anointed with the holy spirit" in 4QD^e 2 ii 14 as a reference to "inspired teachers of the community."[55] It seems more likely to me, however, that this expression refers to the prophets as is the case in CD 2:12-13. Such an identification is suggested by a number of biblical passages, esp. Ps. 105:15.[56] Moreover, the reference to the offence of revealing a secret of his people to the nations in 4QD^e 2 ii 13 clearly reflects a national perspective.[57]

---

[53] Stegemann, "Towards Physical Reconstructions of the Qumran Damascus Document Scrolls," 177-200.

[54] Cf. Baumgarten, DJD 18.145-46; O. Betz, "The Qumran Halakhah Text Miqṣat Maʿaśe Ha-Tôrah (4QMMT) and Sadducean, Essene, and Early Pharisaic Tradition," *The Aramaic Bible. Targums in Their Historical Context* (ed. D. R. G. Beattie and M. J. McNamara; Sheffield: JSOT, 1994) 176-202; and Schiffman, "Place of 4QMMT."

[55] Baumgarten, DJD 18.146.

[56] Cf. M. A. Knibb, *The Qumran Community* (Cambridge: Cambridge University Press, 1987) 27.

[57] A similar offence is found in 11QT^a 64:6-9 and the Ein Gedi inscription; see

As far as the literary growth of the Laws of the Damascus Document is concerned, two alternatives seem possible to me. Either this list was a pre-existent document that was incorporated into the Laws, and a number of issues were spelt out in more detail subsequently; or the list of transgressions is a kind of summary of the topics dealt with in the halakhic stratum of the Laws of D. The former seems more likely to me. It seems less likely that we are dealing with a summary of halakhic points that was composed at a late stage in the development of the halakha stratum since not all the material mentioned in the catalogue is dealt with elsewhere, although because of the fragmentary nature of both the catalogue and the rest of the Laws it is difficult to be sure.

If the catalogue of transgressions pre-dated the rest of the Laws it could be of central importance for our understanding of the growth of the Laws, or at least for the literary growth of the halakhic component of the Laws. It may have served as a skeleton parts of which were subsequently fleshed out. Moreover, the largest number of thematic correspondences between the Laws of D and the halakhic portion of 4QMMT can be traced to this catalogue of transgressions.[58]

1 4QD^e 2 ii 6 as read and partly restored by Baumgarten deals with the fourth year produce. This topic is dealt with again in 4QD^a 6 iv 4 and in 4Q396 1-2 iii 2b-3a, and both passages were briefly dealt with above.

2 4QD^e 2 ii 7-8 is partially preserved and as plausibly completed by Baumgarten deals with the tithe of cattle and sheep, an issue referred to also in 4Q396 1-2 iii 3b-4a.

3 Skin disease is mentioned in the catalogue in 4QD^e 2 ii 12, taken up in the body of the Laws of D in 4QD^a 6 i par. as well as in 4Q396 1-2 iii 4b-11 - iv 1a par.

4 Slaughtering pregnant animals is referred to as a contentious issue in 4QD^e 2 ii 15 as well as in 4Q396 1-2 i 2-4 par.[59]

Baumgarten, DJD 18.146 and M. Weinfeld, *The Organizational Pattern and the Penal Code of the Qumran Sect. A Comparison with Guilds and Religious Associations of the Hellenistic-Roman Period* (Göttingen: Vandenhoeck & Ruprecht; Fribourg: Éditions Universitaires, 1986) 25.

[58] The overlap between the catalogue of transgressions and 4QMMT is noted also by Baumgarten, DJD 18.13.

[59] See also 11QT^a 52:5, cf. Schiffman, "*Miqṣat Maʿaśe Ha-Torah* and the Temple Scroll," 448-51; idem, "Place of 4QMMT," 88 and 93. Further, J. M. Baumgarten, "A Fragment on Fetal Life and Pregnancy in 4Q270," *Pomegranates and Bells. Studies in Biblical, Jewish, and Near Eastern Ritual, Law, and Literature in Honor of Jacob Milgrom* (ed. D. Wright, D. N. Freedman and A. Hurvitz; Winona Lake: Eisenbrauns, 1995) 445-48.

In sum, the relatively small amount of text preserved of the list of transgressions in 4QDᵉ deals with four issues that are paralleled in the halakhot in MMT.

Conclusion

By way of conclusion let me sum up the results of these comparative remarks as well as offer a number of further reflections. Rather than comparing the Laws of the Damascus Document *in toto* to 4QMMT I have focused on those parts of both documents that resemble each other most closely, i.e. the halakha stratum of the Laws of D and the halakhic portion of 4QMMT. Correspondences of various kinds (theological, halakhic, formal, and thematic) between the halakha stratum in the Laws of D and the halakhic portion of MMT were identified. Priestly concerns were seen to lie behind a substantial portion of the Laws of D and virtually all of the halakhot in MMT. The priestly character of the latter is widely acknowledged,[60] and I hope to have been able to show that a considerable portion of the Laws of D shares such concerns. A concentration of thematic over-lap was noted between the halakhot listed in 4QMMT and the cata-logue of transgressions in 4QDᵉ. On the negative side 4QMMT's focus on Jerusalem and the Temple is more pronounced than in the halakhic parts of D. Moreover, MMT's characteristic references to the practice of opponents distinguishes the way its halakhot are pre-sented from the Laws of D.

It seems to me that the close relationship between the halakha stratum of D, particularly the catalogue of transgressions, and the halakhic portion of MMT is beyond doubt. I would like to end by attempting to relate these results to the literary and compositional history of both documents. As far as the Laws of the Damascus Document are concerned I suggest that the compiler of that corpus made use of a body of halakhic traditions and incorporated these into the Laws as we know them today alongside a variety of other material most notably a sizeable amount of communal legislation. I have argued elsewhere that 4Q159 constitutes an example of the kind of source used by the compiler of the Laws of D.[61] Moreover, I noted above that the list of transgressions fragmentarily preserved in 4QDᵉ may well constitute an important witness to the growth of the halakha stratum of D. Turning to 4QMMT, the excitement over the

---

[60] Cf., for example, the observations offered by Y. Sussman in "History of the Halakhah," 187.

[61] See my "4QOrdᵃ (4Q159) and the Laws of the Damascus Document."

initial assessment of it as a letter by the Teacher of Righteousness to the wicked priest, still held by some[62] and questioned by others,[63] may have prevented us from thinking in terms of a compositional history of 4QMMT. An exception is the much debated question of the relationship of the calendric section to the rest of the work.[64] I see no reasons to believe that the compositional history of 4QMMT is any less complex than is increasingly taken for granted for other Dead Sea Scrolls. It seems probable to me that its author(s) made use of earlier collections of halakhot of the kind that lie behind the Laws of D.[65]

---

[62] This position has been restated recently by H. Eshel, "4QMMT and the History of the Hasmonean Period," *Reading 4QMMT*, 53-65.

[63] See, for example, Schiffman, "New Halakhic Letter," and Strugnell, "Second Thoughts," 70-73.

[64] Cf. F. García Martínez, "Dos notas sobre 4QMMT," *RevQ* 16 (2993) 293-97; Schiffman, "Place of 4QMMT," 82-86; Strugnell, "Second Thoughts," 61-62; J. C. VanderKam, "The Calendar, 4Q327, and 4Q394," *Legal Texts and Legal Issues*, 179-94.

[65] As this paper was going to press I became aware of the recent study of 4QMMT by M. Pérez Fernández ("4QMMT: Redactional Study," *RevQ* 18 [1997] 191-205). This excellent study argues on linguistic grounds that MMT is a composite text and its results complement the conclusions reached in this paper.

THE RELATIONSHIP BETWEEN THE DAMASCUS DOCUMENT AND THE COMMUNITY RULE

SARIANNA METSO

University of Helsinki

There has not been a great deal of discussion specifically about the rules in the Damascus Document and the Community Rule over the past two decades. When Essene rules were discussed, understandably 1QS and CD[a,b] were virtually the only manuscripts cited. But with the publication of the Cave 4 copies of those rules,[1] it is time to inaugurate a new investigation, to determine whether commonly held views are in the main correct and simply need a bit of updating or whether the Cave 4 copies indicate that a significant re-evaluation is required, leading possibly to a new synthesis.

Even the early stages of analysis of the Cave 4 material already convince me that simple supplementation will not be sufficient for the conventional theories regarding either the textual development of the documents or the history of the community as depicted in them. A re-evaluation at a deeper level is necessary, and it needs to be asked whether the old theories stand the test of the new evidence. The textual basis of the individual documents must be sorted out before beginning to analyze the function of the rule texts within the Essene movement or attempting the reconstruction of the history of the community on the basis of the rule texts. The task here appears to be a major one.

---

[1] J. M. Baumgarten and M.T. Davis, "Cave IV, V, VI Fragments Related to the Damascus Document (4Q266-273 = 4QD[a-h], 5Q12 = 5QD, 6Q15 = 6QD)," *The Dead Sea Scrolls. Hebrew, Aramaic and Greek Texts with English Translation. Vol. 2: Damascus Document, War Scroll, and Related Documents* (ed. J. H. Charlesworth; Tübingen: Mohr-Siebeck; Louisville: John Knox, 1995) 59-79; J. M. Baumgarten, *Qumran Cave 4.XIII. The Damascus Document (4Q266-273)* (DJD 18; Oxford: Clarendon, 1996); E. Qimron and J. H. Charlesworth, "Cave IV Fragments (4Q255-264 = 4QS MSS A-J)," *The Dead Sea Scrolls. Hebrew, Aramaic, and Greek Texts with English Translations. Vol. 1: Rule of the Community and Related Documents* (ed. J. H. Charlesworth; Tübingen: Mohr-Siebeck; Louisville: John Knox, 1994) 53-103; C. Martone, *La "Regola della Comunité." Edizione critica* (Quaderni di Henoch 8; Torino: Silvio Zamorani Editore, 1995); S. Metso, *The Textual Development of the Qumran Community Rule* (STDJ 21; Leiden: E. J. Brill, 1997); P. S. Alexander and G. Vermes, *Qumran Cave 4.XIX. Serekh Ha-Yaḥad and Two Related Texts* (DJD 26; Oxford: Clarendon, 1998).

In the attempt to understand the history of the Qumran community and that of the larger Essene movement the data from the rule
texts and Josephus' reports about the Essenes were pivotal. Although
"consensus" might be an overstatement, a dominant perspective
emerged early and was shared by many Qumran scholars that the
Community Rule describes the life of the Qumran community
specifically, whereas the Damascus Document was composed with
the members of the larger Essene movement in mind. There were,
of course, different nuanced views within this general perspective:
Baumgarten, for example, concluded that celibacy was practiced at
Qumran by those who aspired to the "perfection of holiness,"[2] while
Schiffman believed that the majority were either not yet married or
already married before they came to the community but had (at
least temporarily) left their families.[3] It may well turn out that the
Essene movement included groups which differed in their beliefs
and practices, perhaps many scholarly views will be sustained. But
the availability of the new material—both additional copies of works
that were published earlier and documents previously unknown—
challenges us to aim at a sharper understanding. Not only content
but methodology needs re-examination. In light of the new evidence, it is imperative to submit to fresh tests not only the current
hypotheses and views, but also the method by which scholars have

---

[2] J. M. Baumgarten, "The Qumran-Essene Restraints on Marriage," *Archaeology
and History in the Dead Sea Scrolls. The New York University Conference in Memory of Yigael
Yadin* (ed. L. H. Schiffman; JSPSup 8; Sheffield: JSOT, 1990) 13-24. Baumgarten
writes in his analysis of CD 6:11-7:7 about the passage in 7:6-7: "...the editor of CD
placed this provision after the promise to those who walk in perfect holiness quite deliberately. Its adversative formulation beginning with the conditional 'And if' indicates that the previously mentioned aspirants to perfect holiness did not dwell in
scattered dwelling places in the conventional manner of the land, did not take wives,
and did not get children" (18), and "...if our interpretation is valid, we have here an
important attestation in a Qumran source of the bifurcation in the practice of
celibacy among the Essenes. The writer refers to sectarians who followed a normal
way of life, residing in various camps, marrying and having children, but he also
knew of those who never married or at a late stage of life renounced the continuation of marital relations because they aspired to the 'perfection of holiness'" (19).
Note, however, Baumgarten's remark on p. 20: "The foregoing discussion suggests
that celibacy at Qumran was never made into a universal norm. It was confined to
those who emulated a 'perfection of holiness' requiring uninterrupted purity, and
even for them perhaps only in the later stages of their lives." While I would like to
leave the question of celibacy at Qumran open, I find it interesting that in numerous places in the Community Rule, a person joining the community or living as its
member is expected to live his life in "perfection" or according to a "perfect way."
The term תמים is used a total of eighteen times, but see esp. 2:2; 3:3; 8:10, 18, 20
(אנשיתמי קודש corr. אנשי תמים הקודש), 21; 9:5-9.
[3] L. H. Schiffman, *Sectarian Law in the Dead Sea Scrolls. Courts, Testimony and the
Penal Code* (BJS 33; Chico: Scholars Press, 1983) 12-13.

made use of the rule texts to reconstruct the history of the Qumran community and the Essenes in general.

In light of the new material, I find it problematic to reckon with only two monolithic groups: the community behind the Damascus Document, on the one hand, and the community behind the Community Rule, on the other. First, the recently published Cave 4 documents—4Q265 (Serek Damascus), 4Q477 (Decrees), 4Q275 (Communal Ceremony; previously 4QS$_c$ or Tohorot B$_a$) and 4Q279 (Four Lots; previously 4QS$_b$ or Tohorot D$_a$)[4] —appear to present a more complex picture, not two clearly defined groups. Moreover, the manuscripts of the Damascus Document and the Community Rule from Cave 4 show even more clearly the composite nature and complex redactional histories of these documents.

It should be stressed that the composite character of the texts needs to be taken seriously when different documents are compared with each other. Often the comparison is done between documents as a whole; the separate components, however, of the documents should be analyzed first. Textual similarities and differences must be studied and the logical inferences from them must be considered, before the historical conclusions may be drawn from the manuscripts, for it is possible and even likely that there were contacts between the different groups responsible for various sections. They may have used common sources and borrowed material from each other. Quite naturally, the manuscripts found at Qumran functioned as whole documents, and individual sections may have gained new focuses in their new contexts. But if the purpose of study is to reach the historical reality of the groups behind the texts, a more detailed analysis is needed, viz., analysis of the compositional history of the text rather than reckoning only with the final redactional stage.

The methodological difficulty regarding the interrelationship of the groups behind the rule texts emerges sharply in the case of the parallel penal codes between the Community Rule and the Damas-

---

[4] J. M. Baumgarten, "The Cave 4 Versions of the Qumran Penal Code," *JJS* 43 (1992) 268-76. J. T. Milik appears to have presumed a third group in addition to those behind the Damascus Document and the Community Rule, for he speaks of "tertiaries" in connection with 4Q265. See his *Ten Years of Discovery in the Wilderness of Judaea* (SBT 26; London: SCM, 1959) 90. The original French publication was *Dix ans de découvertes dans le Désert de Juda* (Paris: Cerf, 1957); E. Eshel, "4Q477: The Rebukes by the Overseer," *JJS* 45 (1994) 111-22. According to Eshel "the text preserves remnants of a legal record, compiled by the sect's Overseer (מבקר), of those members who were rebuked after committing a sin. It appears that, although it is an official written text, it was probably read out in public by the Overseer" (111); for 4Q275 and 279, see Alexander and Vermes, DJD 26.209-16 and 217-23.

cus Document. The Cave 4 version of the Damascus Document witnessed by 4QD^a (4Q266) and 4QD^e (4Q270), includes a section of a penal code which is clearly based on the same text as the one in 1QS.[5] Many of the regulations are identical in both, though 1QS contains some that are not found in 4QD^{a,e}. The order, however, of those regulations that are shared is the same. Thus, it must be the case either that the same source was used by the authors of the Community Rule and the Damascus Document or that one of the sections is directly dependent on the other. The transgressions are in most cases expressed in an identical way, the differences, when they occur, being mainly orthographic or morphological.[6] The punish-

---

[5] Joseph Baumgarten has dated 4QD^a (4Q266) to the first half or the middle of the first century BCE and 4QD^e (4Q270) to the early first century CE (DJD 26.30, 140). The penal code is located toward the end in both manuscripts, before the expulsion ceremony which concludes the work. What catches one's attention is that the section parallel to the material in 1QS forms only a part of a larger penal code in 4QD; it is surrounded and preceded by penal regulations which have no parallel in 1QS. Similarly, the shared portion of the penal regulations forms only a part of a larger penal code in 1QS. The penal code begins at the end of column 4, but the first case that has a parallel in the 4QD manuscripts is to be found in 7:8 and, at the end of column 7, there are penal regulations which have no parallel in 4QD. The manuscript 1QS is generally dated to 100-75 BCE; see F. M. Cross, *The Ancient Library of Qumran and Modern Biblical Studies. The Haskell Lectures* (London: Duckworth, 1958) 58; N. Avigad, "The Palaeography of the Dead Sea Scrolls and Related Documents," *Aspects of the Dead Sea Scrolls* (Scripta Hierosolymitana 4; Jerusalem: Magnes, 1958) 56-87, esp. 57; G. Bonani, M. Broshi, I. Carmi, S. Ivy, J. Strugnell, W. Wölfli, "Radiocarbon Dating of the Dead Sea Scrolls," *Atiqot* 20 (1991) 27-32. The material reconstruction of two manuscripts of the Community Rule from Cave 4 (4QS^b and 4QS^d) based on the physical characteristics of the remaining fragments indicates, however, that there existed a shorter version of the penal code of 1QS columns 6 and 7. There is very little material left of the penal code in 4QS^{b,d}, but generally these manuscripts have preserved a more original text than 1QS, although they are palaeographically younger than 1QS; see J. T. Milik, "Numérotation des feuilles dans le scriptorium de Qumran (Planches X et XI)," *Semitica* 27 (1977) 75-81, esp. 78; G. Vermes, "Preliminary Remarks on Unpublished Fragments of the Community Rule from Qumran Cave 4," *JJS* 42 (1991) 250-55, esp. 255; Metso, *The Textual Development*, 74-90, esp. 89. The manuscripts 4QS^b and 4QS^d have been dated to the second half or the last third of the first century BCE; see Milik, "Numérotation," 75-81, esp. 76-78; F. M. Cross, "Paleographical Dates of the Manuscripts," *The Dead Sea Scrolls. Hebrew, Aramaic, and Greek Texts with English Translations. Vol. I: Rule of the Community and Related Documents* (ed. J. H. Charlesworth; Tübingen: Mohr-Siebeck; Louisville: Westminster John Knox Press, 1994) 57; A. J. T. Jull, D. J. Donahue, M. Broshi, E. Tov, "Radiocarbon Dating of Scrolls and Linen Fragments from the Judaean Desert," *Radiocarbon* 37 (1996) 11-19.

[6] The parallel sections—1QS 7:8-21, 4Q266 (4QD^a) 10 ii 2-15 and 4Q270 (4QD^e) 7 i 1-11—that I will discuss below cover sixteen cases of transgression and punishment. Thirteen of them are found both in the Community Rule and the Damascus Document, and the cases in common occur in identical order in the manuscripts. In 1QS there are three additional cases, however, located in between the shared regulations. The cases that are absent in the Damascus Document involve avenging oneself (1QS 7:9), spitting in the meeting of the *rabbim* (1QS 7:13),

ments, however, tend to differ in a interesting way. Many of the punishments in 4QD, in contrast to those in the Community Rule, consist of two parts: punishment (נענש) and exclusion (הובדל).[7] In most cases the length of the punishment in 1QS corresponds to that of the exclusion in 4QD.[8]

J. M. Baumgarten has studied these sections both in his article of 1992[9] and in his DJD edition of the 4QD manuscripts,[10] and C. Hempel has discussed the parallels extensively in her article of 1997.[11] Baumgarten comments on these sections in the edition in the

and murmuring against the foundations of the community (1QS 7:17). It is remarkable that the transgressions have often been expressed in exactly the same terms in both documents (there are four such cases: 4QDᵃ 10 ii 3-4/1QS 7:9; 4QDᵃ 10 ii 5-6/1QS 7:10; 4QDᵃ 10 ii 13-14/4QDᶜ 7 i 5/1QS 7:15; 4QDᶜ 7 i 7-8/1QS 7:17-18). Once a transgression has been listed using synonymous words (4QDᵃ 10 ii 2-3/1QS 7:8). Three times the same basic transgression has been defined in one of the documents slightly differently, e.g., more accurately (4QDᵃ 10 ii 4-5/1QS 7:9-10; 4QDᵃ 10 ii 6-9/1QS 7:10-12; 4QDᵃ 10 ii 9-10/4QDᶜ 7 i 1-2/1QS 7:12). In addition, there are orthographical differences and a number of morphological and syntactical differences between the documents (for morphological differences, see 4QDᵃ 10 ii 4-5/1QS 7:9-10; 4QDᵃ 10 ii 10-12/4QDᶜ 7 i 3-4/1QS 7:13-14; 4QDᵃ 10 ii 12-13/4QDᶜ 7 i 4/1QS 7:14-15; 4QDᵃ 10 ii 14-15/4QDᶜ 7 i 5-6/1QS 7:15-16; 4QDᶜ 7 i 7-8/1QS 7:18-21; syntactical differences: 4QDᵃ 10 ii 2-3/1QS 7:8; 4QDᶜ 7 i 6-7/1QS 7:16-17).

[7] In three cases it can be stated with certainty that both 4QD and 1QS had the same punishment: for interrupting a neighbour's speech (4QDᵃ 10 ii 4-5/1QS 7:9-10) and for gesticulating with the left hand (4QDᵃ 10 ii 13-14/4QDᶜ 7 i 5/1QS 7:15) the transgressor was to be fined, whereas the one who slandered the *rabbim* was to be sent away without possibility of return (4QDᶜ 7 i 6-7/1QS 7:16-17). There are three other cases where one could ask whether the punishment in 4QD was the same in 1QS; the text in 4QD is very fragmentary and Baumgarten's reconstructions are largely based on 1QS. These cases concern leaving in the middle of the *rabbim* meeting (4QDᵃ 10 ii 6-9/1QS 7:10-12; it is unsure whether the verb used in Dᵃ actually was נענש [2x]), indecent exposure (4QDᵃ 10 ii 10-12/4QDᶜ 7 i 3-4/1QS 7:13-14; 4QDᵃ has a double punishment but Baumgarten has reconstructed a single punishment in 4QDᶜ on the basis of 1QS) and murmuring against a neighbour (4QDᶜ 7 i 7-8/1QS 7:17-18; Dᶜ here is wholly reconstructed on the basis of 1QS).

[8] A special characteristic of the penal code of the Damascus Document is the use of double punishment consisting of exclusion and a fine. The double punishment occurs in five cases: insulting one's neighbour (4QDᵃ 10 ii 2-3/1QS 7:8), foolish speech (4QDᵃ 10 ii 3-4/1QS 7:9), falling asleep at the meeting of the *rabbim* (4QDᵃ 10 ii 5-6/1QS 7:10), indecent exposure (4QDᵃ 10 ii 10-12/4QDᶜ 7 i 3-4/1QS 7:13-14), and deviating from the fundamental principles of the community (4QDᶜ 7 i 8-10/1QS 7:18-21). Apparently the nature of the transgression, i.e., whether the transgression was minor or more severe, was not decisive in using the double punishment, for double punishment occurs in connection with both foolish speech and deviating from the fundamental principles of the community. Interestingly, in all of these cases the length of the exclusion in 4QD corresponds to the length of the fine in 1QS.

[9] J. M. Baumgarten, "The Cave 4 Versions of the Qumran Penal Code," *JJS* 43 (1992) 268-76.

[10] Baumgarten, DJD 18.7-9, 74-75 and 162-66.

[11] C. Hempel, "The Penal Code Reconsidered," *Legal Texts and Legal Issues:*

following way: "It thus appears that the penal code, which in the Community Rule seems to reflect the discipline of an all male order, was capable of being also applied to a society in which both men and women took part in communal life."[12] Hempel considers the relationship to be more complex, speaking of a parent movement.[13] Indeed, the relationship between the penal codes does not seem to be one of direct dependence, such that the author of D would have borrowed and modified the penal code of S, or vice versa. The variants—both of content and of grammar—point rather in the direction of a common source, since both the section in D and the section in S seem to have undergone redaction independently.[14]

Proceedings of the Second Meeting of the International Organization for Qumran Studies, Cambridge, 1995 Published in Honour of Joseph M. Baumgarten (ed. M. J. Bernstein, F. García Martínez and J. Kampen; STDJ 23; Leiden: Brill, 1997) 337-48.

[12] Baumgarten, DJD 18.8. Baumgarten discusses in the same context (p. 8) penalties for improper marital relations and for murmuring against the Mothers, absent in 1QS: "We have now in the cave 4 manuscripts of D an extensive pericope from the sectarian penal code which closely parallels that of 1QS both verbally and in substance. However, it has a more consistent pattern of dual punishment, exclusion from purities and penance, each for a specified length of time. It also includes offences such as 'fornication' with one's wife and murmuring against the Fathers and Mothers of the community, which are absent in the *Rule*. Clearly these offences presuppose family life with marriage and children."

[13] Hempel, "Penal Code," 345 and 348.

[14] Two of the cases of comparison are particularly interesting. First, in the case of deviating from the fundamental principles of the community (4QD^e 7 i 8-10/1QS 7:18-21) 4QD lists a double punishment of two years' exclusion and sixty days' fine. 1QS reads a single punishment, two years' fine, but there is an an additional clause indicating that the two year period of punishment consisted of different stages: in the first year the transgressor was not allowed to touch the the purity of the *rabbim*. In the second year he was not permitted to touch the drink of the *rabbim*, and he had to sit behind all the men of the community. An inquiry of the *rabbim* after the two-year period is attested both in 1QS and 4QD. After the punishment both texts develop, but in different ways. In 1QS the regulation is expanded by two rules, the first of which regards a community member who has betrayed the community after having been in the council of the community for ten full years, and the second of which regards any other member who is contact with such transgressor. In 4QD^e, on the other hand, there follows a regulation regarding the transgression of despising the law of the *rabbim*. Both the regulation in 1QS and in 4QD^e deal with the member's conduct towards the *rabbim*, but where 1QS speaks about "betraying the community" (לבגוד ביחד) and "leaving the *rabbim*" (ויצא מל־ הרבים) after ten years, 4QD^e speaks about "despising the law of the *rabbim*" (ימאס א[ת משפט הרבים) and makes no differentiation between a new member and a member who has been in the community for a longer period. Although it is not fully clear whether "leaving the *rabbim*" should be understood literally or figuratively (the member would not necessarily want to resign but he would no longer want to commit himself to the rules of the community), it is most likely that 1QS and 4QD^e speak about two different things. Moreover, in 4QD^e there is no rule about a member who is in contact with the transgressor. The rule was presumably inserted in the Community Rule only secondarily. The comparison between the 4QD manuscripts and 1QS may thus shed further light on the redaction of the penal code in 1QS. The second interesting case is the one of slandering the neighbour (4QD^a 10

The conclusions resulting from a comparison of the penal codes have methodological implications for the study of the rule texts: if different groups were using common sources and borrowing material from each other, how is it possible to identify the specific groups behind the manuscripts? If extensive sections of text from various manuscripts are borrowed and modified, what are the criteria that enable us to assign whole manuscripts to particular groups (e.g. a celibate community versus a community where marriage was common)? The case of the penal codes in S and D, in my view, shows clearly that the composite character of the documents must be considered in any attempt to reconstruct the life and history of the Essene communities.

A second major topic in the discussion of 1QS and CD has been the question of how the rules that were included in the documents originated. Schiffman takes as his starting point that the doctrine of oral transmission of law, and more generally, the concept of oral law was absent at Qumran. According to him the Qumranic legal traditions were derived only through scriptural exegesis.[15] Philip Davies and Moshe Weinfeld have criticized his views from different angles. Davies emphasizes the differences between the two rules. He thinks that the Damascus Document indeed, save one or two exceptions, is based on scriptural exegesis, whereas the laws recorded in the Community Rule have not been presented as, or were not intended to be understood as, derived from scriptural exegesis. From this Davies concludes that the group behind the Damascus Document must have been different from that behind the Community Rule.[16] Moshe Weinfeld's criticism of Schiffman's views stems from his observation that the rules regulating the community organization and admission of new members are very similar to those found in hel-

---

ii 14-15/4QD^c 7 i 5-6/1QS 7:15-16). A double punishment of fine and exclusion is attested both in D and S, and this is the only occurrence of a double punishment in 1QS. However, although the length of the exclusion is defined, the length of the period when the member is fined is unclear. 1QS reads: "The man who goes about slandering his neighbour shall be excluded from the purity of the *rabbim* for one year and fined." The regulation is not fully preserved in D^a, so the length of the fine is not known from there either. According to Baumgarten, Milik suggested a restoration "six months" for D^c, but Baumgarten does not relate the basis for Milik's restoration. D^a and D^c specify only that the transgressor is to be expelled from "the purity," whereas 1QS emphasizes that the transgressor is to be expelled from "the purity of the *rabbim*."

[15] L. H. Schiffman, *The Halakhah at Qumran* (SJLA 16; Leiden: E. J. Brill, 1975) 19-20.

[16] P. R. Davies, "Halakhah at Qumran," *A Tribute to Geza Vermes. Essays on Jewish and Christian Literature and History* (ed. P. R. Davies and R. T. White; JSOTSup 100; Sheffield: JSOT, 1990) 37-50, esp. 43-49. See also his contribution to this volume, 27-43.

lenistic and Roman religious groups. He argues that we must distinguish between rules sanctified by the Torah and those arising only within the community itself: the laws of Torah belong to the realm of the covenant between God and Israel, whereas community regulations concern social organization, the members of which were bound by a voluntary commitment to the rules approved by the group. Weinfeld does not subscribe to Schiffman's conclusion that a member of the community who did not obey an order given by a superior was, by rejecting a communal rule, ultimately rejecting a divine commandment.[17]

A new element should be entered into this discussion. The newly published Cave 4 texts, when compared with 1QS, illuminate a development in the redactional history of the Community Rule. The need to find a scriptural legitimation for the regulations of the community apparently arose only at a secondary stage of the rule's history, presumably in a situation where the community's strict rules had been questioned.[18] Thus, the process appears to have been the reverse of what has been often presumed, at least in some cases. The laws regulating "matter of fact" details of the community life especially seem not to have emerged as a result of scriptural exegesis, but rather scriptural quotations or allusions were inserted into the text due to the need to justify the rules already in practice. The section in 1QS 6:8-13 dealing with the session of the *rabbim* provides quite a detailed picture of a situation where community legislation was created. Remarkably, there is no reference to the Torah or other written rules. Whenever the community authority is discussed in the Community Rule, the decisions are said to be made על פי הרבים, on the basis of the word of the *rabbim* or, as in 9:7, on the word of the sons of Aaron.

Thus, in the redactional process of the Community Rule scriptural quotations were inserted as proof-texts for certain community regulations. This fact argues for the assumption that, ultimately, the community regarded its own regulations as resting on the Old Testament authority. The inserted formula "for thus it is written" (כיא כן כתוב, 1QS 5:15/כאשר כתוב, 1QS 5:16, 8:14) is a clear indication of this. Therefore, the hypothesis that the community would

---

[17] M. Weinfeld, *The Organizational Pattern and the Penal Code of the Qumran Sect. A Comparison with Guilds and Religious Associations of the Hellenistic-Roman Period* (NTOA 2; Göttingen: Vandenhoeck & Ruprecht, 1986) 71-76.

[18] Metso, *The Textual Development*, 76-90. The quotations that are absent in 4QS[b,d] occur in 1QS 5:13-16, 16-19 and 8:12-16. The rule of separation governing the community life has been legitimized by references to Exod. 23:7, Isa. 2:22 and 40:3.

have made a distinction between its own rules and the regulations of the Torah does not seem plausible. From the point of view of a modern reader, the connection between a regulation and a citation supporting it may be artificial. The community, however, considered its laws to be in accordance with the Torah.

YOSE BEN YOEZER AND THE QUMRAN SECTARIANS ON PURITY LAWS: AGREEMENT AND CONTROVERSY[*]

Eyal Regev

Bar-Ilan University

Introduction

For the last twenty years the relationship between Qumran halakha and rabbinic sources has been dealt with extensively. Many scholars have compared the laws in the Damascus Document, the Temple Scroll and, recently, also 4QMMT to rabbinic halakha, and most have emphasized the fact that the Qumran sectarians were stricter than the Pharisees in observing the laws.[1] But this comparison has a minor chronological and methodological problem: it compares the Qumran scrolls, dated to the Hasmonean and Herodian period, on the one hand, to the Tannaitic corpus, which is obviously a much later composition, on the other. Naturally, scholars have to face the fact that only a few halakhot are ascribed to Pharisaic figures from the Hasmonean period, and some of them have no relation to the laws mentioned in the Qumran writings.[2]

Considering this difficulty in comparing Pharisaic and Qumran halakha and its historical implications, it would be appropriate to point out a few halakhot which are ascribed to a well-known Pharisaic sage, Yose ben Yoezer. This may help us to understand better not only the differences and disagreement between the Pharisees and Qumran sectarians in the early days of their activity, but also their common interest in certain issues of purity in the early Hasmonean period. We are familiar with four of Yose ben Yoezer's halakhot that dealt with purity. The significance of these purity laws

---

[*] I would like to thank the participants of the Symposium for their helpful remarks during and after the discussion in this paper, especially Dr. H. Eshel for his help with the material discussed in nn. 20 and 27.

[1] See the bibliography and discussion in L. H. Schiffman, *The Halakhah at Qumran* (SJLA 16; Leiden: E. J. Brill, 1975) 77 ff.; E. Qimron and J. Strugnell, *Qumran Cave 4.V. Miqsat Maʿaśe Ha-Torah* (DJD 10; Oxford: Clarendon, 1994) 124 ff.

[2] On the use of Qumran halakha to date rabbinic law to the Hasmonean period, see L. H. Schiffman, "Pharisaic and Sadducean Halakhah in Light of the Dead Sea Scrolls: the Case of *Ṭevul Yom*," *DSD* 1 (1994) 285-99.

is derived from the fact that very close issues, sometimes even identical ones, are mentioned in the Dead Sea Scrolls, especially in the
Damascus Document. Thus, we shall juxtapose Yose ben Yoezer's
halakhot with the relevant purity laws from the Damascus Document, the Temple Scroll, and other fragments from Cave 4. First we
shall examine the relationship between the positions of Yose ben
Yoezer and the Qumran sectarians, and then we shall offer some
tentative historical conclusions pertaining to the relationship between the Pharisees and the Qumran sect in the early Hasmonean
period.

Before we discuss halakhic matters, it should be mentioned that
Yose ben Yoezer of Zereda is the earliest sage whose halakhot are
given in rabbinic literature. He and Yose ben Yoḥanan of Jerusalem
are the first of the five "pairs" (זוגות), and it seems that he was the
Pharisaic leader during the Maccabean revolt against the Seleucids.[3]
It is also probable that he was active in the days of Jonathan and
Simon.[4] Thus, it is significant that Yose ben Yoezer probably represents the Pharisaic views in the period in which the Pharisees and
the Essenes are first introduced by Josephus (Ant. 13.171-173) and
during which the Qumran sect is active.[5] Bearing that in mind, we
shall now examine four purity laws of Yose ben Yoezer and their relation to Qumran halakha in the Damascus Document and other
compositions.

Impurity of Gentile Land

Yose ben Yoezer decreed (along with Yose ben Yoḥanan) on the impurity of foreign territory (b. Shab. 14b; j. Shab 1:4, 3d).[6] A ruling
which is very close to this decree is found in a fragment of the

---

[3] The only evidence for this is, however, the legend about Yose ben Yoezer and
יקים איש צרורות (Alcimus) in Gen. Rabba 65:22 (ed. Theodor-Albeck, 742 ff.). See
the discussion of J. A. Goldstein, *I Maccabees* (AB 41; Garden City: Doubleday,
1976) 334-36, 393. This tradition was considered historical by M. Hengel, *Judaism
and Hellenism* (Philadelphia: Fortress, 1974) 1.80. Hengel supposed that Yose ben
Yoezer was one of the Hasideans killed by Alcimus (cf. 1 Macc. 7:12; Hengel,
Judaism and Hellenism, 1.175 ff.).
[4] In contrast to the common scholarly view, the legend in Genesis Rabba does
not hint that Yose ben Yoezer died. Assuming that he was one of the Hasideans (cf.
m. Ḥag. 2:7) there is no reason to include him with the sixty Hasideans that were
killed by Alcimus, for some of the Hasideans probably survived. On the chronological difficulty that underlies this widespread assumption, see A. Guttman, *Rabbinic
Judaism in the Making* (Detroit: Wayne State University Press, 1970) 34.
[5] Cf. E. Schürer, *The History of the Jewish People in the Age of Jesus Christ (175
B.C.–A.D. 135)* (ed. G. Vermes, F. Millar and M. Goodman; Edinburgh: T. & T.
Clark, 1986) 3.400f., 560, 585 ff.

Damascus Document from Cave 4 (4Q266 and some parallels in 4Q267 and 4Q273), which deals with the disqualifications of priests from serving in the Temple. Joseph Baumgarten has already determined that one of the reasons listed in these fragments for such disqualification is defilement by the Gentiles.[7] According to the Damascus Document there are two situations in which priests are defiled by this form of impurity:

1) אחו הכהנים בעבודה [ואן]ל [...איש] מבני אהרון אשר ישבה לגואים [...] לחללה בטמאתם אל יגש לעבודת [הקודש.

his brethren, the priests in the service, but he shall n[ot ...Any one] of the sons of Aaron who was in captivity among the Gentiles... to profane it with their uncleanness. He may not approach the [holy] service.

2) איש מבני אהרון אשר ינדד לעבונד את הגואים...] להורות עמו בישוד עם וגם לבגונד]

Any one of the sons of Aaron who migrates to se[rve... the Gentiles...] <to teach> his people the foundation of the nation and also to betray [...

Consequently, Baumgarten has concluded that priests who had been in foreign captivity could not minister in the sanctuary or partake of the offerings and that priests who migrated into pagan lands, as well as apostates, were regarded as no longer belonging to the "council of the people" and were thus likewise excluded from partaking of the offerings.[8]

According to Baumgarten's understanding of these fragments, the connection of this law with the decree on the impurity of Gentile land is quite obvious: both Yose ben Yoezer and the author of the Damascus Document argue that foreign land is defiled, although it

---

[6] See, Hengel, *Judaism and Hellenism*, 1.52-53; D. T. Ariel and A. Strikovsky, "Appendix," in Y. Shiloh and D. T. Ariel, *Excavations at the City of David, 1978-1985* (Qedem 30; Jerusalem: Institute of Archaeology, Hebrew University of Jerusalem, 1990) 25-28, and bibliography. On the halakhic concept of the impurity of Gentile territory, see G. Alon, "The Levitical Uncleanness of Gentiles," *Jews, Judaism and the Classical World* (tr. I. Abrahams; Jerusalem: Magnes, 1977) 183-86. The Talmuds also attribute to the first "pair" the decree on the impurity of glass, but this has no parallel in the Qumran writings. See also the halakhic controversy in m. Hag. 2:2.

[7] 4Q266 (4QD^a) frg. 5 ii ll. 4-5, 8-9. Parallels: 4Q267 frg. 5 iii, 4Q273 2 and 3. See J. M. Baumgarten, *Qumran Cave 4.XIII. The Damascus Document (4Q266-273)* (DJD 18; Oxford: Clarendon, 1996) 49-52, 102, 195; idem, "The Disqualifications of Priests in 4Q Fragments of the Damascus Document, a Specimen of the Recovery of Pre-rabbinic Halakha," *The Madrid Qumran Congress* (ed. J. Trebolle Barrera and L. Vegas Montaner; STDJ 11; Leiden: E. J. Brill, 1992) 2.503-13.

[8] Baumgarten, "Disqualifications of Priests," 509.

seems that the Pharisees did not share the Qumran view concerning the defilement of captured priests. It is interesting that to illustrate this halakhic concept, Baumgarten mentions the departure of a renegade High Priest from the land of Israel, in order to be nominated by Demetrius I (2 Macc. 14:3, 7).[9] One may even suggest that the historical background for the law of the impurity of Gentile land should be traced to the time of Menelaus and Alcimus. This corresponds to the period in which Yose ben Yoezer was active, and thus the basic agreement between the first "pair" of the Pharisees and the Damascus Document should be explained by their common reaction to the rise of a hellenized priest in Jerusalem.

The three other halakhot which are attributed to Yose ben Yoezer are listed in m. 'Ed. 8:4:

העיד רבי יוסי בן יוער איש צרידה על איל קמצא, דכי; ועל משקה
בית מטבחיא, דאנון דכין; ודיקרב במיתא מסתאב. וקראו לה יוסי שריא.

> R. Yose b. Yoezer of Zereda testified that the *Ayil-locust* is clean, and that the liquid [that flows] in the shambles [in the Temple] is not susceptible to uncleanness and he that touches a corpse becomes unclean and they called him "Yose the Permitter."[10]

This Mishnah has not yet been compared with what we know from the Dead Sea Scrolls, although the content of Yose ben Yoezer's statements has historical importance since not only are they the most ancient halakhic views in rabbinic sources, but their Aramaic language gives them a reliable character.[11] By juxtaposing these three halakhot with the relevant laws from the Qumran writings, we would like to offer a new understanding of the specific issues which are being dealt with in these particular sources. Thus we may clarify somewhat the halakhic atmosphere of the early Hasmonean period and the points of contrast between the Pharisees and Qumran.

The Question of Pure Locusts

Yose ben Yoezer argues that a certain kind of locust called an *Ayil-locust* is pure and therefore permitted for consumption. Although it is

---

[9] Baumgarten, "Disqualifications of Priests," 512.

[10] H. Danby, *The Mishnah* (London: Oxford University Press, 1949) 436. S. Safrai, "Halakha," *The Literature of the Sages* (ed. S. Safrai; CRINT 2/3; Assen/Maastricht: Van Gorcum; Philadelphia: Fortress, 1987) 1.146, n. 142, omits the word "Rabbi."

[11] See the exceptional agreement between J. N. Epstein, *Prolegomena ad Litteras Tannaiticas* (Jerusalem/Tel Aviv: Magnes and Dvir, 1957) 505-06 (Hebrew), and J. Neusner, *The Rabbinic Traditions about the Pharisees before 70* (Leiden: E. J. Brill, 1971) 1.64-66, and cf. 62. See also: Safrai, "Halakha," 146, 154.

almost impossible to identify the locust to which Yose ben Yoezer referred,[12] it is interesting to mention another law concerning kosher locusts in CD 12:14-15:

וכל החגבים יבאו באש או במים עד הם חיים כי הוא משפט בריאתם.[13]

And all species of locusts shall be put into fire or water while still alive, for this is the precept of their creation.

Of course, there is no direct connection between these two food regulations, and no conclusion can be drawn from them concerning a controversy between Yose ben Yoezer and the Damascus Document. However, it is interesting that both Yose ben Yoezer and the author of the Damascus Document were concerned with the problem of kosher locusts.[14] Additionally, it is clear from Tannaitic sources that the Pharisees could not accept the position of the Damascus Document, for the Tosefta (t. Ter. 9:6) permits eating a live locust, although the Rabbis themselves seem to doubt whether anyone would dare to do so.[15] Hence, it is possible that the Pharisees and the author of the Damascus Document did not agree on this point.

Impurity of Liquids of the Temple Canal

Yose ben Yoezer states that the liquids of the Temple canal, namely, the blood of the sacrifices and the water used for washing the altar, cannot defile. An opposite observation is made in the Temple Scroll 32:12-15:

ועשיתה תעלה סביב לכיור אצל מזבח העולה הולכת לנתחת הכיור ומחלה
יורדת למטה אל תוך הארץ אשר יהיו המים נשפכים והולכים אליה
ואובדים בתוך הארץ ולא יהיו נוגעים בהמה כול אדם כי מדם העולה
מתערב במה ...[16]

---

[12] But see b. 'Abod. Zar. 37a-37b and Rashi *ad shoshiba*.

[13] See also the parallel in 4Q266, frg. 9 ii (Baumgarten, DJD 18.68-70). According to L. Ginzberg, *An Unknown Jewish Sect* (New York: JTS, 1976) 80, 348-49, since locusts have no blood they may be cooked or roasted without further ado. In contrast to Ginzberg, it seems that the prohibition against eating live locusts is implied here. See A. Büchler, "Schechter's 'Jewish Sectaries'," *JQR* 3 N.S. (1912-13) 444-45 and n. 15 below.

[14] As Prof. A. I. Baumgarten suggested, although locust regulations are common in rabbinic sources, it may be that the interest in this kind of food in the early Hasmonean period should be connected to the distress of the rebels against the Seleucids during their hiding in the desert. See 2 Macc. 5:27 and compare 1 Macc. 1:62-63, Mark 1:7; A. I. Baumgarten, *The Flourishing of Jewish Sects in the Maccabean Era: An Interpretation* (JSJSup 55; Leiden: Brill, 1997) 92 f.

[15] See the discussion of S. Lieberman, *Tosefta ki-Peshuta* (Jerusalem: JTS, 1992²) 1.451-53. We may also assume that the Qumran sectarians did not agree with the permission of Yose ben Yoezer to eat the *Ayil-locust*.

[16] E. Qimron, *The Temple Scroll. A Critical Edition with Extensive Reconstructions* (Beer

[And] you shall make a conduit(?) around the laver near its house. And the condui[t] shall lead [from the house of] the laver into a pit, [extend]ing downwards into the land, which the water will be flowing into it and will lost in the land, and it (the water) shall not be touched by anyone, for it is mixed with the blood of the burnt offering...[17]

It is here, no doubt, that there is a controversy between Yose ben Yoezer and the Temple Scroll. While Yose ben Yoezer, along with later Rabbis,[18] declares that the liquids that flow from the altar and the laver outside the Temple cannot defile, the Temple Scroll stresses their impurity. It seems that the law of the Temple Scroll emerges from the notion of *sancta contagion*[19]: the holiness of the sacrifice which was offered on the altar is transmitted to the blood and, consequently, transmitted to the other liquids in the canal as well. Of course, like any holy thing it must not be touched by unholy hands or used for unholy purposes. But according to Yose ben Yoezer the holiness of the sacrifices is not as contagious as the Temple Scroll claims, and the blood of the sacrifices does not conduct holiness. Therefore one who touches it does not desecrate it. Indeed, there is a basic divergence of opinion between the Qumran halakha and the Rabbis concerning this notion, namely, how much holiness is contained in holy things, especially the Temple.[20] Thus, the contrast between the Pharisees and the Qumran sect concerning the impurity of liquids in the Temple canal is not insignificant, for it has certain implications concerning a central issue in the Tannaitic sources and in the Dead Sea Scrolls: the purity of Jerusalem and its environs.

Sheva: Ben-Gurion University of the Negev; Jerusalem: Israel Exploration Society, 1996) 47.

[17] Yadin, *The Temple Scroll* (Jerusalem: Israel Exploration Society, Shrine of the Book, Israel Museum, 1983) 2.139.

[18] M. Kel. 16:6. See also J. N. Epstein, *Mavo' le-Nusah ha-Mishnah* (Jerusalem: 1948) 181 (Hebrew); Yadin, *Temple Scroll*, 1.223f. Cf. Neusner, *Rabbinic Traditions*, 61f.

[19] J. Milgrom, "Sancta Contagion and Altar/City Asylum," *Congress Volume, Vienna 1980* (ed. J. A. Emerton; VTSup 32; Leiden: E. J. Brill; 1981) 278-310; idem, *Leviticus 1-16* (AB 3; New York: Doubleday, 1991) 976-85.

[20] For examples of this trend in rabbinic sources, see S. Friedman, "The Holy Scriptures Defiled the Hands: The Transformation of a Biblical Concept in Rabbinic Theology," *Minha le-Nahum: Biblical and Other Studies Presented to Nahum M. Sarna in Honour of his 70th Birthday* (ed. M. Bretter and M. Fishbane; JSOTSup 154; Sheffield: Sheffield Academic Press, 1993) 116-32, and cf. Milgrom, "Sancta Contagion," 298, n. 5, and the rabbinic halakhot cited in Yadin, *Temple Scroll*, 1.222-24. Schiffman has suggested another explanation (following Yadin, *Temple Scroll*, 1.224), connecting the impurity to the water of the house of the laver in which the priests were washing themselves; but since they were already pure it is hard to find the cause of impurity in the water. Thanks are due to Profs. M. Kister and J. Milgrom for their helpful remarks on this subject.

Gradual Purification from Corpse Impurity

The third halakha which is listed in M. 'Eduyot deals with corpse impurity: ודיקרב במיתא מסתאב. וקראו לה יוסי שריא "and [one] who touches a corpse becomes unclean." The Mishnah concludes: "and they called him 'Yose the Permitter'." The content of this halakha is obscure since it has two contradicting parts: on the one hand, Yose ben Yoezer argues that one who touches a corpse is impure, but on the other the Mishnah emphasizes that his attitude was lenient, and therefore he was called (the Mishnah does not say by whom) "Yose the Permitter." Another problem which emerges from this is, why does Yose ben Yoezer bother to repeat a basic notion which is already known from Numbers 19? These problems have been addressed by the Amoraim (b. 'Abod. Zar. 37b) and modern scholars. Two alternative explanations have been suggested:

1. Yose ben Yoezer does not refer to the person who touched the corpse itself (אב הטומאה), but only to one who has come into contact with another person already defiled by a corpse (ראשון לטומאה). Thus, Yose ben Yoezer states that this person is impure only for one day (and not for seven days like one who has touched a corpse). But since this view does not correspond to the view of the Rabbis, the Amoraim had to argue that although this was the decree of Yose ben Yoezer, later Sages decreed that one who touched a person defiled by a corpse (ראשון לטומאה) is also impure for seven days.[21]

2. Yose ben Yoezer refers to the simple case of obvious contact with a corpse but his main focus is the case of ספק, where there is doubt whether a person touched a corpse. Yose ben Yoezer rules that this person is impure but for only one day instead of seven, and thus his statement pertains only to this scenario.

The difficulties with these two explanations are clear. In trying to harmonize Yose ben Yoezer's statement with the fact that he was considered lenient, the traditional interpreters of this single halakha added complicated conditions to his ruling, although it contains only three words ודיקרב במיתא מסתאב.[22] In light of these difficulties, we suggest interpreting this obscure early Pharisaic halakha according

---

[21] See the discussion of Epstein, *Prolegomena*, 506; Safrai, "Halakha," 153. J. Neusner, *A History of the Mishnaic Law of Damages* (SJLA 35; Leiden: E. J. Brill, 1985) 4.132, implies this explanation in his translation to this Mishnah, but admits that he cannot explain this particular halakha.

[22] Although it is possible that some words are missing in Yose ben Yoezer's laconic statement, and a solution is therefore impossible, it should be observed that its syntactic pattern (i.e., X is דכי/דכין/מסתאב) resembles the two other halakhot in this Mishnah.

to a contemporary halakhic view, rather then harmonizing it with later rabbinic laws. It is also necessary to understand its literal meaning, without reading external halakhic views into Yose ben Yoezer's words. Our suggestion for resolving the paradox of this Mishnah is to juxtapose it with an opposing halakhic view from Qumran and to point to a possible controversy between the Pharisaic leader and the Qumran sectarians.[23]

The halakhic view that we would like to compare with Yose ben Yoezer's assertion deals with a concept that was recognized about two decades ago, as a result of the discovery of the Temple Scroll. According to the 11QT 50:13-16 (also 4Q512, 4Q514, and recently also 4Q414), corpse impurity is removed by gradual purification: in addition to immersion and sprinkling of the ashes of the red heifer upon the defiled person on the seventh day, these texts argue for immersion on the first and third days of impurity, and sprinkling with ashes on the third day. J. Milgrom and J. M. Baumgarten have already asserted that the purpose of this regulation is to ensure that an impure person would not be completely defiled while he eats and drinks, and thus, he would not contaminate his food and drink.[24] Hence, this purity law presumes an intermediate level of impurity: the person is, of course, impure until the seventh day but he may eat and drink without defiling ordinary (unsacred) food. Therefore, although this gradual impurity seems, at first glance, to be a lenient attitude towards purification, since it diminishes the degree of corpse impurity, it is actually a stricter halakha than the common Pharisaic view because it demands a gradual purification procedure before one eats and drinks, even when one is undoubtedly defiled.

The juxtaposition of this halakha concerning gradual purification with Yose ben Yoezer's statement, that one who touches a corpse becomes unclean, leads to an interesting result. If we take his words

[23] Interestingly, Albeck, noting the difficulties of the traditional solutions, has already suggested that this halakha is an anti-Essene polemic, referring to War 2.150, where Josephus depicts the older Essenes avoiding contact with the young ones, and immersing after such contact, considering it as defiling as contact with a stranger (ἀλλοφύλῳ). See C. Albeck, *Shisha Sidrei ha-Mishna* (Jerusalem/Tel Aviv: Bialik Institute, 1958) 4.485 (Hebrew).
[24] J. Milgrom, "Studies in the Temple Scroll," *JBL* 97 (1978) 512-18; idem, *Leviticus 1-16*, 968-76; J. M. Baumgarten, "The Purification Rituals in DJD 7," *The Dead Sea Scrolls: Forty Years of Research* (ed. D. Dimant and U. Rappaport; STDJ 10; Leiden: E. J. Brill; Jerusalem: Magnes Press and Yad Izhak Ben-Zvi, 1992) 199-209. Cf. also: E. Eshel, "4Q414 Fragment 2: Purification of a Corpse-Contaminated Person," *Legal Texts and Legal Issues. Proceedings of the Second Meeting of the International Organization for Qumran Studies, Cambridge, 1995 Published in Honour of Joseph M. Baumgarten* (ed. M. J. Bernstein, F. García Martínez and J. Kampen; STDJ 23; Leiden: Brill, 1997) 3-10.

as a reference to this Qumran halakha, then his statement will not seem obvious or superfluous, and the following note, "and they called him Yose the Permitter," will not contradict his own halakha. Since, unlike the Qumran sectarians, the Pharisees did not allow an impure person to eat ordinary food in a certain state of purity, we suggest that Yose ben Yoezer opposed the gradual purification of corpse impurity; therefore, his claim that one who touches a corpse becomes unclean is opposed to the Qumran view that one purifies oneself gradually by immersing on the first and third day. Furthermore, the conclusion of the Mishnah, that Yose ben Yoezer had lenient halakhic views, may also be confirmed, since the Qumran view is in fact a stricter halakha, for it demands a degree of purification from an impure person, a degree which Pharisaic halakha ignores.[25]

According to our proposed solution to the paradox of the third halakha in m. 'Ed. 8:4, those who disagreed with Yose ben Yoezer (וקראו לו) were not necessarily his fellow Pharisees but members of a competing sect. The justifications for this interpretation of the Mishnah are: a) there is no clue in the Mishnah to the identity of Yose's critics; b) the traditional assumption that they were other rabbis[26] raises great halakhic difficulties that, in our opinion, may be solved by the juxtaposition of the Qumran halakha of gradual purification. Thus, according to our explanation, in this case Yose ben Yoezer denied the need for gradual purification, and held a permissive attitude in opposition to the stricter Qumran halakha. This may be a possible solution to this difficult Mishnah, which one could not raise before the recent discoveries of the Temple Scroll and the relevant fragments from Cave 4.

---

[25] As Prof. D. R. Schwartz has noted, we presume, along with all other commentators and scholars who have dealt with this halakha, that the lenient attitude which is expressed by the term "Yose the Permitter" refers to all three of his statements. But even if we ignore the contradiction between the content of Yose ben Yoezer's third halakha and his reputation as a "permitter," his intention in this halakha is quite unclear (since he repeats the biblical law of corpse impurity) and requires explanation.

[26] Neusner, *The Rabbinic Traditions*, 1.65, supposes that those who called him "Yose the Permitter" were Temple priests or authorities. It is important to note that the concept of gradual purification was held by others besides the Qumran sectarians, such as the author/editor of the Book of Tobit and perhaps also Philo. See the discussion in my forthcoming article, "Non-priestly Purity and Its Religious Perspectives according to Historical Sources and Archeological Findings," *Purity and Holiness* (ed. M. Poorthuis and J. Schwartz; JCP 2; Leiden: Brill).

Tentative Historical Conclusions

In comparing these four halakhot of Yose ben Yoezer to the relevant
laws of the Damascus Document, the Temple Scroll and some 4Q
fragments, we find that there is some agreement between Yose ben
Yoezer and the Damascus Document concerning the impurity of
Gentile land; there is a controversy concerning the impurity of the liquids of the Temple canal; and, according to our reconstruction of
Yose ben Yoezer's view of corpse impurity, he also opposes the
Qumran law of gradual purification. Thus, there is a certain agreement between the Pharisaic leader and the Qumran sectarians in the
one case but controversy and opposition on the other two issues.

What historical implications may be drawn? In the first place, we
should, of course, draw attention to the fact that the problems treated by Yose ben Yoezer were also dealt with by the Qumran sectarians. Considering the common view that Yose ben Yoezer was active
in the days of the Maccabean revolt against the Seleucids and in the
early Hasmonean period, it is possible that similar and opposing
laws of the Qumran sect were created or discussed during the same
period. It is also possible that the importance of these purity laws
and many others are in fact the consequence of the rebellion against
the Seleucids and a reaction to the contamination of the Temple at
that time.

We should remember that although it is not at all surprising that
this Pharisaic leader opposed the Qumran purity laws, he was the
very first Pharisee to have done so. In fact, his views are almost the
only Pharisaic laws of purity attributed by Tannaitic sources to the
early Hasmonean period. Therefore, we should point out that if we
agree that the Qumran sect was already in existence by this time,
then the halakhic divergence between the Pharisees and the
Qumran sectarians had begun in the days of Yose ben Yoezer. But
these controversies were not merely theoretical. The Damascus
Document and the pesharim mention strong arguments with the
Pharisees and their leaders, and also raise serious accusations against
דורשי החלקות, the "Seekers of Smooth Things," not to mention the
halakhic argument in 4QMMT.

Since the Qumran sectarians confronted the Pharisees and their
leaders in the early Hasmonean period, and since Yose ben Yoezer
was the Pharisaic leader in those days, it is plausible that the sectarians argued with him about halakhic and other religious matters.
But, admittedly, the only clue to a personal encounter and schism
between Yose ben Yoezer and Qumran may lie in the relationship
between Yose ben Yoezer's halakhot and the Qumran laws of puri-

ty. In our view, m. 'Ed. 8:4 may indicate that Yose ben Yoezer actually encountered Qumran sectarians, or at least was familiar with some of their halakhic attitudes. The fact that Yose ben Yoezer opposes two Qumran laws of purity may hint that he was referring to the Qumran halakha, especially concerning gradual purification. In fact, since he is the only Pharisaic figure that we are familiar with who deals with the same problems which interested the Qumran sect, an encounter between Yose ben Yoezer and the sect would seem to be within the realm of possibility. One might even consider identifying Yose ben Yoezer with איש הכזב or איש הלצון, "the Man of Lies," mentioned in the Damascus Document and the pesharim, but we should bear in mind that apart from Yose ben Yoezer's halakhot, we know almost nothing about Pharisaic leaders in that period.[27]

---

[27] Some have identified the Man of Lies with the leader of a group that broke away from the sect. See G. Jeremias, *Der Lehrer der Gerechtigkeit* (Studien zur Umwelt des Neuen Testaments; Göttingen: Vandenhoeck & Ruprecht, 1963); 79 ff., esp. 125 f.; J. Murphy-O'Connor, "The Essenes and their History," *RB* 81 (1974), 234 ff. But many scholars have asserted that the Liar is a Pharisaic leader (connecting him to the Seekers of Smooth Things, cf. CD 1:14-18). See D. Flusser, *Kirjath Sepher* 33 [review on Milik, *Ten Years* (see below)] (1957-58) 458; H. Stegemann, *Die Entstehung der Qumrangemeinde* (Bonn: Rheinische Friedrich-Wilhelms-Universität, 1971) 69 ff., 177 f., 187 f., 200 ff., esp. 229-31; B. Nitzan, *Pesher Habakkuk* (Jerusalem: Bialik Institute, 1996) 13-14, 136-138, 167, 187 (Hebrew). Other scholars doubt whether is it possible to identify the Man of Lies, e.g., P. R. Callaway, *The History of the Qumran Community: An Investigation of the Problem* (doctoral dissertation; Ann Arbor: UMI, 1986) 212. For specific identification of the Man of Lies, see J. T. Milik, *Ten Years of Discovery in the Wilderness of Judaea* (tr. J. Strugnell; SBT 26; London: SCM, 1959) 88 (John Hyrcanus or maybe Jonathan); F. M. Cross, *The Ancient Library of Qumran* (Sheffield: Sheffield Academic Press, 1995³) 116-118 (Simon, whom he also identifies with the Wicked Priest. However, they are probably different persons, cf. Flusser, *Kirjath Sepher*, 457-59; Stegemann, *Die Entstehung*, 99-100); M. H. Segal, "The Habakkuk 'Commentary' and the Damascus Fragments," *JBL* 70 (1951) 146f. (Simon ben Shetah, and see further, Jeremias, *Lehrer der Gerechtigkeit*, 125, n. 4). Cf. Nitzan, *Pesher Habakkuk*, 138. For the identification of Yose ben Yoezer with the Teacher of Righteousness (!) see the bibliography in G. Vermes, *The Dead Sea Scrolls. Qumran in Perspective* (London: SCM, 1994³) 138, n. 7.

In fact, if, for the sake of the discussion, we ignore this major difficulty concerning the lack of information about the early history of the Pharisees, the identification of the Man of Lies with Yose ben Yoezer may seem quite convincing: since the Teacher lived in the early Hasmonean period we should point to a contemporary Pharisaic leader who might have confronted him. That Pharisaic leader probably was not a Hasmonean High Priest and, if the Wicked Priest who persecuted the Teacher was Jonathan (cf. H. Eshel, "4QMMT and the History of the Hasmonean Period," *Reading 4QMMT. New Perspectives on Qumran Law and History* [ed. J. Kampen and M. J. Bernstein; JBLSym 2: Atlanta: Scholars Press, 1996] 61 ff. and bibliography), then it is possible that the Man of Lies was one of the leading Pharisees of Jonathan's time. Additionally, according to 1QpHab 10:5-13, the Man of Lies is accused of establishing a congregation with deceit (הקים עדה בשקר) and this may hint that the Man of Lies had established a sect or a party. This may be connected to our knowledge about the emergent Pharisees and Yose ben Yoezer: Josephus introduces the Pharisees in the days of Jonathan (Ant. 13.171-73); Yose ben Yoezer is the first Pharisee in rabbinic sources who has a halakhic opinion attributed to him.

Regardless of the relations between Yose ben Yoezer and the
Qumran sectarians, we should address the problem of the historical
significance of his halakhot. Were they his personal opinions or were
they authoritative views that influenced popular practice in daily life
and the Temple ritual? Although we have no historical information
from rabbinic literature concerning this problem, we should pay attention to the implicit information about the Pharisaic influence in
the early Hasmonean state, and especially in the Temple. While it
seems that we can conclude from Josephus' account on the rupture
between John Hyrcanus and the Pharisees that before the rift this
party had some control on internal affairs, 4QMMT argues against
the Pharisaic halakha which is dominant in the Temple cult. Hence,
both sources, neither of which can be suspected of sympathy towards the Pharisees, admit that during the early Hasmonean period
the Pharisees had the upper hand.[28] None of these sources, however,
specifies the leaders in charge of this domination. Here we may correlate the evidence about Yose ben Yoezer: since his halakhot are
remnants of Pharisaic halakha in the early Hasmonean period, then
the evidence from Josephus and Qumran may teach us that his
statements reflect not only his own views but are actually the laws
practiced in the Temple by many Jews in this period.[29] If this is the
case, than the supposed opposition of the Qumran sectarians (and
perhaps others as well, cf. n. 26) to Pharisaic leaders such as Yose
ben Yoezer would be self-explanatory.

In summary, our main conclusion is that from the very beginning
the Pharisees and the Qumran sectarians were concerned with the
same problems of purity. Since Yose ben Yoezer is the earliest
Pharisaic figure who deals with halakhic problems, his halakhot re-

Thus, we may regard him as the first (along with Yose ben Yoḥanan?) to establish
Pharisaic halakha and the first leader of the Pharisees as a formal sect. This may
also be the basis of the rabbinic tradition of the first "pair" as grape clusters
(אשכולות). Cf. Neusner, *Rabbinic Traditions*, 62 f.

[28] Schwartz, "MMT, Josephus and the Pharisees," *Reading 4QMMT*, 67-80. Cf.
idem, "Josephus and Nicolaus on the Pharisees," *JSJ* 14 (1983) 157-71. However, it
is interesting that none of Yose ben Yoezer's halakhot are referred to in 4QMMT,
although other laws concerning the impurity of Gentiles and the Temple are dealt
with extensively.

[29] Note that Neusner, *Rabbinic Traditions*, 1.64-66, has denied the possibility that
Yose ben Yoezer had any control in the Temple, as he has underestimated the influence of the Pharisees on formal institutions, especially the Temple, neglecting the
evidence of Josephus (Ant. 13.288-98) and considering Josephus' description of the
Pharisees as unhistorical. See idem, 3.248-55, 301ff. Cf. Schwartz, "Josephus and
Nicolaus." If our explanation is correct, than the term "testified" (העיד) in m. 'Ed.
8:4 is the consequence of a later editing (cf. Neusner, *Rabbinic Traditions*, 1.61 f.) and
it is possible that Yose ben Yoezer decreed (גזר) his three halakhot, such as his decree on Gentile land.

flect Pharisaic law in the early Hasmonean period. It is significant that a concern for the same halakhic problems combined with opposing views, is found in the Damascus Document, the Temple Scroll and other fragments. By juxtaposing the different pieces of evidence from the early days of the Pharisees and Qumran we can confirm the evaluation that purity was indeed among the main issues dividing the Pharisees and the Qumran sect in the early Hasmonean period.

THE DAMASCUS DOCUMENT FROM THE CAIRO GENIZAH: ITS DISCOVERY, EARLY STUDY AND HISTORICAL SIGNIFICANCE

Stefan C. Reif

Geniza Research Unit, Cambridge

What Is History?

"Such a view," declares one of the doyens of modern Jewish historiography, "effectively negates any question of objectivity from even the most capable of historians. [It is] a view I cannot but regard as cynical, if not downright impudent, or, to use the more vigorous Yiddish expression, a *chuzpa*." This is how Jacob Katz responds to the critical advice of one scholar who suggests that, before examining any historical work, one should take a good look at the life, times and outlook of the writer. Such an examination, according to that scholar, will constitute a better guide to the work than the academic theories of the writer himself. At the same time, however, Katz unequivocally acknowledges the importance of the debate about whether any historian is capable of adopting a totally impersonal position with regard to the events of the past. Indeed, having noted the impudence of the extreme version of such a scholarly scepticism, he backtracks more than somewhat and states his own belief that an acquaintance with the life of a writer will assist the reader in assessing the degree to which that writer's views may be regarded as objective. Since, in his opinion, historians would never claim absolute detachment for any of their statements or judgements, they are aware that their personal stories will interest those who are acquainted with their publications. In this way, Katz justifies his decision to compose his own autobiography.[1]

A few more words ought to be said about the importance of personal and even ephemeral data in the study of scholarly views and theories and about the differences in this connection between nineteenth and twentieth century historical research. Until well into this century, it was believed, in common with the Victorian teachers,

---

[1] J. Katz, *With My Own Eyes. The Autobiography of an Historian* (tr. A. Brenner and Z. Brody; Tauber Institute for the Study of European Jewry 20; Hanover: University Press of New England, 1995; original Hebrew: *Bemo Enay*, Jerusalem: Keter, 1989) x. These introductory remarks do not appear in the Hebrew edition.

that the true student of the past was capable of standing outside his own chronology and locality and could, by an enthusiastic and judicious marshalling of progressively more intricate data from chosen sources, replace the folktales of tradition with the scientific analysis of the present, producing a picture of the past precisely as it was. In the amusing and perceptive words of E. H. Carr, "three generations of German, British and even French historians marched into battle intoning the magic words '*wie es eigentlich gewesen ist*' like an incantation—designed, like most incantations, to save them from the tiresome obligation to think for themselves." More recent historians are no less committed to the pursuit of reliable information and fresh sources; but they recognize that neither the historian nor his source can ever be regarded as dispassionate and that academic history is a matter of placing everyone and everything in their contexts and interpreting their significance accordingly and with as little subjectivity as one can manage.[2]

Current scholars are more at home with the humanity of history than with its grander sweeps. Testimonies to the petty incident, details of the underprivileged group and remnants of the unconventional text are given a status once denied them and there is an almost voyeuristic obsession with individuals, their lives and their motivations. Today's intense interest in both the most obscure contents of the Genizah Collection itself and in the people associated over the years with its discovery and exploitation is to a considerable degree due to such changes in scholarly outlook. What Schechter and his colleagues set aside in their day as unimportant today attracts fresh attention, whether it is economic data, printed matter or magical charms. *Wissenschaftsgeschichte* is now a flourishing science and it is widely felt that enthusiasm for an academic subject must also entail a fascination with those who have promoted it. Here, too, it has become as important to know about the personal involvement as it is to be *au fait* with the technical data.[3]

---

[2] Some of the relevant issues are touched on in the entry, "History," *New Encyclopaedia Britannica* 20 (1991) 572-74, and much of the debate was fired by the controversial study of the subject by E. H. Carr, *What is History? The George Macaulay Trevelyan Lectures Delivered in the University of Cambridge, January-March 1961* (London: Vintage, 1961; 2nd ed: ed. R. W. Davies; London: Macmillan, 1986), especially 1-24. The quotation is from p. 3.

[3] Such an interest in mundane details and in personalities is exemplified in two recent exhibitions mounted at the Israel Museum, Jerusalem, and at Cambridge University Library, to mark the centenary of Solomon Schechter's famous and successful visit to Cairo early in 1897; see the exhibition catalogues *The Cairo Genizah: A Mosaic of Life* (ed. D. Raccah-Djivre; Jerusalem: Israel Museum, 1997) and *History in Fragments: A Genizah Centenary Exhibition* (ed. S. and S. C. Reif; Cambridge, 1998).

Ben Sira Case

I recently applied this approach, I believe with some success, to a close study of Schechter's involvement with the textual history of the book of Ben Sira. An examination of his earlier scholarly work and the way it related to that of his colleagues in Oxford revealed theological as well as historical and literary reasons for his deep interest in finding an authentic Hebrew version of the work. These undercurrents explained the almost paroxysmal excitement generated in him in May, 1896, when he identified a manuscript folio brought to him by Mrs. Agnes Lewis and Mrs. Margaret Gibson as a tenth century fragment of just such a version.[4] When later, as a widow, Mrs. Mathilde Schechter reminisced about the years that she had spent with her husband in Cambridge, she recalled how very keen he had been to locate the original Hebrew of Ben Sira. "The subject interested him very much," she wrote, "and occupied his mind intensely, for the great savant who lived 200 ... years before Christ had been the subject of argument among biblical critics and Christian theologians throughout the century." After he had made his identification of the Lewis-Gibson fragment, Dr. Schechter would, according to his wife's testimony, often say, "If only I had leave of absence and sufficient money, I would go in search of that lost Hebrew original."[5]

In my article, I pointed out that Schechter's trip to Cairo was privately financed by Charles Taylor, the Master of St. John's College, and not by the University of Cambridge, because of the fear that any formal announcement would lead to alternative bids to uncover the manuscript source. This, in Mathilde Schechter's frankly expressed statement, "would have brought Oxford University and probably other places into competition, and might have spoiled any chance of Dr. Schechter's success." She also cited her husband's conviction that "if the original Hebrew of Jesus Ben Sira was in existence, it could be found only in the Genizah of old Cairo, as Saadya Gaon, the last person to quote Jesus Ben Sira, hailed from Cairo, and his manuscripts would naturally be hidden there, as it was the old Jewish custom never to destroy but to hide or bury Hebrew writings, mostly in synagogues." According to my analysis, the subse-

---

[4] S. C. Reif, "The Discovery of the Cambridge Genizah Fragments of Ben Sira: Scholars and Texts," *The Book of Ben Sira in Modern Research* (ed. P. C. Beentjes; Berlin/New York: de Gruyter, 1997) 1-22.

[5] These and the following quotations from Mrs. Schechter are to be found in her memoirs, located in the Schechter Papers at the Library of the Jewish Theological Seminary of America in New York. I am grateful to the Library for permission to use and cite this and similar material.

quent jockeying for scholarly prominence in the subject was the inspiration for many discoveries and publications and it was not difficult to identify the human motivations, some more honourable than others, that lay behind the academic enterprises.[6]

Searching for a Background

When kindly invited by the organisers of this symposium to make a novel contribution to the current discussions about the Damascus Document (= CD), particularly in connection with Schechter's discovery of the Genizah manuscripts, it occurred to me that it would be interesting for me, as well as for my listeners and, ultimately, my readers, if I could subject this topic to an analysis that was in essence similar to that undertaken in the case of the Ben Sira Genizah fragments.[7] One could once again uncover the personal feelings and controversies that inspired the discovery, locate earlier treatments of the subject, and place Schechter's work in the context of earlier historical research. Alas, as the Scots poet, Robert Burns, wisely concluded, no doubt at the end of an especially abortive effort at one literary composition or another, "the best-laid schemes o' mice an' men gang aft a-gley [= often go awry]."[8] Had he been born in Galicia rather than Ayrshire, he would no doubt have expressed it as "a mensch tracht und Gott lacht." None of Schechter's pre-Genizah publications reveals any particular interest in Jewish sectarian literature. He was not at the time of his discovery of CD engaged in any controversy about the existence of Hebrew literature that appeared to originate in non-rabbinic circles. There was no reason, at least none that I could identify, why he might have a burning ambition to locate the theological and exegetical ideas of a previously unknown sect. In sum, I was unable to place the discovery of CD in the kind of human context that I had successfully found for the explosion of Ben Sira research at the same period.

But today's scholars also have motivations for their studies. If one is scheduled to give a paper at a conference, a topic has to be developed. If one's expenses are to be paid, they have to be justified by the treatment of a fresh theme. If a *curriculum vitae* is to be updated

---

[6] Reif, "The Discovery," 3-11.

[7] I welcome the opportunity of recording my gratitude to Prof. Michael Stone and Dr. Esther Chazon for organising the symposium and for their kind invitation to me to participate in it.

[8] The line occurs in his poem *Ta a Mouse. On turning her up in her nest with the plough, November, 1785* (Kilmarnock edition, 1786), the first line of which reads: "Wee, sleeket, cowrin, timrous beastie."

for a research assessment exercise, it had better include some additional items. The questions might have to be different for CD than they were for Ben Sira but a closer look at personal and institutional archives, at the interpretations offered by Schechter and his supporters and critics, and at the results of broader studies relating to the scholarly interaction with Genizah materials, would undoubtedly produce some worthwhile findings. When did Schechter discover the manuscripts of CD and why did it take him so long to publish them? Was there any development in his theories about CD and, if so, under whose influence? Are there any obviously personal elements in the scholarly controversies? Does current research about the earliest Genizah discoveries contribute anything to the discussions about CD? How do Schechter's views, and those of his contemporaries, compare with post-Qumranic interpretations? The fresh treatment of these questions will make it possible to assess the degree to which George Margoliouth of the British Museum is justified when he claims in 1910 that Schechter "has added glory to his name by bringing to light a document which will, in the opinion of many, take an even higher rank than the Hebrew text of Ecclesiasticus, which owes its identification to the same ingenious and practised scholar."[9]

Gradual Revelations

Although Schechter published CD in the first volume of his *Documents of Jewish Sectaries* in Cambridge in 1910, he had discovered and identified it many years earlier.[10] When he left Cambridge for New York in 1902, he arranged to borrow both manuscripts of CD; he had obviously made his exciting find, therefore, during the years of his intensive Genizah research in Cambridge. The personal excitement and the human progress of these five years, from 1897, when he returned from Cairo with his famous "hoard of Hebrew manuscripts," until 1902 when he sailed for the United States to take over the leadership of the Jewish Theological Seminary, are well documented in his archives and those of his academic colleagues, as well as in more formal University documents. The team of enthusiastic specialists that Schechter gathered around him are

---

[9] G. Margoliouth, "The Sadducean Christians of Damascus," *The Athenaeum* no. 4335 (26 November, 1910) 659.

[10] S. Schechter, *Documents of Jewish Sectaries. Vol. I: Fragments of a Zadokite Work* (Cambridge: Cambridge University Press, 1910). The classmarks of the two CD manuscripts at Cambridge University Library are T-S 10K6 and T-S 16.311.

seen to be busy making all manner of discoveries and sharing the details with each other. A picture emerges of industrious activity relating to the study, transcription, conservation and publication of the fragments presented by Schechter and Taylor, and to the possible purchase and acquisition of other Genizah material. Scholarly and popular articles appear in considerable number and there are times when Schechter makes a positive nuisance of himself by bombarding his colleagues with information about his latest revelations.[11]

Given such a situation, it is more than a little surprising that his first encounters with CD are not trumpeted from the ramparts of the records. Not only is there no major publicity about his revelations; there seems to be a positive reticence about reporting and explaining them, and it is only with some difficulty that one can ascertain when they occurred. The first hint that he had identified such items is offered in an article that he published in *The Jewish Chronicle* of London on 1 April, 1898. Continuing the general report on the Genizah Collection's broad contents that he had commenced in *The Times* of London on 3 August, 1897, he promises the historian a wealth of new material relating to forgotten groups and their religious writings:

> And what raptures of delight are there in store for the student when sifting and reducing to order the historical documents which the Genizah has furnished in abundance, *including even the remains of the sacred writings of strange Jewish sects that have long since vanished* [emphasis mine]. Considerations of space, however, forbid me to enter into detailed descriptions; these would require a whole series of essays.[12]

Clearly Schechter is aware that has uncovered texts that are of major significance for Jewish sectarian history but he is loath to describe them in detail. No mention is made of them either in the report prepared by the University Library's Cairo Subsyndicate in 1899 or, perhaps even more strangely, in the summary of the Collection drawn up in 1900 by Herman Leonard Pass, the young convert from Judaism to Christianity employed by Schechter to identify and describe a broad range of biblical and apocryphal items.[13] It is of course possible that Schechter was anxious to keep the discovery to himself

---

[11] Details are given in S. C. Reif, "Jenkinson and Schechter at Cambridge: An Expanded and Updated Assessment," *Transactions of the Jewish Historical Society of England* 32 (1993) 279-316. See also the first paragraph of the article by "an occasional correspondent" under the title "Facts and Fictions about Aquila," *Jewish Chronicle* (15 October, 1897) 21.

[12] S. Schechter, "Work in the Cambridge-Cairo Genizah," *Jewish Chronicle* (1 April, 1898) 26.

[13] Papers prepared for the Cambridge University Library Syndicate and presented to them at their meetings of 24 October, 1900 (minute 10; data prepared by Pass) and 14 November, 1900 (minute 7; data prepared by N. McLean and A. T.

but, given that he had publicised so much else that he was researching or planned to research, such a motivation is by itself insufficient to explain his behaviour. It is also known that Schechter held things back for publication in America in order to bring prestige to his new institution[14] but in this case the edition of CD did not appear until 1910, eight years after he arrived at the Seminary. Taken together, however, with a hesitation on his part to commit himself to a definitive identification of historical provenance, theological context and literary importance, these motivations become more convincing. Schechter undoubtedly had the imagination, the flair and the enthusiasm to locate manuscripts of outstanding significance for Hebrew and Jewish studies, but it was sometimes left to others to complete the detailed scholarly process. As his student and friend Norman Bentwich, in his famous biography of the master, put it: "After his first editions he was outstanding rather as the discoverer than the commentator, a master of intuition rather than erudition. He was the explorer reporting his travels in the land of manuscripts as he went."[15]

Early Interpretation

This theory about his overall hesitation is borne out by the fact that Schechter begins to allude to CD in slightly more detail in his own reports on the Taylor-Schechter Collection as University Reader in Talmudic, and as Curator in Oriental Literature at the University Library, published as appendices to the Library Syndicate's reports between 1900 and 1902. In his statement of 6 May, 1900, he is more explicit than he had been in a letter to Cyrus Adler of two weeks earlier, [16] this time not only noting CD's borrowings from the Book of Jubilees but also favouring a Samaritan origin, via the Dosithean sect. He knew that he was looking for a sect that had survived from Second Temple times into the Middle Ages; the one that was referred to by rabbinic, early Christian and medieval Islamic

Chapman); and *Cambridge University Reporter*, no. 1360 (12 June, 1901), 1088 and 1107-8.

[14] J. D. Sarna, "Two Traditions of Seminary Scholarship," *Tradition Renewed: A History of the Jewish Theological Seminary of America. Vol. 2: Beyond the Academy* (ed. J. Wertheimer; New York: JTS, 1997) 62. His comments are based on Schechter to Sulzberger, 5 November 1901, in M. Ben-Horin, "Solomon Schechter to Judge Mayer Sulzberger," *JSS* 25 (1963) 285, and J. Jacobs, "Solomon Schechter as Scholar and as Man," *Jewish Theological Seminary Students Annual* 3 (1916) 99.

[15] N. Bentwich, *Solomon Schechter. A Biography* (Philadelphia: JPS, 1938) 263.

[16] C. Adler, "Solomon Schechter: A Biographical Sketch," *American Jewish Year Book* 5677 [1916-17] 53.

sources and was linked with the personal name Dosa, Dostai, Dusis
or Dustan (Dositheos in Greek), seemed to be an obvious candidate:

> We have now fragments of the original Hebrew of Ben Sira repre-
> senting three different manuscripts, which have been edited by the
> Master of St. John's and Dr. Schechter. The Megillath Antiochus is
> represented in many copies. Mr. Pass has lately discovered an
> Aramaic fragment, similar in character to a Targum, which probably
> formed the original of the Testament of the Twelve Patriarchs. *In this
> connection may be mentioned a larger fragment of Samaritan origin (probably em-
> anating from the sect of the Dostaim) which gives many quotations from the Book
> of Jubilees and which on further study should help to solve the problem of this
> Apocryphon.*[17] [emphasis mine]

By the time that he was about to leave Cambridge for Seminary
pastures, he had clear-cut plans to publish his various fragments relating to Jewish sects and he reported on 25 February, 1902, that
"the fragments of Anan's book will form part of a volume on Jewish
Sectaries which is being printed by the Cambridge University
Press."[18] At that time, however, the link he had made was still primarily with the Samaritans, as is made clear by the notes prepared
in the University Library at that time, no doubt with Schechter's involvement, and relating to the loan being made to him of those
items required for the preparation of his volume:

> Dr. Schechter took with him from Cambridge March 14/02
> (Returned by Dr. Schechter 1910):
>
> T-S 16.311 Samaritan paper
> T-S 10K6 Samaritan paper 8 leaves
> Anan (Karaites Polemics) Vellum T-S 16.359-367 (returned by Dr.
> Schechter 1910 July 13)[19]

Apparently, soon after he settled in the United States, he had a discussion about the CD fragments with Kaufmann Kohler, the distinguished scholar and leader of Reform Judaism who presided over
the Hebrew Union College from 1903. From that discussion, Kohler
concluded that the Samaritan and Dosithean connections were still

---

[17] Appendix II of Library Syndicate's report for 1899, entitled "Report of the
Reader in Talmudic on the Taylor-Schechter Collection," dated 6 May, 1900, published in the *Cambridge University Reporter*, no. 1308 (15 June, 1900), 1082-83.
   [18] Appendix II of Library Syndicate's report for 1900, entitled "Report of the
Curator in Oriental Literature on the Taylor-Schechter Collection," dated 18
March, 1901, published in the *Cambridge University Reporter*, no. 1360 (12 June, 1901)
1107-8.
   [19] These details appear on the copy of a typed sheet relating to the Loan
Collection that Schechter took to New York and bound together with the fragments
in binder T-S Misc. 35.1-57.

central to Schechter's theories, as he reported when he wrote a review of *Documents of Jewish Sectaries* in 1911 and complained about
the author's alteration of these:

> Indeed, eight years ago, Professor Schechter was far nearer the truth,
> when, in conversation with the writer, he spoke of the Dosithean
> character and origin of the manuscript he had brought from
> Cambridge. The very opening words of the document show it to have
> been the messianic *pronunciamento* of the Samaritan heresiarch ...[20]

Not only Kohler's report but also an account of a lecture given by
Schechter to a well attended meeting of the Society of Biblical
Literature and Exegesis at Columbia University in New York City
on 30–31 December, 1902, attest to an evolution in the lecturer's
thoughts about CD. The Samaritan connection is replaced by a
Karaite link and, perhaps even more importantly, Schechter acknowledges the tentative nature of his hypothesis:

> Prof. Solomon Schechter of the Jewish Theological Seminary of
> America then spoke on "A Newly-Discovered Document of an Old
> Jewish Sect." From the Cairo Genizah he had brought several MSS.,
> *whose meaning he was at a loss to explain.* As he is publishing the text, he
> believed that some scholar to whose attention the subject might be
> brought would be able to solve the mystery. The MS. contains refer-
> ences to a Samaritan city. It speaks of the three cardinal sins and of
> polygamy, against which it makes a novel argument. *Professor Schechter
> claims that this MS. must be the laws of some Jewish sect, like the Karaites, per-
> haps, surely midway between the Jews and the Samaritans. The sect is not like the
> Samaritans, for it acknowledges certain prophets as authorities; besides, it lives in
> Damascus at the period of the destruction of the second temple, and not in
> Gerizim.*[21] [emphasis mine]

It may hardly be doubted that Schechter was a very busy man at the
Seminary during the next few years with many administrative bur-
dens, a heavy teaching load, and a demanding agenda in the wider
Jewish and non-Jewish communities. This took its toll on the time
available for research and inevitably led to a delay in the appearance of the volumes devoted to CD and Anan. At the same time, I
believe that there may have been other factors that also contributed
to that delay. If, as has been suggested, Schechter was slowly adjust-
ing his views, or reaching the conclusion that only a tentative hy-

---

[20] K. Kohler, "Dositheus, the Samaritan Heresiarch, and His Relations to Jewish
and Christian Doctrines and Sects," *American Journal of Theology* 15 (1911) 406.

[21] *Jewish Comment* 16, no. 12, Baltimore (2 January, 1903) 11. I am grateful to Dr.
Michael Grunberger of the Library of Congress for kindly providing me with a
copy of this page.

pothesis was possible, this would have created a hesitancy on his part to commit himself to print. His earlier work had been of a considerably different character, more concerned with establishing critical texts on the basis of manuscript comparisons, and less demanding of historical and theological theorising.[22] His other Genizah work was in fields with which he was thoroughly familiar and where he could feel confident about his interpretations. CD represented a singularly different challenge and it is possible that the team of distinguished scholars of Judaica that now surrounded him in New York, and that he had indeed newly added to the Seminary's faculty, had both a favourable and a less than favourable effect on his project.

Collegial Influences

In his preface to *Fragments of a Zadokite Work*, Schechter acknowledges the assistance three of his colleagues, Israel Friedlaender and Alexander Marx at the Seminary, and Henry Malter at Dropsie College.[23] Although no more details are given about Friedlaender's contribution to Schechter's research, it seems likely that he made more than a minor impact on its direction. A graduate of the Hildesheimer Rabbinical Seminary in Berlin and an expert Semitist who had studied with Theodor Nöldeke in Strasbourg, Friedlaender functioned as the Seminary's professor of Bible.[24] He had little enthusiasm for this role and preferred to concentrate his efforts on medieval Jewish and Islamic sects, with the focus, as his biographer puts it, on "popular movements, not elitist philosophies, religious enthusiasm rather than conventional piety, heterodoxy more than orthodoxy."[25] His published studies of medieval sectarianism and his views on the religious interchange between Islam and Judaism have left their mark on scholarship and he presupposed, without being able to identify the route, a movement of religious ideas from the ancient world to the philosophies of medieval sects. I find it hard to believe that he provided Schechter only with translations of Arabic texts but am not yet in a position to cite documentary evidence for my suspicions. Both Marx and Malter, encouraged by Schechter's

---

[22] Compare his *Aboth de Rabbi Nathan* (Vienna, 1887); *Agadath Shir Hashirim* (Cambridge, 1896); and (with S. Singer) *Talmudical Fragments in the Bodleian Library* (Cambridge, 1896).

[23] Schechter, *Documents of Jewish Sectaries. Vol. I*, preface.

[24] For biographical details, see B. R. Shargel, *Practical Dreamer: Israel Friedlander and the Shaping of American Judaism* (New York: JTS, 1985).

[25] Shargel, *Practical Dreamer*, 68.

example and assistance, specialized in various aspects of Genizah research and it is hardly surprising to find their names mentioned in Schechter's CD volume.[26]

A name that is, however, conspicuous by its absence from that study is that of the scholar who was undoubtedly the most distinguished among the Judaic experts whom Schechter had brought to the Seminary, namely, Louis Ginzberg. Some further attention should therefore be given to the relationship that these two outstanding teachers and researchers enjoyed during Schechter's presidency of the Seminary. Ginzberg's son, Eli, has described that relationship as mutually warm and supportive. They admired each other's scholarship to such a degree that Schechter entrusted to Ginzberg whole areas of Genizah research that he himself could not find the time to undertake, and Ginzberg was genuinely distraught when faced with a Seminary without Schechter on the latter's untimely death in 1915.

At the same time, there were clearly some tensions between them. Eli Ginzberg must have had some specific discussions and situations in mind when he claimed that "Schechter could not have escaped moments of disquietude when he realized that my father's single-handed devotion to scholarship was propelling him into a position of international renown."[27] One such tense situation was undoubtedly created when Schechter asked Ginzberg whether the fragments of the Talmud Yerushalmi that he had found in the Genizah had any special value. His younger colleague's less than modest reply was "Yes, when I have added my notes and commentary."[28]

In my view, such tensions are also manifest in the matter of CD and help to explain the differences between Schechter and Ginzberg with regard to its interpretation. Schechter had already passed enough Genizah material to Ginzberg to ensure that he would overtake his chief in the matter of the quantity of his Genizah publications and was anxious to retain exclusive control of CD. Perhaps the acknowledgements in his preface imply that Ginzberg's views were receiving little or no attention. Schechter saw the work as decidedly non-Pharisaic and in opposition to the talmudic Judaism in which Ginzberg was so expert. Ginzberg was convinced that Schechter's

---

[26] On various aspects of Schechter's Genizah initiatives with his Seminary colleagues, see S. C. Reif, "The Cambridge Genizah Story: Some Unfamiliar Aspects" (Hebrew) in *Te'uda* 15 (ed. M. A. Friedman; in press).
[27] E. Ginzberg, *Louis Ginzberg: Keeper of the Law—A Personal Memoir* (reprint of 1966 edition with "afterword" by EG; Philadelphia: JPS, 1996) 90 and 95-96.
[28] Ginzberg, *Keeper*, 119.

identification of the sect was mistaken and that the sect represented by CD was essentially Pharisaic, and he published a lengthy set of German articles, in many instalments, saying precisely why.[29] The impression given by his corrections to Schechter's readings and interpretations, and presumably intended by the author, is that he is the greater talmudist and more brilliant expounder of manuscripts. For his part, Schechter declared that he had "an inveterate objection to reading scientific matter in instalments." This situation created hurt feelings on both sides, with remorse about the clash subsequently being felt by the two academics. Schechter was loath to produce his second edition and take on the task of refuting Ginzberg, while Ginzberg stalled for the rest of his life in the matter of the publication of an English edition of his work. He was willing to disagree with his senior colleague during the latter's lifetime but reticent about carrying on the battle after the Seminary President's death.[30]

Schechter's Hypothesis

The views that Schechter finally adopted were therefore in a number of ways a reflection of ten years' discussion and human interplay, as well as the result of strictly scientific enquiry and deep personal contemplation. He concluded that his work would prove to be a valuable contribution to the history of early Jewish sects, revealing as it did the religious law and theology of a sect long extinct that once enjoyed its own sacred literature, its own calendar and its own interpretation of the Hebrew Bible, and that fathered later traditions at variance with rabbinic Judaism. He saw the special loyalty to the Prophets and the close connections with apocryphal and pseudepigraphical books in general, and with Jubilees, Testaments of the Twelve Patriarchs and Enoch in particular, as indicative of adherence to a form of Jewish faith and practice at variance with "official" Pharisaic and rabbinic Judaism and, indeed, distinctly hostile to it. Important parallels could be drawn with aspects of Samaritanism and Karaism and with the re-

---

[29] Ginzberg's response to Schechter's publication first appeared in a series of articles entitled *"Eine unbekannte jüdische Sekte"* in *MGWJ* 55 (1911) 666-98; 56 (1912) 33-48, 285-307, 417-48, 546-66, 664-89; 57 (1913) 153-76, 284-308, 394-418, 666-96; and 58 (1914) 16-48, 143-77 and 395-429. It was then published in one volume as *Eine unbekannte jüdische Sekte* (New York: [privately published], 1922) and in a posthumous English edition entitled *An Unknown Jewish Sect* (New York: G. Olms, 1976), with a foreword by Eli Ginzberg.
[30] S. Schechter, "Reply to Dr. Büchler's Review of Schechter's 'Jewish Sectaries'," *JQR* 4 N.S. (1913-14) 474; Adler, "Schechter," 50-51; *An Unknown Jewish Sect*, EG's foreword, x.

ligious traditions of the Falashas but he had to admit that "the annals of Jewish history contain no record of a Sect agreeing in all points with the one depicted in the preceding pages." He was aware that the state of knowledge in his day was such that only a workable hypothesis was possible and he claimed that he would be delighted if further discoveries would further elucidate the history of the sect, and even upset his own theories.[31] Cyrus Adler, who was close to him while he was working on CD, was able to testify soon after his death that Schechter "went about this edition with the greatest caution, as was his custom, and wrote his introduction, and stated his theory with the full realization of the fact that it was an hypothesis and that his conclusions might be attacked, but he deemed it cowardly to simply issue a text with philological notes and not be courageous enough to endeavor to present it in its proper historical and literary setting."[32]

Schechter's workable hypothesis was that the limited available evidence indicated that CD constituted extracts from the writings of the Zadokites, whose existence is noted in Karaite writings, notably those of Qirqisani. The origins of such a sect were likely to be among the Sadducees, not the Pharisees, and the various reports about the Dositheans justified the conclusion that it amalgamated with the Zadokite group and made more proselytes among the Samaritans than among the Jews. The characteristic features of such groups were not, however, wholly clear or consistent and the versions of earlier works presupposed in CD often did not tally with the texts known to us from elsewhere.[33] In addition, the readings and interpretations offered for the manuscripts were in no way definitive. Schechter's own words summarize the situation neatly, modestly and cautiously:

> The defective state of the MS. and the corrupt condition of the text in so many places make it impossible to draw a complete picture of the Sect. Yet what remains offers us a few distinct features and salient points enabling us to catch a few glimpses of the history of the sect, its claims and its relation to the rest of the nation.[34]

Responses to the Publication

When Schechter had formally arranged with the University of Cambridge to borrow a set of Genizah manuscripts on which he was working and to remove them to New York, the intention had

---

[31] Schechter, *Fragments*, especially xii, xvi, xviii, xxi-xxii, xxv-xxix.
[32] Adler, "Schechter," 51.
[33] Schechter, *Fragments*, xxi-xxii, xxv-xxix.
[34] Schechter, *Fragments*, xii.

been, according to his fellow donor, Charles Taylor, to return these within two or three years.[35] It was, however, not until July, 1910, that the CD and Anan manuscripts were returned to the University Library by Schechter, during an extended visit to Europe and, indeed, a further fifteen years were to pass before the remaining items found their way back to Cambridge. When he handed the CD fragments over to the University Librarian, Francis Jenkinson, he stipulated—one wonders precisely by what authority, since no special conditions had earlier been attached to CD—that they should not be made available to any other scholar for another five years. Jenkinson did as he was bade but five years to the day later he swiftly had the CD codex bound up, re-attached the two manuscripts to the remainder of the Genizah collection, and made them fully available.[36]

It seems reasonable to suggest that Schechter was again motivated by his doubts and hesitations. Once he had received the comments and criticisms of his peers, he would be in a position to respond to them, and then he could afford to allow them full access. Not that he was not proud of what he had achieved; he was delighted when Jenkinson expressed interest in reading his two volumes on Jewish sectarians and quickly regaled him with copies of the work. The Librarian dutifully read them but confided to his diary that they were rather out of his depth. When the Jewish philanthropist, musician and bibliophile, Mr. James Loeb (founder of the Loeb Classical Library), was in Cambridge, during Schechter's visit to his old academic hunting ground, he welcomed the opportunity of viewing the CD fragments in their editor's presence.[37]

Schechter's edition was, as Cyrus Adler succinctly put it, "followed by a trail of admiration, criticism, and discussion."[38] A host of alternative identifications were made of the sect and the whole

---

[35] One of the conditions of the gift of the Genizah collection made by Taylor and Schechter was that the donors should have exclusive access to the fragments of Ben Sira and the Greek palimpsests until they had completed their editions of them but Taylor had indicated that this would be done within two or three years; see *Cambridge University Reporter*, no. 1215 (14 June, 1898) 968-69. For the whole story of the Loan Collection, see S. C. Reif, "The Cambridge Genizah Story: Some Unfamiliar Aspects" (Hebrew) in *Teʿuda* 15 (in press).

[36] See the bound volumes catalogue in the Manuscripts Reading Room at Cambridge University Library under T-S 10K6 and the personal diary of Jenkinson for 20 July, 1910 (Add. 7433) 201.

[37] See the personal diary of Jenkinson for 19-20 and 31 December, 1910 (Add. 7433) 353-54 and 365, and for 16 January, 1911 (Add. 7434) 16; also Schechter's letters to Jenkinson from the Kingsley Hotel in London dated 27 December, 1910, and 11 January, 1911 (Add. 6463.7061 and 7072).

[38] Adler, "Schechter," 51

subject preoccupied what would today be called the field of Jewish studies, particularly for the remaining five years of Schechter's life. Ginzberg at the Jewish Theological Seminary in New York insisted that CD represented an earlier and purer form of Pharisaism than that familiar to the Rabbis and offered numerous alternative readings and interpretations of the texts.[39] For Kaufmann Kohler at the Hebrew Union College, the fragments were a remnant of that religious system of the Zadokites, Sadducees, Samaritans and Karaites which preserved ancient and elitist traditions and practices, in contrast to the progressive and populist notions of the Pharisees, and had been reliably transmitted by the Dositheans.[40]

The CD fragments were seen by Adolph Büchler, Principal of Jews' College, the Orthodox Rabbinical Seminary in London, as containing the fabricated history of a sect living in Damascus in the seventh or eighth century and as belonging not to an earlier period but to the period of the religious upheavals that preceded the emergence of the Karaite movement.[41] It was the link with early Christianity that appealed to George Margoliouth of the British Museum and he dated CD around the time of the destruction of the Second Temple, the work of the "Sadducean Christians of Damascus."[42] George Foot Moore, the Presbyterian but ecumenical professor of religious studies at Harvard, found himself substantially in agreement with Schechter, equally hesitant about a precise identification but tending to the view that earlier ideas championed by Samaritans and Sadducees had survived long enough "to be gathered ... into the capacious bosom of Karaism" and consigned to the Genizah by way of "some Rabbanite controversialist in Egypt."[43] The Jewish hebraist, Moses Hirsch Segal, then in England but later at the Hebrew University of Jerusalem, added his notes to the text but felt that Schechter's overall interpretation still left scholars in the dark about the sect's origins, relationships with other groups, and place in Jewish history.[44]

---

[39] Ginzberg, *Unknown Jewish Sect*, xviii.

[40] Kohler, "Dositheus," 404-35.

[41] Büchler, "Schechter's 'Jewish Sectaries,'" *JQR* 3 N.S. (1912-13) 429-85.

[42] G. Margoliouth, "The Sadducean Christians of Damascus," *The Athenaeum*, no. 4335, 26 November, 1910, 657-59; *The Expositor* 2 (1911) 499-517.

[43] Moore, "The Covenanters of Damascus: A Hitherto Unknown Jewish Sect," *HTR* 4 (1911) 331-77, especially 377.

[44] Segal, "Additional Notes on 'Fragments of a Zadokite Work'," *JQR* 3 N.S. (1912-13) 301-11.

Since part of our remit in this treatment of the subject is, as explained at the outset, to uncover the human angle on the scholarly developments, it is relevant to draw attention to the possibility that a
number of those who responded to Schechter's publication had, even
if perhaps only subconsciously, their own religious or personal agen-
das. Was Ginzberg at least partially motivated by a desire to associate
CD with proto-rabbinic Judaism so that his own impressive compe-
tence in the talmudic field would become more directly relevant and
provide him with the opportunity of bettering Schechter in finding
parallels to CD? Given that Kohler was engaged in religious polemics
about the validity of Reform Judaism, did he not welcome the opportunity of demonstrating that talmudic Judaism was the reforming element in its day and that the more ancient and authentic voice was to
be found among those groups who took the Scriptures more literally?
Did Margoliouth, from a Jewish family who had converted from
Judaism and become leading Anglicans, have a special interest in finding kindred spirits who were both Jewish and Christian as long ago as
the first century CE? Could there be some substance in the suggestion
that Moore's favourable response to Schechter's theories was part of
his friendly approach to rabbinic Judaism as a whole, arising out of
the liberal nature of his modern Christian convictions?[45] I wonder also
if Büchler harboured a grudge against Schechter for having stolen the
Genizah limelight from himself and his uncle, Adolph Neubauer,
given that the two of them had actually published fragments from that
source before their Cambridge colleague and competitor.[46]

---

[45] In addition to the biographical details about Ginzberg contained in his son
Eli's volume, see also essays by M. J. Kohler and D. Philipson in Kohler's *Festschrift*
entitled *Studies in Jewish Literature* (Berlin: Reimer, 1913) and the new introduction by
J. L. Blau to the reprint of Kohler's *Jewish Theology Systematically and Theologically Con-
sidered* (New York: Ktav, 1968); the entry for George Margoliouth in *Who Was Who
1916-1928* (London: A. & C. Black, 1929) 540, with general information on the
Margoliouth family that may be found in W. T. Gidney, *The History of the London
Society for Promoting Christianity among the Jews, from 1809 to 1908* (London: London
Society for Promoting Christianity Amongst the Jews, 1908) 16-17, 216, 247, 281,
399, 534-35 and 626, and in D. S. Katz, *The Jews in the History of England* (Oxford:
Clarendon, 1994) 379-80; and M. Smith's appreciation of "The Work of George
Foot Moore," *Harvard Library Bulletin* 15 (1967) 169-79.

[46] For an account of the degree to which they pre-empted Schechter, see S. C.
Reif, "Fragments of Anglo-Jewry," *The Jewish Year Book 1998*, lviii-lxvii.
Biographical details of Büchler by I. Epstein appear in his posthumously published
Studies in Jewish History (ed. I. Brodie and J. Rabbinowitz; London: Oxford Uni-
versity, 1956) xiii-xxii.

Angry Reactions

What surely cannot be gainsaid is that the two Oxford scholars, Robert Charles[47] and David Margoliouth,[48] were angry with Schechter and barely hid their feelings in their publications. Distinguished rabbinic scholars such as Schechter and Ginzberg were never slow in demonstrating their contempt for the Christian professors who tackled the history of the Jews and Judaism in the Second Temple period without what they regarded as the necessary mastery of post-biblical Hebrew and the earliest rabbinic sources. In this case, too, they had scant respect for Charles' work. He, for his part, occupied as he was with preparing the classic English edition of the Apocrypha and Pseudepigrapha, bitterly resented the exclusive access to the Genizah manuscripts of CD that Schechter had arranged for himself and the restriction of facsimiles to only one folio. According to the Oxford biblical scholar and Christian cleric, Schechter deserved the reprobation of scholars for his selfishness and their criticism for his careless editing and dubious translations.[49]

Margoliouth was, of course, Schechter's sparring partner in the whole matter of the Hebrew of Ben Sira[50] and the rabbinic specialist's new publishing venture called forth the bitterest invective from the Laudian Professor of Arabic at the University of Oxford. CD was no more than the remains of a Karaite essay dating from no earlier than the eighth century that should have been permitted to remain in its obscurity and the whole Genizah was virtually without value. He expressed himself in the following forthright fashion:

> About a score of years ago the University of Cambridge was presented with the contents of a huge waste-paper basket, imported from Egypt, where such stores abound. The material contained in these repositories is almost always valueless, like the gods of the Gentiles unable to do good or harm, and so neither worth preserving nor worth destroying; and the first great product of the *Genizah* [the Hebrew of Ben Sira] corresponded with this description ...

[47] In his obituary of Charles published in the *Proceedings of the British Academy* 17 (1931) 437-45, the Cambridge palaeographer who had worked with Schechter on the Genizah fragments, Francis Burkitt, referred to the fact that Charles "was not very patient of adverse criticism."
[48] There is an apprecation of D. S. Margoliouth by G. Murray in the *Proceedings of the British Academy* 36 (London: Oxford University Press for the British Academy, 1940) 389-97; see also n. 45 above regarding the Margoliouth family.
[49] R. H. Charles, *Fragments of a Zadokite Work Translated from the Cambridge Hebrew Text and Edited with Introduction, Notes and Indexes* (Oxford: Clarendon, 1912), especially the preface and the introduction, xvi-xvii.
[50] Reif, "The Discovery," 4-8.

In 1910 Dr. Schechter produced another of these treasures—
"Fragments of a Zadokite Work," being some twenty pages of Hebrew text...the ignorance of Hebrew and of the Bible which is dis-
played by these documents is intolerable ... this document also might
have slept in its obscurity without serious loss, except perhaps to specialists in the controversy between Rabbanites and Karaites.[51]

Despite a controversy that Norman Bentwich called "fiercer and
more voluminous than that about Ben Sira,"[52] what virtually all the
experts were nevertheless agreed about was that Schechter had laid
all scholars of Judaism under his debt by his discovery and publication of CD, had inspired his colleagues to apply themselves afresh to
Jewish life and thought from the axial period to the rise of Karaism,
and had added even more glory to his name by this work than by
his famous contributions to Ben Sira studies. As is well known,
Schechter expressed the intention of publishing a second edition,
with corrections and additions, with a full facsimile and with a detailed response to all his critics.[53] Alas, he failed to do so before he
was prematurely summoned to the heavenly academy and scholars
had to wait until the Qumran discoveries before the subject was
again extensively covered.

Dating of Genizah Manuscripts

In the final part of this paper, it will be appropriate to offer some remarks about how some of the issues raised and the theories offered
by Schechter, as well as a number of the responses that they attracted from his contemporaries, compare with the conclusions being
reached about CD by a consensus of specialists who have been able
to benefit from the discoveries made in the Judean desert since
1947, precisely fifty years ago and fifty years after Schechter's own
forays in the Cairo Genizah. The first question to be asked in this
connection is whether the recent developments in Hebrew palaeography provide any indication of the accuracy of Schechter's dating
of the Genizah manuscripts of CD. The problem that immediately
confronts us in this connection is that we are here dealing with a literary and not a documentary text. At the same time, it is neither
biblical nor rabbinic. There is therefore a distinct lack of parallels
that might assist us in dating and we shall have to wait for further

---

[51] D. S. Margoliouth, "The Zadokites," *The Expositor* 6 (1913) 157-64, especially
157, 159 and 164.
[52] Bentwich, *Schechter*, 159.
[53] Schechter, "Reply," 474; Adler, *Schechter*, 51.

studies to be completed before a more definitive assessment can be made.

A few points are, however, worth stressing in the meantime. There are close similarities between our CD manuscripts and texts written in the square oriental style and dated from the eighth to the tenth century. There are no more than a few scribal characteristics that would point to a sophisticated and developed system of transcription.[54] On the other hand, there is a standard number of lines and a larger number of folios than is common for many codices of the period. There is the occasional indication (as has been suggested recently by Beentjes with regard to the Genizah manuscripts of Ben Sira) that the transcription may have been done on the basis of an oral recitation, or one recalled from memory, rather than copied from an exemplar.[55] Comparison with a biblical text from 933 CE and with an Egyptian square script from a similar period indicates that Schechter's estimate of the tenth century for the fuller manuscript is fairly accurate and that, if any adjustment is to be made, it should be towards the ninth rather than the eleventh century. The situation with regard to the other manuscript is clearer, parallels being found among numerous Genizah texts and indicating that a twelfth, or possibly thirteenth century oriental provenance is highly likely.[56]

Issue of Canonicity

Schechter did not clearly indicate whether he thought that the appearance of the CD manuscripts in the Genizah pointed to their canonicity in rabbinic or, indeed, in any other circles, although he did seem to place them in the context of apocryphal and pseudepigraphical literature, rather than what he referred to as "official Judaism." The difficulty of using the Genizah provenance to support

---

[54] An excellent facsimile is now available in the edition of M. Broshi, *The Damascus Document Reconsidered* (Jerusalem: Israel Exploration Society, Shrine of the Book, Israel Museum, 1992).

[55] Many commentators have drawn attention to what they regard as the poor transmission, either oral or textual, of the Genizah CD versions. See also P. C. Beentjes, "Reading the Hebrew Ben Sira Manuscripts Synoptically: A New Hypothesis," *The Book of Ben Sira*, 95-111.

[56] S. A. Birnbaum, *The Hebrew Scripts*, 2 parts (London: Palaeographia/Leiden: E. J. Brill, 1954-57, 1971) plates 91*-93 and 185-86; M. Beit-Arié, *Hebrew Codicology: Tentative Typology of Technical Practices Employed in Hebrew Dated Medieval Manuscripts* (Paris: Centre national de la recherche scientifique, 1976; Jerusalem: Israel Academy of Sciences and Humanities, 1981) plate 21; and the general treatment of the subject by B. Richler, *Hebrew Manuscripts: A Treasured Legacy* (Cleveland: Ofek Institute, 1990).

an assumption of rabbinic canonicity is categorically and even somewhat mischievously highlighted by Louis Ginzberg:

> A famous historian of religion has declared in the chief organ of
> German Oriental studies that the fragments should not be attributed
> to a particular sect in as much as their discovery in the Genizah of the
> community of Cairo shows that they were there regarded as canoni-
> cal. Following out this line of reasoning, the begging letters, the pre-
> scriptions for gout and anaemia, the invoices of merchandise and the
> exercises of schoolboys learning their ABC's, which are all abundant-
> ly represented in the Genizah, must have enjoyed canonical status in
> the community. All that now remains is for the genizah of a commu-
> nity in Lithuania to come to light, and our historians of religion will
> make the happy discovery that Karl Marx's *Das Kapital* and Eugene
> Süe's novel *The Mysteries of Paris* enjoyed a canonical dignity among
> the Lithuanian Jews of the nineteenth century. Fragments of these
> works will inevitably be found in the genizot, which are the ultimate
> repositories of everything that is written or printed in Hebrew charac-
> ters; in the eleventh century it may be a sectarian book, and in the
> nineteenth a novel translated from the French.[57]

More modern awareness of the problem of drawing conclusions
about the rabbinic canonicity of Genizah texts is to be found in recent suggestions made by Menahem Ben-Sasson and Mark Cohen.
The Polish Karaite leader, Abraham Firkovich, who was an enthusiastic collector of manuscripts, appeared on the Egyptian scene in
1864–65 and a substantial proportion of his extensive collection undoubtedly came from the Karaite synagogue in Cairo. Firkovich was
neither explicit about the provenances of his finds nor averse to doc-
toring what he found to support an early date for the emergence of
Karaism. It therefore remains unclear, even after much recent investigation of the matter by Ben-Sasson, whether or not some of his
haul, including many choice historical items, came from the Ben
Ezra synagogue. What is clear is that he knew of the importance of
its *genizah* and that, if his financial situation had permitted it, he
might have persevered longer in Cairo and pre-empted Schechter's
extensive discoveries of more than thirty years later.[58]

In a paper co-authored with Yedida Stillman, Mark Cohen has

---

[57] Ginzberg, *Unknown Jewish Sect*, xvii.
[58] The origins of the Firkovich collection and its relationship to Genizah collec-
tions in general are analysed by Menahem Ben-Sasson in an article entitled
"Firkovich's Second Collection: Remarks on Historical and Halakhic Material," in
Jewish Studies 31 (1991) 47-67, with an update in a lecture prepared by himself and
Ze'ev Elkin for the Ben Zvi Institute in February, 1997, and entitled "Abraham
Firkovich and the Cairo Genizah: New Evidence." The text of this lecture is ex-
pected to be published shortly in *Pe'amim*.

pointed out that what is referred to as Genizah material may not all have originated in one depository or in the same synagogue. The nature and location of the *genizah* in the Ben Ezra synagogue changed from time to time and there were various communal centres in Cairo, Karaite as well as Rabbanite, where such material was stored. Use was also made of the Bassatin cemetery and some items were acquired from local dealers in antiquities, with no information being provided about their previous provenance. Perhaps even more significantly, during the renovations carried out in the Ben Ezra in 1890, manuscripts from its *genizah* were buried in the synagogal grounds and what was later returned to the inside of the building may have come from various sources.[59] Who can therefore be certain about where a particular text was stored, let alone how it was regarded by the community that consigned it to such storage?

Interestingly, the same serious doubts about the definition and extent of canonicity are entertained by contemporary scholars with regard to the manuscripts found at the Dead Sea. It is now widely recognized that some of that precious collection may reflect wider Jewish beliefs and practices and not only those of the groups that settled in and around Qumran. What is being uncovered may consequently testify to a lack of consistency in the matter of the sacred or authoritative status of particular pieces of literature. It is likely that CD enjoyed a greater theological respect among some Jews than it did among others. Indeed, the later evidence of talmudic literature is again somewhat ambivalent. Does the citation of verses from Ben Sira indicate a canonical status, a tolerance of the text as readable but not formally in the synagogue, or the remnant of an earlier approach that preceded its classification as heretical? What also remains open to question is whether one is entitled to draw parallels between the function occupied by texts of Ben Sira and the Testament of Levi on the one hand and those of CD and the apocryphal psalms on the other. It is possible that only those more closely concerned with what Haran has called "the biblical vision" could have been transmitted by rabbinic circles. Alternatively, the rabbinic tradition was less central than it later imagined itself to have been and found room at that stage for a wider variety of theological expression. The matter remains almost as open now as it was in Schechter's day.[60]

---

[59] M. Cohen and Y. Stillman, "The Cairo Geniza and the Custom of Geniza among Oriental Jewry: An Historical and Ethnographical Study," *Pe'amim* 24 (1985) 3-35.

[60] M. Haran, *The Biblical Collection: Its Consolidation to the End of the Second Temple Times and Changes of Form to the End of the Middle Ages* (Jerusalem: Mosad Bialik, Magnes, 1996) especially chs. 3 and 5, 141-200 and 276-303 (Hebrew); S. C. Reif,

Historical links

As far as the establishment of direct historical links between CD and known sects is concerned, it will be recalled that Schechter drew the obvious Samaritan, Karaite and Falasha parallels but was hesitant about precise dates and identifications. He opted for a faith and practice at variance with Pharisaic and rabbinic Judaism and originating in some form of Sadducean and Zadokite Judaism, albeit transmitted by a Dosithean sect. He saw the literary context as that of the apocryphal and pseudepigraphical writings and looked forward to further discoveries that would elucidate the history of those who wrote and transmitted it. Somewhat remarkably, if one examines the latest scholarly views on such matters, they are not so much at variance with what Schechter proposed and with the cautious approach he advised. Some see the Nestorian Patriarch Timotheus' report of around 800 CE as the clue to the adoption by the Karaites of earlier views, as found in the caves,[61] while others argue that other historical and theological factors must have been more dominant. There are scholars who trace ideas found in Second Temple literature and among the Manicheans, through early Muslim groups (both in Iraq and the Holy Land) and aspects of rabbinic thought, to their successful incorporation, not necessarily with consistency or theological intent, into Karaism. There is also opposition to such an interpretation on the part of those who prefer to see the novelty of some Karaite traditions and a direct debt to Islam in the case of others, and point to the fact that Karaites themselves did not claim a Sadducean origin and expressed themselves in all manner of ways.[62]

If one reads carefully the conclusions of those who have recently summarized the content and significance of the Dead Sea Scrolls, one can hear echoes of some of Schechter's remarks of almost a century ago. Such a comprehensive, careful and balanced treatment as that offered three years ago by Larry Schiffman talks of the leading role of the Zadokite priests and the major impact of the Sadducean approach. He refers to the presence of Samaritan traditions, to the common heritage of apocryphal literature, and to the presence among the Judean scrolls of works originating among a number of Jewish groups. Although he argues that sectarian groups such as the Essenes and the Sadducees disappeared as independent entities after

"Cairo Genizah," *Encyclopedia of the Dead Sea Scrolls* (ed. L. H. Schiffman and J. C. VanderKam; forthcoming).
    [61] P. Kahle, *The Cairo Geniza* (Oxford: Blackwell, 1959²) 16.
    [62] For a useful summary of the issues and arguments, see the exchanges, in Hebrew, between Y. Erder and H. Ben-Shammai, *Cathedra* 42 (1987) 54-86.

the destruction of the Second Temple, he acknowledges that some of their traditions remained in circulation long enough to influence the Karaites and that some of the texts found at Qumran circulated in different versions among the Jews of the early Middle Ages.[63] Specifically about CD, Schiffman writes:

> From the very first discovery of what we now know to be a Qumran text—the *Zadokite Fragments* found in the Cairo *genizah*—it was clear that the new material would be of great importance for our understanding of the history and development of Jewish law. When the Qumran library itself was discovered, the presence of multiple copies of that text, as well as other halakhic material, made clear that the new texts had much to teach us in this area of research... The nine copies of the *Zadokite Fragments* found at Qumran confirm the general reliability of the medieval copies of this text. At the same time, the Qumran texts have doubled the size of the preserved text known to us.[64]

Given that achievement, and the additional realization that his interpretations have retained more than a little value, we can, in conclusion, express wholehearted agreement with the evaluation of his CD edition offered by Büchler who unabashedly opted for the medieval Karaite hypothesis but nevertheless noted, as have a number of today's specialists in the field,[65] scholarship's debt to Schechter:

> Let us be grateful to Professor Schechter for his discovery and for the thoroughness with which he has elucidated many of the most difficult points; and especially for the many-sided commentary and the learned introduction in which he has drawn our attention to the numerous problems awaiting solution. Even if his find should not prove to be an early Zadokite book ... it has drawn the attention of the literary world to a chapter of Jewish history which has rightly invited the collaboration of many great minds and will long continue in attracting and captivating our best scholars.[66]

---

[63] L. H. Schiffman, *Reclaiming the Dead Sea Scrolls. The History of Judaism, the Background of Christianity, the Lost Library of Qumran* (Philadelphia: JPS, 1994), especially 76, 89, 101, 113, 130, 167, 178, 185-86, 192, 195, 198, 253, 274, 403, and 408-9.

[64] Schiffman, *Reclaiming the Dead Sea Scrolls*, 245 and 273-74.

[65] See, for example, P. R. Davies, *The Damascus Covenant: An Interpretation of the "Damascus Document"* (JSOTSup 25; Sheffield: JSOT, 1983) 5-7, where he favourably assesses Schechter's work and argues that the Dosithean theory is "one of the few elements ... that has not borne fruit in subsequent research."

[66] Büchler, "Schechter's 'Jewish Sectaries'," 485.

THE RELATIONSHIP OF THE ZADOKITE FRAGMENTS TO THE TEMPLE SCROLL

Lawrence H. Schiffman

New York University

The recent publication of the Cave 4 fragments of all the Zadokite Fragments (more generally known as the Damascus Document) by J. M. Baumgarten[1] has made available to us important material for reevaluating the relationship of this central sectarian text to the Temple Scroll.[2] Such a study is significant because a number of legal rulings are shared between these two texts and 4QMMT.[3] Other rulings are shared by other halakhic texts which also exhibit parallels with the Temple Scroll. At the same time, it is clear that the sectarian orientation of the Zadokite Fragments differs extensively from the priestly, sacrificial nature of the Temple Scroll and its irenic tone.[4] Further, in the legal section, the Zadokite Fragments for the most part, though not entirely, consist of exegetically derived apodictic laws, whereas the Temple Scroll is based on biblical material much more directly. Actually, one can compare the relationship of the Zadokite Fragments and the Temple Scroll, from a literary point of view, with that of the Mishnah and the halakhic midrashim.

This paper will investigate the relationship of these two Qumran texts from a number of perspectives. First, we shall discuss the literary structure of these texts and their relation to their biblical and post-biblical sources. We shall then comment on the contrast between these texts regarding the use of sectarian technical terminology. The main thrust of this paper is a thorough listing and discussion

---

[1] J. M. Baumgarten, *Qumran Cave 4.XIII. The Damascus Document (4Q266-273)* (DJD 18; Oxford: Clarendon, 1996).

[2] Y. Yadin, מגילת המקדש (3 vols.; Jerusalem: Israel Exploration Society, 1977) and its English edition, *The Temple Scroll* (3 vols.; Jerusalem: Israel Exploration Society, 1983). Yadin's edition must be supplemented with the readings of E. Qimron, *The Temple Scroll, A Critical Edition with Extensive Reconstructions* (Beer Sheva: Ben-Gurion University of the Negev; Jerusalem, Israel Exploration Society, 1996).

[3] E. Qimron and J. Strugnell, with Y. Sussman and A. Yardeni, *Miqṣat Ma'aśe ha-Torah* (DJD 10; Oxford: Clarendon, 1994); cf. Baumgarten, DJD 18.7.

[4] Cf. L. H. Schiffman, "The Temple Scroll and the Nature of Its Law: The Status of the Question," *Community of the Renewed Covenant: The Notre Dame Symposium on the Dead Sea Scrolls* (ed. E. Ulrich and J. C. VanderKam; Christianity and Judaism in Antiquity Series 10; Notre Dame: University of Notre Dame Press, 1994) 37-55.

of the parallel legal rulings found in these two texts. Relevant aspects of the relationship of these two texts to other manuscripts of the Qumran corpus will be briefly surveyed. Finally, we will discuss the implications of our observations for the wider issues arising from the study of these texts.

1. *The Literary Character of the Texts*

The Zadokite Fragments consist of two major sections, each of which is, in turn, a composite work, both from the literary and historical points of view. The text begins with an Admonition, a series of what must have originally been separate speeches interspersed with biblical interpretations. Some of these interpretations are pesharim, and show the interpretive strategies and even literary forms of this genre. Other interpretations represent halakhic exegesis—a type of halakhic midrash. In these cases, there is sometimes direct allusion to biblical verses just as there is in the pesher interpretations. The Admonition, while presenting the self-image of the sectarians and their aspirations for a life of purity and holiness, covers only a few halakhic topics, most of which are presented in the course of polemics against the opponents of the sect. These polemics are, for the most part, directed against the Pharisees.

The halakhic section of the Zadokite Fragments is the largest part of the text. Today, after the publication of the Cave 4 manuscripts, it is clear that the laws must have covered some three-quarters of the text in its original form. If we had the entire document, we might find that the laws constituted an even larger percentage. One thing is clear: the Admonition is intended as an introduction to the complete work, which is predominantly a compilation of Jewish law on a variety of topics.[5] Investigation of the laws as presented both in the genizah manuscripts,[6] as well as in the Qumran texts, indicates that this section is constituted of what were originally separate units of text. Each unit itself consisted of a series of laws on a given topic that had been compiled into a collection, known in Qumran sectarian terminology as a *serekh*.[7] We have argued that these *serakhim* were originally formulated as collections of laws which emerged from sec-

[5] Cf. J. M. Baumgarten, "The Laws of the *Damascus Document* in Current Research," *The Damascus Document Reconsidered* (ed. M. Broshi; Jerusalem: Israel Exploration Society, Shrine of the Book, Israel Museum, 1992) 52, 61.

[6] The most reliable reading of the genizah MSS is E. Qimron, "The Text of CDC," *Damascus Document Reconsidered*, 9-49.

[7] L. H. Schiffman, *The Halakhah at Qumran* (SJLA 16; Leiden: E. J. Brill, 1975) 60-68.

tarian study sessions which were a regular part of the life of the community.[8]

One of the most significant characteristics of the laws of the Zadokite Fragments is the fact that they are divided into sections by subject classification. These sections, clearly the result of a collector or collectors who brought together material on one subject, often have titles such as, "regarding the Sabbath, to observe it according to its regulation" (CD 10:14). We can assume that if the entire work were intact, most of the laws would appear underneath such section headings. Such a heading, "regarding forbidden sexual relations," occurs in 4QHalakha[a] 17 1.[9] These headings help to indicate the literary units from which the larger text was composed.

The laws contained in the Zadokite Fragments are mostly based on language derived from biblical verses.[10] It is those verses which are being interpreted, although only rarely are the verses themselves explicitly quoted. It is only by detailed investigation of the apodictic legal statements that one can determine what biblical passages served as the basis of which laws. Nevertheless, some of the prescriptions found in the Zadokite Fragments are actually sectarian regulations, rules dealing with entry to the sect and its particular way of life, not laws based on the Bible.

By contrast, the Temple Scroll is of a very different literary character. Like the Zadokite Fragments, the Temple Scroll is a composite work made up of preexisting documents brought together by an author/redactor. These documents were probably composed over a long period of time but share a general literary structure.[11] Because they stem from a common ideological and literary background, they follow set patterns which they share to some extent with the Rewritten Pentateuch,[12] and especially with the 4Q365a material[13]

---

[8] L. H. Schiffman, *Sectarian Law in the Dead Sea Scrolls; Courts, Testimony and the Penal Code* (BJS 33; Chico: Scholars Press, 1983) 9.

[9] See the forthcoming edition of by E. Larson, M. Lehmann and L. H. Schiffman in the DJD series. We have numbered this frg. 17, but it was formerly frg. 12.

[10] Cf. D. Dimant, "בין מקרא למגילות: ציטטות מן התורה במגילת ברית דמשק," *Sha'arei Talmon, Studies in the Bible, Qumran, and the Ancient Near East Presented to Shemaryahu Talmon* (ed. M. Fishbane and E. Tov, with W. W. Fields; Winona Lake, Ind.: Eisenbrauns, 1992) 113*-122*.

[11] Cf. Schiffman, "The *Temple Scroll* and the Nature of Its Law," 46-48; A. Wilson and L. Wills, "Literary Sources of the Temple Scroll," *HTR* 75 (1982) 275-88; M. O. Wise, *A Critical Study of the Temple Scroll from Qumran Cave 11* (Studies in Ancient Oriental Civilization 49; Chicago: The Oriental Institute of the University of Chicago, 1990) 21-23.

[12] E. Tov and S. White, in H. Attridge, et al., *Qumran Cave 4.VIII. Parabiblical Texts Part I* (DJD 13; Oxford: Clarendon, 1994) 187-318, 335-51.

[13] S. White in DJD 13.319-33.

which may even have originally served as source material for the author of one of the sources of the Temple Scroll.[14] The various laws
presented in the Temple Scroll seem at first glance to be rehashes of
biblical law but, in fact, the Bible has been rewritten to express a variety of legal views held by the respective authors. Modifications and
expansions which are designed to convey these views have been
made, following a variety of literary and exegetical strategies.[15] Yet
the overall character of the document is that of a virtual Torah, an
impression heightened by the utilization in this text of most of the
canonical Torah from the end of Exodus through Deuteronomy. If
the Zadokite Fragments, with its apodictic law, has the feel of the
Mishnah, the Temple Scroll, with its scriptural character, has some
of the feel of midrash.

We may characterize the relation of the various laws in the
Temple Scroll to the text of the Bible in an ascending order of the
extent of modification of the biblical *Vorlage*. Some passages essentially reflect quotations of the Pentateuch according to the readings
available to the authors in contemporary manuscripts. Other texts
reflect slight exegetical additions designed to indicate the interpretations of the author. More complicated are passages in which commands found in different places in the Torah are merged together to
form a unified, harmonious text. Somewhat more complex are passages which show evidence of midrashic interpretation, in which one
passage is understood in light of another. Furthest from the biblical
text are those passages which reflect original composition by the author but which are couched in biblicizing language, and which in-
variably allude to specific biblical texts.[16]

From this basic outline, it should already be clear that the Temple
Scroll and the Zadokite Fragments do not share a common literary
form. While the laws in both texts are closely related to their biblical
counterparts, the nature of their formulation and organization is
markedly different. It would be a great mistake, however, not to notice
that some texts in the Zadokite Fragments resemble to some extent the
character of the Temple Scroll.[17] Indeed, some of the smaller halakhic
compositions—or at least those which appear smaller in their state of
preservation—share with the Temple Scroll the use of paraphrase in

---

[14] As suggested by J. Strugnell, quoted by B. Z. Wacholder, *The Dawn of Qumran,
the Sectarian Torah and the Teacher of Righteousness* (Cincinnati: Hebrew Union College
Press, 1983) 205-6.

[15] Yadin, *Temple Scroll*, 1.71-88; D. D. Swanson, *The Temple Scroll and the Bible, The
Methodology of 11QT* (STDJ 14; Leiden: E. J. Brill, 1995).

[16] Cf. L. H. Schiffman, "The Deuteronomic Paraphrase of the Temple Scroll,"
RevQ 15 (1992) 543-67.

setting forth halakhah. Similar paraphrase occurs in 4Q251 (Halakha[a]), which should probably be called "Halakhic Paraphrase." Other halakhic texts, such as Serekh-Damascus (SD), display a formulation resembling the more apodictically-oriented Zadokite Fragments.

2. *Terminology and Language*

The Temple Scroll lacks both the sectarian terminology and animus which is familiar from the Zadokite Fragments and from the sectarian scrolls as a whole. In the Admonition and in those laws which pertain to sectarian procedure, such as joining the sect, the Zadokite Fragments employs the very same terminology found in the Rule of the Community and other such documents. It was this similarity that led E. L. Sukenik to conclude early on that the Zadokite Fragments and the other sectarian scrolls stemmed from the same provenance.[18] Although the Temple Scroll shares many of the characteristics of language generally associated with the texts of the Qumran sect, such as the use of long endings, Qumranic forms are less extensive here, perhaps due to the early date of the sources of the Temple Scroll. Similarly, the absence of sectarian animus in this text may result from the fact that its sources came into being even before the sectarian schism had taken place.[19] Certainly, we can explain the absence of technical terminology pertaining to the way of life and teachings of the sect as resulting from the composition of the documents which make up the Temple Scroll before the sect had taken shape. We may note parenthetically that 4QMMT occupies a middle position here. It is certainly evidence of the beginnings of the sectarian polemic, but it is not yet affected by the bitterness and self-perception of the incipient sectarian group.

One of the more interesting comparisons to be made between the Zadokite Fragments and the Temple Scroll relates to their use of terminology that we generally recognize from Tannaitic sources. The Zadokite Fragments generally makes use of biblical substitutes for post-biblical legal terminology.[20] It appears that this terminology was

---

[17] E. L. Sukenik, מגילות גנוזות מתוך גניזה קדומה שנמצאה במדבר יהודה, סקירה שנייה (Jerusalem: Bialik Institute, 1950) 21. See also the pioneering study of S. Iwry, *The Damascus Document and the Dead Sea Scrolls* (diss.; Johns Hopkins University, 1951), especially 130-48.

[18] See H. Stegemann, "The Origins of the Temple Scroll," *VTSup* 40 (1988) 237-46. We cannot, however, accept his dating of the sources of the scroll to the Persian period (246-56).

[19] C. Rabin, *Qumran Studies* (Scripta Judaica 2; Oxford: Clarendon, 1957) 108-11.

[20] Yadin, *Temple Scroll*, 1.36-38.

known to the authors of the Zadokite Fragments but that as part of their anti-Pharisaic polemic they eschewed its use. The substitution of biblicizing terminology was intentional and close to consistent. To some extent this pattern is also observable in other sectarian texts, like the Rule of the Community and the War Scroll, but the legal content of the Zadokite Fragments makes this phenomenon more prominent. The Temple Scroll, on the other hand, while certainly using much biblical terminology, shows evidence of the influence of the very same post-biblical terminology which typifies the later mishnaic corpus. Numerous terms of the post-biblical legal vocabulary are evident in this scroll and seem to have been used without hesitation.[21]

3. *Parallel Laws*

The Zadokite Fragments and the Temple Scroll display many instances of parallel laws. In what follows, we list and analyze these cases, making an attempt to present an exhaustive list:

a. *Polygamy*

CD 4:19-5:2, in the Admonition, includes a prohibition of polygamy.[22] The same prohibition directed, however, only at the king is found in 11QT 57:17-19.[23] This passage indicates that the king may only be married to one wife unless she dies, in which case he may remarry. We should note as well that the passage from the Zadokite Fragments also appealed to the Law of the King in Deut. 17:14-20, to support its requirement of monogamy. From the passage in the Temple Scroll, however, it is impossible to know if the prohibition would have extended to the rest of the people. It seems, from the common proof text, that the difficult language of the Zadokite Fragments (בחייהם) should be understood to mean that one may not take a second wife as long as the first is alive, even in the event of divorce. This same rule, then, would probably have been intended by the Temple Scroll.[24] The prohibitions regarding consanguineous

---

[21] For a sampling of the many studies on this passage, see F. García Martínez, "Damascus Document: A Bibliography of Studies 1970-1989," *Damascus Document Reconsidered*, 66. Cf. L. Ginzberg, *An Unknown Jewish Sect* (New York: JTS, 1970) 19-20.

[22] Cf. Yadin, *Temple Scroll*, 1.355-57.

[23] Cf. L. H. Schiffman, "Laws Pertaining to Women in the *Temple Scroll*," *The Dead Sea Scrolls. Forty Years of Research* (ed. D. Dimant and U. Rappaport; STDJ 10; Leiden: E. J. Brill/Jerusalem: Magnes and Yad Izhak Ben-Zvi, 1992) 216-18.

[24] Cf. Yadin, *Temple Scroll*, 2.299-300. Cf. the similar laws contained in 4QHalakhaᵃ frg. 17 (previously numbered 12) and our forthcoming DJD commentary on it.

marriage found at the end of the Temple Scroll, in the last preserved column (66:11-16), do not prohibit polygamy, but we must
remember that the text is fragmentary.[25]

b. *Marital impurity*
CD 12:1-2 (= 4Q271 5 i 17-18) indicates that it is prohibited to have
sexual relations in the City of the Sanctuary[26] because this would
render the holy place impure. A similar prescription is found in the
Temple Scroll in which one who has had a seminal emission may
not enter the Temple until after a three-day purification period
(11QT 45:7-12).[27]

4Q266 6 ii 1-4 indicates that a woman who has had relations while
menstrually impure, or while experiencing a non-menstrual blood
flow, must go through a seven-day purification period.[28] She must remain outside the Temple and may not eat sacred food. The text emphasizes that her purification is not complete until the sun has set on
the eighth day. This passage is one of several in which the Zadokite
Fragments polemicize against the Pharisaic concept of *ṭevul yom*, according to which purification is attained for certain purposes even before the completion of the final day. The Temple Scroll follows the
same view as our text (11QT 45:9-12, 49:19-21, 51:2-5).[29] The same
issue recurs in the Zadokite Fragments (4Q269 8 ii 3-6 = 4Q271 2 10-
13),[30] regarding one who sprinkles waters of purification from the impurity of the dead who must wait until sunset before he is considered
to be pure. A parallel to this law is found in 4QMMT B14-16, and in
general 4QMMT also rejects the concept of *ṭevul yom*.[31]

c. *Prohibited marriage*
CD 5:7-9 legislates the prohibition of marriage to one's niece,
whether on the side of one's brother or sister.[32] The very same re-

---

[25] On this disputed term, see L. H. Schiffman, "*Ir Ha-Miqdash* and Its Meaning in the Temple Scroll and Other Qumran Texts," *Sanctity of Time and Space in Tradition and Modernity* (ed. A. Houtmans, M. J. H. M. Poorthuis and J. Schwartz; JCP 1; Leiden: Brill, 1998) 95-109.
[26] Cf. Yadin, *Temple Scroll*, 1.285-89.
[27] See the comments in Baumgarten, DJD 18.56.
[28] Cf. J. M. Baumgarten, "The Pharisaic Sadducean Controversies about Purity and the Qumran Texts," *JJS* 31 (1980) 157-70; L. H. Schiffman, "Pharisaic and Sadducean Halakhah in Light of the Dead Sea Scrolls: The Case of Ṭevul Yom," *DSD* 1 (1994) 285-99.
[29] Baumgarten, DJD 18.131-32, 174-75.
[30] Cf. Qimron and Strugnell, DJD 10.152-4; L. H. Schiffman, "Miqṣat Maʿaśeh ha-Torah and the Temple Scroll," *RevQ* 14 (1990) 438-42.
[31] Cf. Ginzberg, 2-4.
[32] Cf. Yadin, *Temple Scroll*, 1.371-72, 2.299-300.

striction seems to be repeated in a different passage in 4Q270 2 ii
16. In the early days of research on the Zadokite Fragments, it was
noted that this was a polemic against the practice of the Pharisees
who, as we know from later Talmudic sources, permitted such marriages and even praised them. The very same proscription appears
in 11QT 66:15-17[33] and in 4QHalakha[a] 17 2-3.[34]

d. *The law of testimony*

From the complex laws of testimony found in CD 9:16-23, it can be
deduced that the text understood the commands of Deut. 17:6-7
and 19:15 regarding "two or three witnesses" to require two witnesses for financial matters but three for capital matters.[35] 11QT 64:8-9
refers to these passages in discussing the law of the informer who is
to be put to death, apparently by crucifixion. This passage, however,
also seems provide that two witnesses only might be involved in tes-
tifying against such a criminal.[36] In this respect, the Temple Scroll
may differ from the Zadokite Fragments.

The Zadokite Fragments contains detailed laws pertaining to the
judiciary which, while derived from biblical law, extend it considerably.[37] The Temple Scroll, however, in alluding to the biblical command to establish courts (11QT 51:11-12), basically recapitulates the
biblical laws on this matter with only small changes.

e. *Magic and necromancy*

CD 12:1-3 (cf. 4Q267 4 11-12; 4Q270 2 i 10; 4Q271 5 i 18-19) mentions the prohibition of עוב and ידעוני, two types of necromancy. The
Temple Scroll lists these practices among a variety of prohibitions regarding magic (11QT 61:18-19). The scroll generally describes these
practices as abominations before God on account of which He removed the Canaanites from the land. This motif is derived directly
from the biblical text.[38] The Zadokite Fragments, however, in referring to practitioners of necromancy, describes them as "any person
over whom spirits of Belial rule and who speaks with apostasy ..." (CD
12:2-3; 4Q271 5 i 18). While these concepts are not necessarily con-
tradictory, they do indicate the independent formulation of these rules.

---

[33] Previously frg. 12. See our forthcoming DJD edition.
[34] Cf. L. H. Schiffman, *Sectarian Law in the Dead Sea Scrolls. Courts, Testimony and the Penal Code* (BJS 33; Chico: Scholars Press, 1983) 73-78.
[35] Cf. Yadin, *Temple Scroll*, 1.379-82. Yadin, 381, n. 14, notes that his interpreta-
tion differs from mine.
[36] Cf. Schiffman, *Sectarian Law*, 23-40.
[37] Cf. Lev. 20:27 and Deut. 18:11.
[38] L. H. Schiffman, "Legislation Concerning Non-Jews in the Zadokite Fragments and in Tannaitic Literature," *RevQ* 11 (1983) 379-89.

f. *Idolatry*

CD 12:8-11 contains a series of laws forbidding the sale to non-Jews of items which may be used for pagan sacrifices. These descriptions have clear parallels in Tannaitic literature, as we have shown in a detailed study.[39] Despite recapitulation of the prohibitions of idolatry from Exodus and Deuteronomy, the Temple Scroll contains no parallels to these laws.[40] The same is the case regarding the law of the Zadokite Fragments (4Q269 8 ii 2-3; 4Q270 3 ii 20-21; 4Q271 2 8-10 and parallels) pertaining to the use of metals which have been used for idolatrous purposes,[41] which has no parallel in the Temple Scroll.

g. *Impurity of the dead*

CD 12:15-17 (= 4Q266 9 ii 2-3), referring to impurity of the dead, indicates that stones and earth which become impure through contact with oil may transmit impurity.[42] The Temple Scroll, in the same case, states the necessity of cleansing the house of any defilement of oil as part of the process of purifying the house of its ritual impurity.[43] Apparently, both texts regarded oil as a transmitter of ritual impurity.[44]

CD 12:17-18 (= 4Q266 9 ii 4-5) mentions that a nail or peg in the wall of a house which has been affected by impurity of the dead, that is, by the presence of a dead body in the house, shall be considered impure like a vessel found in the house. This law is totally consistent with 11QT 49:14-16 that lists items which do, in fact, become impure in these circumstances. Among the items listed there are vessels of metal (49:15). The text clearly intends to say that there is no minimum size requirement for such a vessel and that even a nail or peg, which does not actually serve as a container, becomes impure.[45]

---

[39] Cf. L. H. Schiffman, "Laws Pertaining to Idolatry in the Temple Scroll," *Uncovering Ancient Stones: Essays in Memory of H. Neil Richardson* (ed. L. M. Hopfe; Winona Lake: Eisenbrauns, 1994) 159-75.

[40] Cf. Baumgarten, DJD 18.131, 174.

[41] Cf. Baumgarten, DJD 18.70.

[42] Cf. L. H. Schiffman, "The Impurity of the Dead in the *Temple Scroll*," *Archaeology and History in the Dead Sea Scrolls. The New York University Conference in Memory of Yigael Yadin* (ed. L. H. Schiffman; JSOT/ASOR MS 2; JSPSup 8; Sheffield: JSOT, 1990) 142-44.

[43] See J. M. Baumgarten, "The Essene Avoidance of Oil and the Laws of Purity," *RevQ* 6 (1967) 183-92.

[44] Schiffman, "Impurity of the Dead," 144-46. See Hahan Eshel's contribution (45-52).

[45] Cf. L. H. Schiffman, *Halakhah at Qumran* (SJLA 16; Leiden: E. J. Brill, 1975) 66-67.

h. *Proselytes*

CD 14:4 (= 4Q267 9 v 10; 4Q268 2 1-2) lists classes of members of the sectarian group. These include priests, Levites, Israelites, and proselytes.[46] The notion that proselytes are in some way not fully Israelites is parallel to the notion in the Temple Scroll (40:6).[47] Therefore, the scroll mandates that until the fourth generation proselytes may not enter the middle court of the Temple precincts.[48] This idea was not accepted as the dominant view in Tannaitic law, but is preserved as a minority point of view.[49]

i. *Oaths and vows*

We have previously published a lengthy comparison of the laws of oaths and vows in the Zadokite Fragments and the Temple Scroll.[50] While both of these treatments are dependent on the same biblical material, the Zadokite Fragments treats additional cases not directly specified by the Torah. While no contradiction can be observed between the two documents, their presentations are incongruent, so that detailed comparison is impossible.

j. *Priestly gifts*

4Q266 6 iv 1-5, a fragmentary passage, seems to require that fourth-year produce be presented to the priests. This notion is clearly stated in 4Q270 2 ii 6.[51] This view is explicit in 11QT 60:3-4 and in Jub. 7:35-7.[52] In contrast, rabbinic law required that fourth-year produce be eaten in Jerusalem.[53] The disagreement results from the general approach of the sectarians who treated fourth-year produce like first fruits, whereas the Pharisaic-rabbinic approach equated this produce to the second tithe which is eaten by the owners in Jerusalem.

A list of priestly gifts appears in 4Q266 2 ii 7-9.[54] This list includes the first fruits, tithes of animals, redemption of the first born of humans and animals, first shearing of the sheep, and assessments for redemption of human vows and their valuation. This list is essentially parallel to that of 11QT 60:3 as well as to that of 4QMMT B63-64.[55]

---

[46] Cf. Yadin, *Temple Scroll*, 2.170.
[47] See Qimron, *Temple Scroll*, 56 for a fuller restoration.
[48] Schiffman, "Exclusion from the Sanctuary," 303-5.
[49] L. H. Schiffman, "The Law of Vows and Oaths (Num. 30, 3-15) in the Zadokite Fragments and the Temple Scroll," *RevQ* 15 (1991) 199-214.
[50] Baumgarten, DJD 18.145.
[51] Schiffman, "Miqṣat Maʿaśeh ha-Torah," 452-56.
[52] Rashi to Lev. 27:30.
[53] Baumgarten, DJD 18.145-46.
[54] Cf. Qimron and Strugnell, DJD 10.164-66.
[55] Baumgarten, DJD 18.146.

k. *Offering of the loaves*

The Zadokite Fragments provide that only after the offering of the first fruits in the Temple is it permissible for the people of Israel to partake of their own crops (4Q270 3 ii 19-21).[56] The reference here is to the first fruits of wheat which are offered in the form of two loaves on the holiday of Shavuot (Lev. 23:17). The Temple Scroll presumes exactly the same law in col. 19, with one difference. According to the Zadokite Fragments, each loaf is to be made of one-tenth of an ephah of wheat. The Temple Scroll expects each loaf to be made of two-tenths (18:15). This difference results from varying interpretations of Lev. 23:17.

l. *Informing against and cursing one's people*

4Q279 2 ii 12-15 refers to one who reveals the secret of his people to the nations, curses his people or speaks against the prophets.[57] This passage parallels 11QT 64:10 which prescribes punishment by crucifixion for one who informs against his people or curses them.[58] But the Zadokite Fragments makes no mention of this rather uncharacteristic penalty.

m. *Slaughter of pregnant animals*

4Q270 2 ii 15 prohibits the slaughter of an animal and its living embryo.[59] In other words, the text prohibits the slaughter of a pregnant animal. This same prescription is found in 11QT 52:5[60] as well as in 4QMMT B38.[61] All these texts share the notion that the slaughter of a pregnant animal violates the Torah's prohibition on slaughter of an animal and its young on the same day.[62]

4. *Relationship to Other Texts*

We have identified a number of laws in which the Zadokite Fragments and the Temple Scroll share the same ruling. In a few cases, such as the *ṭevul yom*, it appears that the shared material constitutes part of the priestly tradition labeled by the Rabbis as Sadducean. Yet much of the material found in Zadokite Fragments finds no

---

[56] Cf. Baumgarten, DJD 18.146.
[57] Cf. Yadin, *Temple Scroll*, 1.373-79.
[58] Cf. Baumgarten, DJD 18.146.
[59] Cf. Yadin, *Temple Scroll*, 1.312-14.
[60] Qimron and Strugnell, DJD 10.157-58.
[61] Schiffman, "Miqṣat Maʿaśeh ha-Torah," 448-51.
[62] Cf. J. M. Baumgarten, "The Cave 4 Versions of the Penal Code," *JJS* 43 (1992) 268-76.

place at all in the Temple Scroll. This is certainly true for all the material pertaining to the sectarian way of life. The vast majority of the regulations of the Zadokite Fragments concern questions of Jewish law, such as Sabbath law and legal procedures, which are beyond the purview of the Temple Scroll and so can have no parallel in that document. Conversely, most laws found in the Temple Scroll are not represented in the Zadokite Fragments. This is certainly the case with laws pertaining to Temple and sacrifice—the main subject of the Temple Scroll—which seem to have played virtually no role in the Zadokite Fragments as they are currently constituted.

In addition to the relationship that the laws in these two texts have to one another, they are related to other texts as well. Despite the many parallels that we have cited between the Zadokite Fragments and the Temple Scroll, the Zadokite Fragments displays closer literary affinities to other texts in the Qumran corpus.

Specifically, we should note that the Zadokite Fragments and the Rule of the Community share numerous sectarian regulations such as a common penal code which appears in differing recessions in the two texts.[63] These regulations cannot be parallel with the Temple Scroll because it has no such sectarian content. These laws are only tangentially dependent on Scripture. It has even been argued that they may have derived from the practices of hellenistic societies.[64] The absence of sectarian regulations from the Temple Scroll has been explained on chronological grounds[65] or as resulting from the unique intention of the author/redactor.

Parallels may be noticed also between the Zadokite Fragments and the so-called SD document,[66] Serekh-Damascus, as well as with 4Q251 (Halakha[a]). These parallels indicate literary dependence of a kind which cannot be demonstrated for those laws we have cited between the Zadokite Fragments and the Temple Scroll. The relationship between the Zadokite Fragments, the Temple Scroll and 4QMMT is based on their common legal heritage rather than on literary parallels.

It seems to be the case, therefore, that the Temple Scroll, dating

---

[63] M. Weinfeld, *The Organizational Pattern and the Penal Code of the Qumran Sect* (NTAO 2; Fribourg: Éditions Universitaires; Göttingen: Vandenhoeck & Ruprecht, 1986) 7-80.

[64] See B. Z. Wacholder and M. G. Abegg, *Preliminary Edition of the Unpublished Dead Sea Scrolls. The Hebrew and Aramaic Texts from Cave Four* (Washington, DC: Biblical Archaeology Society, 1995) 3.72-78.

[65] Schiffman, "*Temple Scroll* and the Nature of its Law," 46-48.

[66] Schiffman, "*Temple Scroll* and the Nature of its Law," 48-51.

to the early Hasmonean period,[67] and its sources dating to even before the Maccabean Revolt,[68] provide a legal and historical backdrop against which the slightly later Zadokite Fragments can be understood. We do not deal here with literary dependence, but rather
with the derivation of halakhic norms from what must have been a
more widespread priestly tradition practiced by some Second
Temple Jews, even beyond the confines of the Temple. This tradition, in turn, shares much with the legal traditions which underlie
the book of Jubilees written in about 180 BCE. The same traditions
helped to shape the sectarian controversy which led to the founding
of the Dead Sea sect in about 152 BCE and which is reflected in
4QMMT.[69] These same prescriptions, therefore, appear in the
Zadokite Fragments and closely related SD and Halakha[a]. These
texts, and the Rule of the Community, originated within the fully
formed Dead Sea sect after the schism was complete. Accordingly,
the Zadokite Fragments, Serekh-Damascus and Halakha[a] share numerous sectarian regulations with the central rule book of the community—the Rule of the Community. Further points of contact exist
with the War Scroll and the eschatological Rule of the Congregation. We deal here therefore, with a fundamental halakhic tradition reflected in a variety of sources.

To return, then, to the question with which we began: the shared
halakhic material in the Zadokite Fragments and the Temple Scroll
reflects the shared priestly legal tradition which served as the basis of
the halakhic system for the sectarian community at Qumran. Common terminology found in these documents likewise stems from that
tradition. Along with the sectarian self-image, terminology, and regulations, this priestly halakhic tradition was one of the pillars of the
sect of the scrolls. But for us, the recovery of this shared priestly legal
tradition—almost definitely that of the Sadducean priesthood—provides additional significance to the rediscovery of the ancient library
of Qumran.

---

[67] L. H. Schiffman, "The New Halakhic Letter (4QMMT) and the Origins of the
Dead Sea Sect," *BA* 53 (1990) 64-73.

QUMRAN POLEMIC ON MARITAL LAW:
CD 4:20—5:11 AND ITS SOCIAL BACKGROUND

ADIEL SCHREMER

Bar-Ilan University

I

In a well known and often cited passage (CD 4:20-5:11) the author of the Damascus Document accuses his opponents, the "Builders of the Wall," of several violations of the law. This text has been used by scholars mainly as a source reflecting the sect's views on some major halakhic and social issues. Its polemical character, however, makes it also a valuable source from which the social historian may obtain some pieces of important information, regarding the norms prevailing among those whom the author attacks, namely, the bulk of Palestinian Jewry of that era.[1]

The text poses several difficulties, not all of which have received equal scholarly attention. In what follows I do not pretend to solve all these problems; rather, I wish to address the question of the social reality among Palestinian Jewry which the author was facing when addressing his accusations. For the sake of convenience I shall represent here the whole passage:

בוני החיץ אשר הלכו אחרי צו ... הם ניתפשים בשתים בזנות לקחת
שתי נשים בחייהם ויסוד הבריאה זכר ונקבה ברא אותם ובאי התבה
שנים שנים באו אל התבה ועל הנשיא כתוב לא ירבה לו נשים ...

---

* I wish to express my gratitude to Prof. Daniel R. Schwartz, for his comments on the draft of this paper.

[1] While some scholars have identified "the builders of the wall" with the Pharisees, others viewed this appellation as referring to the Jewish society of the author's time in general. On the first possibility see: S. Schechter, *Documents of Jewish Sectaries: Fragments of a Zadokite Work* (Cambridge: Cambridge University Press, 1910) 36, n. 22; R. H. Charles, *The Apocrypha and Pseudepigrapha of the Old Testament* (Oxford: Clarendon, 1913) 2.818; J. Grintz, "אנשי היחד – איסיים – בית סין," *Sinai* 32 (1953) 37; A. S. van der Woude, *Die messianischen Vorstellungen der Gemeinde von Qumran* (Assen: van Gorcum, 1957) 240; J. Tomson, *Paul and Jewish Law* (Assen/Maastricht/Minneapolis: van Gorcum, 1990) 111. The other view is held by J. Murphy-O'Connor, "An Essene Missionary Document? CD II,14—VI,1," *RB* 77 (1970) 220; P. R. Davies, *The Damascus Document* (JSOTSup 25; Sheffield: JSOT, 1983) 111-13; M. A. Knibb, *The Qumran Community* (Cambridge: Cambridge University Press, 1987) 42; J. G. Campbell, *The Use of Scripture in the Damascus Document 1-8, 19-20* (BZAW 228; New York and Berlin: de Gruyter, 1995) 120.

וגם מטמאים הם את המקדש אשר אין הם מבדיל כתורה ושוכבים
עם הרואה את דם זובה ולוקחים איש את בת אחיה(ם)ן ואת בת
אחותו ומשה אמר אל אחות אמך לא תקרב שאר אמך היא ומשפט
העריות לזכרים הוא כתוב וכהם הנשים ואם תגלה בת האח את
ערות אחי אביה והיא שאר.

> The builders of the barrier ... are caught by two. By unchastity—tak-
> ing two wives in their lives, while the foundation of creation is "male
> and female he created them." And those who entered the ark went
> two by two into the ark. And of the prince it is written: "Let him not
> multiply wives for himself"... And they also pollute the sanctuary by
> not separating according to the Torah. And they lay with a woman
> who sees blood of flowing. And they marry each one his brother's
> daughter or sister's daughter. And Moses said "To your mother's sis-
> ter you may not draw near, for she is your mother's near relation."
> And the precept of incest is written from the point of view of males,
> but the same applies to women, so if a brother's daughter uncovers
> the nakedness of a brother of her father, she is a relationship.[2]

The author accuses his opponents of [1] taking two wives in their
lives; [2] defiling the sanctuary; and [3] marrying one's niece. Most
of the scholars who dealt with this passage have concentrated on the
first accusation. While the majority of the text's readers tend to understand it (at least at first glance) as a statement against polygamy,[3]
other interpretations were offered as well. Some scholars have argued that divorce is strictly forbidden in our text.[4] Others have suggested that the text opposes not only polygamy, but also second

---

[2] The translation is based on J. M. Baumgarten and D. R. Schwartz,
"Damascus Document," *The Dead Sea Scrolls: Hebrew, Aramaic, and Greek Texts with
English Translations* (ed. J. H. Charlesworth; Tübingen: Mohr-Siebeck/Louisville:
John Knox Press, 1995) 2.19-21, with some minor modifications.

[3] This is the view held by L. Ginzberg, *Eine unbekannte jüdische Sekte* (New York:
[privately published], 1922) 26; C. Rabin, *The Zadokite Document* (Oxford:
Clarendon, 1954) 17; Y. Heinemann, *Darke ha-Agada* (Jerusalem: Magnes, 1954) 177
(Hebrew); E. E. Urbach, "The Drasha as a Basis of the Halakha and the Problem
of the Soferim," *Tarbiz* 27 (1958) 176 (Hebrew); Y. Brand, "The Scroll of the
Covenant of Damascus and Date of Composition," *Tarbiz* 28 (1959) 21 (Hebrew);
D. Flusser, "The Jewish Origin of Christianity," *I. F. Baer Jubilee Volume* (Jerusalem:
Historical Society of Israel, 1960) 81, n. 20 (Hebrew); Z. W. Falk, *Marriage and
Divorce* (Jerusalem: Mifal ha-shikhpul, 1961) 8 (Hebrew); O. J. R. Schwarz, *Der erster
Teil der Damaskusschrift und das Alte Testament* (Diest: Lichtland, 1965) 142; G. Vermes,
"Sectarian Matrimonial Halakhah in the Damascus Rule," *JJS* 25 (1974) 198; M.
D. Herr, "Continuum in the Chain of Torah Transmission," *Zion* 44 (1979) 53
(Hebrew); S. Z. Havlin, "The Aramaic Translation of *Ruth*—a Vulgate
Translation?," *Sidra* 2 (1986) 27 (Hebrew); Knibb, *Qumran Community*, 43; D. R.
Schwartz, *Studies in the Jewish Background of Christianity* (Tübingen: Mohr, 1990) 3, n.
6.

[4] See, for example, R. H. Charles, *The Apocrypha and Pseudepigrapha of the Old
Testament* (Oxford: Clarendon, 1913) 2.796.

marriage after divorce (while the first wife is still alive).[5] Others went a step further and contended that the text prohibits any second marriage, even after the death of the first wife.[6]

I shall return to this question later on; at this stage I would like to reexamine one aspect of the text which, although mentioned here and there in scholarly literature, nevertheless to the best of my knowledge has not received the full attention it deserves, that is, the problem of the structure of the passage and the connections between its components.

In its present form, the text places the accusation of marriage with one's niece [3] after the accusation of defilement of the sanctuary [2]. Yet, since the author's subsequent claim, "They also pollute

[5] Scholars who have interpreted the text in this way are listed by Vermes, "Sectarian Matrimonial Halakhah," 198. See also J. R. Mueller, "The Temple Scroll and the Gospel Divorce Texts," *RevQ* 10 (1980) 247-56; B. Z. Wacholder, *The Dawn of Qumran* (Cincinnati: Hebrew Union College Press, 1983) 25; Y. Yadin, "L'attitude essénienne envers la polygamie et le divorce," *RB* 79 (1972) 98-99; idem, *The Temple Scroll* (Jerusalem: Israel Exploration Society, 1983) 1.355-57; 2.258; L. H. Schiffman, "Laws Pertaining to Women in the Temple Scroll," *The Dead Sea Scrolls. Forty Years of Research* (ed. D. Dimant and U. Rappaport; STDJ 10; Leiden: E. J. Brill, 1992) 217; idem, *Reclaiming the Dead Sea Scrolls. The History of Judaism, the Background of Christianity, the Lost Library of Qumran* (Philadelphia: JPS, 1994) 130. It seems that J. M. Baumgarten too now accepts this interpretation; see his "The Qumran-Essene Restraints on Marriage," *Archaeology and History in the Dead Sea Scrolls. The New York University Conference in Memory of Yigael Yadin* (ed. L. H. Schiffman; JSPSup 8; Sheffield: JSOT, 1990) 14-15; idem, *Qumran Cave 4.XIII. The Damascus Document (4Q266-273)* (DJD 18; Oxford: Clarendon, 1996) 71, note to line 5. Compare his view in his *Studies in Qumran Law* (Leiden: E. J. Brill, 1977) 34, n. 80.

[6] This interpretation has been suggested already by J. Hempel, in an editorial note appended to Paul Winter's "Sadoqite Fragments IV 20, 21 and the Exegesis of Genesis 1:27 in Late Judaism," *ZAW* 68 (1956) 84. It was articulated most emphatically by Murphy-O'Connor, "Essene Missionary Document?," 220; idem, "Remarques sur l'exposé de Professeur Y. Yadin," *RB* 79 (1972) 99-100. In a similar way the text has been understood by M. Burrows, *More Light on the Dead Sea Scrolls* (New York, 1958) 98-99; G. Jeremias, *Der Lehrer der Gerechtigkeit* (Göttingen: Vandenhoeck & Ruprecht, 1963) 96; J. M. Baumgarten, *Studies in Qumran Law*, 34, n. 80; Davies, *Damascus Document*, 116; idem, *Behind the Essenes* (BJS 94; Atlanta: Scholars Press, 1989) 75-85. The essence of this interpretation rests on the insistence to read the masculine suffix of the word בחייהם at face value, and consequently to understand it as referring to the man (not to the woman), who are condemned, according to this interpretation, for marrying more than once during their lives.
Some scholars, starting with Hempel, have hinted at 1 Tim. 3:2 as a possible parallel to the ruling of our text according to this interpretation: "A Church leader must be a man without fault; he must be *a man of one wife*." This, however, is far from convincing; as noted by Saucy, the question regarding the precise meaning of the phrase μιᾶς γυναικὸς ἄνδρα ("a man of one wife") in that verse "is impossible to answer simply from the words involved" (R. L. Saucy, "The Husband of One Wife," *Bibliotheca Sacra* 131 [1974] 229). It is therefore doubtful whether it really refers to second marriage as such (even after the death of one's first spouse). It is true, as noted by Jeremias, *Lehrer der Gerechtigkeit*, 98-100, that among the western Church Fathers it was usually understood as referring to any second marriage.

(מטמאים) their holy spirits," uses the same verb ("pollute" מטמאים) as the second accusation, one naturally assumes that they are related to one another, and therefore expects this claim to be preceded by the accusation of defilement of the sanctuary [2], not by that of marriage with one's niece [3] as the text stands before us now.

Similarly, as has long been noted, the accusation of marrying one's niece [3] does not seem to be related to the accusation of defilement of the sanctuary [2], which precedes it[7] but, in fact, to the accusation of marrying two women [1],[8] for both share the common subject of marital issues.

Moreover, a linguistic consideration might support this contention as well. According to the translation quoted above, the text says that "The builders of the barrier ... have been caught *in two*" of the nets of Belial, mentioned a few lines earlier.[9] This translation understands the word בשתים (in two) as an adverb, related to נתפשים ("they are caught"). However, many other scholars tend to view בשתים ("in two") as an adjective related to בזנות ("in fornication"), which immediately follows it, and therefore translate the phrase: "The builders of the barrier ... they have been caught in fornication *in two respects*." This understanding is the one preferred by Rabin and shared by many other scholars, among them Dupont-Sommer, Maier, Cothe-

---

However, among the eastern Church Fathers it was understood simply as rejecting polygamy, and this meaning is the one preferred by most modern translations and commentaries. See W. Lock, *The Pastoral Epistles* (ICC; Edinburgh: T. & T. Clark, 1936) 36-38; M. Dibelius and H. Conzelmann, *The Pastoral Epistles* (Philadelphia: Fortress, 1977) 52. On the debates regarding marriage within the early Church in general, see E. H. Pagels, "Adam and Eve, Christ and the Church—A Survey of Second Century Controversies Concerning Marriage," *The New Testament and Gnosis* (ed. A. H. B. Logan and A. J. M. Wedderbaum; Edinburgh: T. & T. Clark, 1983) 146-75.

[7] Schwarz, *Damaskusschrift*, 141; Jeremias, *Lehrer der Gerichtigkeit*, 96; Davies, *Damascus Document*, 113; and Campbell, *Use of Scripture*, 120, assume that the accusation of marriage with one's niece is one of two (or three) explanations of the accusation of defilement of the sanctuary. While the accusation that "they lay with a woman who sees blood of flowing" can fit such an understanding (though not without difficulty, since it has not been stated that "they *enter* the sanctuary"), it seems to me extremely difficult to see how an accusation of illegitimate marriage can be regarded as an example of defiling the sanctuary. Moreover, if one would argue that for some reason this is indeed so, is marriage with two woman not a similar issue?! This has been admitted, after all, by Davies, *Damascus Document*, 115.

[8] See, for example: Rabin, *Zadokite Document*, 17, n. 2; Schwarz, *Damaskusschrift*, 142-43; Murphy-O'Connor, "Essene Missionary Document?," 221; Vermes, "Sectarian Matrimonial Halakhah," 197; Knibb, *Qumran Community*, 41. The way in which Mueller has presented the whole passage (according to which the third accusation immediately follows the first one) indicates that he too understood it in a similar way. See Mueller, "Temple Scroll and Gospel Divorce Texts," 252. Cf. Davies, *Damascus Document*, 114-15.

[9] So too Jeremias, *Lehrer der Gerichtigkeit*, 96; Schwarz, *Damaskusschrift*, 141; Davies, *Damascus Document*, 114-15.

net, Murphy-O'Connor, Vermes, Mueller, Wacholder, Knibb, Betz, Brin, Shemesh and Werman, and many others.[10] And, as Fitzmeyer put it, "this is almost certainly the correct understanding of the text."[11] According to this reading, we should look for *two* issues under the title of "fornication," and these will undoubtedly be marriage with two women, on the one hand, and marriage with one's niece, on the other.

In order to solve the difficulty presented by the unexpected structure of the passage I would suggest surgery, according to which the second accusation, that of defiling the sanctuary [2], is removed from the text altogether.[12] Alternatively, one may prefer to relocate it after the accusation of marriage with one's niece [3] and before the accusation of defiling the holy spirit, where it is expected since, as I have noted above, it uses the same verb (מטמאים) as the subsequent attack.[13] By doing one or the other, the difficulty is resolved.

An intrinsic consideration supports the assumption that the accu-

---

[10] See Rabin, *Zadokite Document*, 17, n. 1 (on line 20); A. Dupont-Sommer, *Die essenischen Schriften vom toten Meer* (tr. W. W. Muller; Tübingen: Mohr-Siebeck, 1960) 141; J. Maier, *Die Texte vom toten Meer* (München/Basel: E. Reinhardt, 1960) 1.52; É. Cothenet, "Le Document de Damas," *Les Textes de Qumran* (ed. J. Carmignac, É. Cothenet and H. Lignée; Paris: Letouzey et Ané, 1963) 1.162; Murphy-O'Connor, "Essene Missionary Document?," 220; Vermes, "Sectarian Matrimonial Halakhah," 197; Mueller, "Temple Scroll and Gospel Divorce Texts," 253; Wacholder, *The Dawn of Qumran*, 120; Knibb, *Qumran Community*, 42; H. D. Betz, *The Sermon on the Mount* (Minneapolis: Fortress, 1995) 252; G. Brin, "Divorce at Qumran," *Legal Texts and Legal Issues. Proceedings of the Second Meeting of the International Organization for Qumran Studies, Cambridge, 1995 Published in Honour of Joseph M. Baumgarten* (ed. M. J. Bernstein, F. García Martínez and J. Kampen; STDJ 23; Leiden: Brill, 1997) 236; A. Shemesh and C. Werman, "Hidden Things and their Revelation," *RevQ* 18 (1998) 423.

[11] See J. A. Fitzmyer, "The Matthean Divorce Texts and Some New Palestinian Evidence," *Theological Studies* 37 (1976) 219.

[12] It is true that according to this suggestion one would be unable to correlate the number of specific accusations to the three nets of Belial mentioned above (4:13). This disjunction, however, which caused much difficulty for readers of our passage exists even if we leave the text as is. As Campbell, *Use of Scripture*, 117, puts it: "It is difficult, if not impossible, to match up coherently 'the three nets' in 4:12-19a with the corresponding sins reported in 4:19 ff." If we take the phrase העולה מזה יתפש בזה והניצלמזה יתפש בזה ("He who escapes from this is caught by that and he who is saved from that is caught by this") to mean that no one can escape *all* the nets, we may assume that the author accuses the builders of the wall of one or two of these nets, not necessarily of all three. Accordingly, the proposed surgery need not be affected by the reference to three nets.

[13] Here I find myself in complete agreement with Knibb, *Qumran Community*, 41-42, who writes: "The first and the third of these accusations are presented as examples of 'fornication' ... the second accusation (making the sanctuary unclean, the third of the nets of Belial) breaks the connection between the two examples of fornication ... it is possible that this accusation was inserted at a second stage, or that it has been misplaced from after v. 11a." See also Schwarz, *Damaskusschrift*, 142; Murphy-O'Conner, "Essene Missionary Document?," 221.

sation of defiling the sanctuary [2] is indeed extraneous to the text, and thus supports the above suggested surgery. For, as pointed out by Davies, this accusation "may be felt to attract suspicion in that unlike the other two specific accusations, it does not cite a biblical text as its basis."[14] It is important to note (and this too has been noted by Davies) that the employment of a biblical proof-text in our text is more than a formal device; for if the law under discussion were disputed by the community and its opponents, as is the case with the other two accusations, the author would surely have been required to base his claim on scripture.[15] Without such a biblical proof text, his argument is baseless. This fact gives rise to the possibility that the second accusation is extraneous to the text. As has been frequently noted, there are traces of secondary expansions within our text—such as 5:1-6—and therefore one may suspect the second accusation to be one of these expansions too.

By removing the second accusation from the text altogether, or by moving it a few lines below, *after* the third accusation, one places the accusation of marriage with one's niece [3] immediately after the accusation of marrying two women [1], to which, according to the suggestion mentioned above, it actually relates. But is there any inherent connection between these two issues? I wish to examine this possibility, in light of some Tannaitic texts from the first chapter of tractate Yevamot.

II

According to biblical law (Deut. 25:5-10), if a married man dies childless, one of his brothers is commanded to marry his widow in levirate marriage (יבום), in order to continue his name after his death. If the living brother refuses to do so, an act of "pulling off the sandal" (חליצה) is to be performed. As long as he does not marry his deceased brother's widow (in the levirate marriage) or performs חליצה, the widow retains the status of a married woman and is not allowed to remarry. There are cases, however, where the duty of יבום may contradict other imperatives (such as incest laws). In such cases, Jewish law gave priority to the latter and exempted the brother, as well as the widow, from the duty of יבום completely. Her status, in such cases, is that of an ordinary widow, who is allowed to remarry whomever she wishes (except, of course, a high priest [Lev. 21:14]).

---

[14] Davies, *Damascus Document*, 115. See also Knibb, *Qumran Community*, 42.
[15] Davies, *Damascus Document*, 115.

The rules of the laws relating to יבום and חליצה are being dealt with mainly in Tractate Yevamot. According to m. Yev. 1:1:

חמש עשרה נשים פוטרות צרותיהן וצרות צרותיהן מן החליצה ומן
היבום עד סוף העולם.

> Fifteen women exempt their co-wives and their co-wives from חליצה and from יבום without limit.

The general principle behind this Mishnah has been explained above, namely, that in cases where the duty of יבום contradicts the incest laws, the latter have primacy over the former. In other words, one would be completely exempt from the duty of יבום. The meaning of this Mishnah's specific ruling is elaborated in the chapter's subsequent halakhot. From these halakhot we learn that the Mishnah deals with the possible problems that might arise when a man married to two women dies childless, and his brother is expected to fulfill the duty of יבום. According to that chapter's halakha, in case the living brother is not allowed to marry one of the wives of his deceased brother (due to their near kinship), he will not be required to perform levirate marriage with her. This woman is free to remarry without recourse to חליצה.

This principle is not disputed. However, the Mishnah is concerned not only with the wife whom the living brother is exempt from marrying (in levirate marriage), but also with her rival. The rival, who has no kinship relation with the living brother, and therefore could have been married to him, is also exempt from יבום (and חליצה). Both women are free to remarry whomever they wish, as if they were ordinary widows. This is, however, the view of the School of Hillel alone; according to the School of Shammai, although the first woman is exempted from the levirate marriage, her rival is not, and she must marry the living brother. Unless they perform the act of חליצה, she cannot remarry.

Unlike other halakhic disputes (such as those which concern the observance of custom), this dispute could have had dangerous social implications. As the *baraita* in t. Yev. 1:8-9 put it:

הלכו צרות אילו וניסו לשוק] —בית שמיי אומ' הן פסולות והולד
פסול. בית הלל או' הן כשירות והולד כשר. נתיבמו – בית שמיי או'
הן כשירות והולד כשר. בית הלל או' הן פסולות והולד ממזר.

> [If] these co-wives went and got married—the School of Shammai say: "They are invalidated and the offspring is invalid"; the School of Hillel say: "They are valid and the offspring is valid." [If] they entered into levirate marriage—the School of Shammai say: "They are valid and the offspring is valid"; the School of Hillel say: "They are invalid and the offspring is a *mamzer*."

This problematic situation is reflected in Rabbi Yoḥanan ben Nuri's complaint, which immediately follows (t. Yev. 1:9):

בא וראה היאך הלכה זו רווחת בישראל: [אם] לקיים כדברי בית
שמיי – הולד ממז' כדברי ב"ה; אם לקיים כדברי בית הלל –
הוולד פגום כדברי בית שמאי.

> Come and observe: can this Halakha be observed among Israel?! [If]
> to act in deed in accord with the opinion of the School of Shammai—
> the offspring will be a *mamzer* according to the opinion of the School
> of Hillel; if it is to act in accord with the opinion of the School of
> Hillel, the offspring is blemished in accord with the opinion of the
> School of Shammai!

There is no doubt that whoever follows the opinion of the School of
Hillel would never marry a woman whose family followed the opinion of the School of Shammai, and vice versa. In other words, this
halakhic controversy could deeply divide Jewish society, leaving it
with no means of overcoming the social rupture.

Tannaitic sources reveal that this problem was quite acute during
the first century. According to a *baraita* "in the days of Rabbi Dosa
ben Harkinas the rival of the daughter has been permitted, and it was
troublesome for the Sages, for he was an old man and a great master"
בימי רבי דוסא בן הרכינס התירו צרת הבת, והיה הדבר קשה לחכמים,
מפני שאדם זקן היה וחכם גדול היה (b. Yev. 16a). And when the sages
asked Rabbi Yehoshua for his opinion on the matter he replied:
"Why do you push my head between two high mountains, between
the School of Shammai and the School of Hillel, that they will crush
my head?" למה אתם מכניסין ראשי לבין שני הרים גדולים, לבין בית שמאי
ובין בית הלל, שיריצו את ראשי? (t. Yev. 1:10). We may sympathize with
Rabban Shimon ben Gamliel's concern: "What shall we do with the
former co-wives?" מה נעשה להם לצרות הראשונות? (t. Yev. 1:10).

The fact that halakhic authorities discussed so emphatically and
emotionally this dispute between the School of Shammai and the
School of Hillel indicates that the issue was of real concern. In
other words, the social reality raised by this halakhic dispute did
indeed exist at the time. This assertion is corroborated also by the
praise of the Mishnah of the School of Hillel and the School of
Shammai for not preventing their followers from marrying one another, despite the halakhic dispute which existed between them.
Had this been only a matter of theoretical importance, it would be
difficult to understand the Mishnah's praise of the Houses for the
liberal stand they took in reality, against their ideal and theoretical
view.

Moreover, it seems unlikely that the issue was considered urgent and acute simply due to one case. On the contrary, Rabbi Yehoshua, for example, testifies that the families of Qifai and Meqoshesh included descendants of levirate marriage with co-wives, some of whom had even been chosen as high priests. Similarly, Abba, Rabban Gamliel's brother, was married to two women, one of whom was Rabban Gamliel's daughter, and after Abba's death Rabban Gamliel married her rival in levirate marriage (in accordance with the opinion of the School of Shammai). It is against this background that we can fully appreciate Rabbi Tarphon's statement: "I crave to have a co-wife of the daughter, and I should marry her into the priesthood" תאיב אני שתהא לי צרת הבת ואסיאנה לכהונה (t. Yev. 1:10, and parallels). We should assume that the problem with which these sources deal was not uncommon.

From the long list of fifteen women who "exempt their rivals and their rivals' rivals from חליצה and from יבום without limit," the case with which the Mishnah illustrates its theoretical halakhic ruling is the one of a man who is married to his brother's daughter: "How do they exempt their rivals [from חליצה and from יבום]? If his daughter was married to his brother, and he [i.e. his brother] had another wife, and he [i.e. his brother] died, etc." , כיצד? היתה בתו נשואה לאחיו ולו אשה אחרת, ומת (m. Yev. 1:2). The situation and the halakhic problem it might pose are clear: if a man has married his brother's daughter and died without leaving any children, his living brother is expected to fulfill the duty of levirate marriage, a duty which he is unable to fulfill since his deceased brother's widow is his own daughter. The same example is used by all the other sources mentioned above, which deal with this problem and the halakhic dispute between the School of Hillel and the School of Shammai over it.

This is no surprise for, as has long been noted, marriage with one's niece was indeed a common practice among Palestinian Jewry during the Second Temple era and even after the destruction of the Temple.[16] Thus, for example, Joseph son of Tobias married his brother's daughter (Josephus, Ant. 12.186-189). Similarly, Herod

[16] See S. Krauss, "Die Ehe zwischen Onkel und Nichte," *Studies in Jewish literature, issued in honor of Professor Kaufmann Kohler, Ph.D., president of Hebrew Union College, Cincinnati, Ohio, on the occasion of his seventieth birthday, May the tenth, nineteen hundred and thirteen* (ed. D. Philipson et al.; Berlin: Reimer, 1913) 165-75; A. Büchler, "Familienreinheit und Familienmakel in Jerusalem vor dem Jahre 70," *Festschrift Adolf Schwarz zum siebzigsten Geburtstage, 15. Juli 1916, gewidmet von Freunden und Schulern* (ed. V. Aptowitzer and S. Krauss; Berlin: R. Lowit, 1917) 136; Ginzberg, *Ein unbekannte jüdische Sekt*, 23-24; Jeremias, *Lehrer der Gerichtigkeit*, 103-4; Herr, "Continuum," 52-53, and n. 64; A. Schremer, "Kinship Terminology and Endogamous Marriage in the Mishnahic and Talmudic Periods," *Zion* 60 (1995) 16-18 (Hebrew).

married his niece (Ant. 17.19), and his sister, Salome, was married to her father's brother (Ant. 15.65). Herod also tried to give his own daughter in marriage to his brother (Ant. 16.194). His granddaughter, Miriam, was married to Antipater, her father's brother (Ant. 17.18), and her sister, Herodias, was first married to Herod's son, Herod, who was her paternal uncle (Ant. 18.136), and secondly to Herod Antipas, who also was her father's brother (Ant. 18.136). Herodias' daughter, Salome, was also married to her paternal uncle, Philipos (Ant. 18.137). The same was the case of Herod of Chalkis, who married his niece Berenikei, Agrippa I's daughter (Ant. 19.277). As we have noted above, Abba, Rabban Gamliel's brother, was married to his niece, Rabban Gamliel's daughter (b. Yev. 16a); similarly Rav Shimon bar Abba, Shmuel's brother, married his brother's daughters (j. Ket. 2:6, 26c).

The fact that, out of the list of fifteen women, the Mishnah illustrated its theoretical ruling with the case of one who married his brother's daughter indicates that this was the social reality which engendered the halakhic dispute under discussion. However, this halakhic dispute could not have arisen unless someone who had married his brother's daughter was also married, simultaneously, to another woman. As the Mishnah itself put it: "If his daughter was married to his brother, and he [that is: "his brother"] *had another wife*" (היתה בתו נשואה לאחיו ולו אשה אחרת [m. Yev. 1:2]).

Indeed, polygamy, as a prevailing norm among Palestinian Jewry during the Second Temple period (and even during the mishnaic and talmudic periods), is attested in many sources. The most important of these is Josephus, who explicitly states that it is customary among Jewish man to marry more than one wife (Ant. 17.14; cf. War 1.477). This is corroborated by Justin Martyr's claim, that the Jews marry many women. Since these testimonies are of a general and observational character, they are of high value. Needless to say, they are confirmed by the specific evidence for the actual practice of polygamy which indeed existed.[17]

The Tannaitic sources of tractate Yevamot reveal a social reality in which there were men who married their nieces while, at the same time, being married to another woman. This is exactly the situation which the author of the Damascus Document sees before his eyes when accusing his opponents of "taking two women in their lifetime," on the one hand, and "marrying each one of them his

---

[17] See my "How Much Polygyny in Jewish Roman Palestine," *Proceedings of the American Academy for Jewish Research* (forthcoming).

brother's daughter and his sister's daughter," on the other. I would suggest, therefore, that the first accusation made by the author of the Damascus Document, that of marrying two women, and the last one, that of marrying one's niece, are closely related one to another and are, in fact, two aspects of the same phenomenon.

III

If our suggestion to view m. Yev. 1:1-4 as a text relating to the same social reality as our passage in the Damascus Document is correct, it might also support the assumption that the first accusation relates to polygamy, not to second marriage, as other interpretations suggest. Regarding the suggestion that the author prohibits not only polygamy or divorce and subsequent marriage but any second marriage (even after the death of one's spouse), it has been frequently argued that a passage in the Temple Scroll (57:17-19) seems to contradict this, since it explicitly rules that the king *may* marry a second wife in a case where his first wife had died:

17 ולא יקח עליה אשה אחרת כי
18 היאה לבדה תהיה עמו כול ימי חייה ואם מתה ונשא
19 לו אחרת

> He shall not take upon her another wife, for she alone shall be with him all the days of her life. But should she die he may take unto himself another (wife).[18]

According to this text, second marriage (after the death of one's spouse) was not forbidden in Qumran. It is true that the Temple Scroll and the Damascus Document are two distinct documents and that the interpretation of the latter should not automatically assume a complete agreement with the former. Nevertheless, a recently published fragment of the Damascus Document itself (4Q271) seems to relate to the case of the marriage of a woman who has previously been married:

10 אל יבא איש
11 [אשה בבריתו](?) הקן]דש אשר ידעה לעשות מעשה מ/בדבר ואשר ידעה
12 [מעשה בבית] אביה או אלמנה אשר נשכבה מאשר התארמלה וכול
13 [אשר עליה ש]ם רע בבתוליה בבית אביה אל יקחה איש כי אם
14 [בראות נשים] נאמנות וידעות ברורות ממאמר המבקר אשר על
15 [הרבים ואח]ר יקחנה ובלוקחו אותה יעשה כמ[ש]פט [ולוא] יגיד עלי[נה]

[18] Y. Yadin, *The Temple Scroll*, 1.258; E. Qimron, *The Temple Scroll—A Critical Edition with Extensive Reconstructions* (Beer Sheva: Ben-Gurion University of the Negev/Jerusalem: Israel Exploration Society, 1996) 82.

10   Let no man bring
11   [a woman into the ho]ly [covenant(?)] who has had sexual experience,
      (whether) she had such
12   [experience in the home] of her father or as a widow who had inter-
      course after she was widowed. And any
13   [woman upon whom there is a] bad [na]me in her maidenhood in her
      father's house, let no man take her, except
14   [upon examination] by trustworthy [women] of repute selected by
      command of the supervisor over
15   [the many. After]ward he may take her, and when he takes her he shall
      act in accordance with the l[a]w [and he shall not t]ell about [her].[19]

The text (line 12) prohibits marriage with a widow who has had sexual experience after she was widowed but not with a widow who ab-
stained from sexual relations since the death of her spouse. Thus, it
makes clear that the author of the Damascus Document did not prohibit second marriage as such.

However, the first and the second suggestions, which interpret our
passage in the Damascus Document as a prohibition of divorce and
second marriage as long as the first wife was still alive, are challenged, too (and this also was mentioned frequently[20]), by the fact
that the Damascus Document (13:16-17) refers to a case in which a
man divorces his wife, and it does not prohibit such an act:

[ ]ח אש[	16 למבקר אשר במחנה ועשה אמנה ולא ישן
[	17] ה]עצה וכן למגרש הוא ישן

16   And so whoever takes a wife
17   And h[e] [   ] council, and to the one who divorces and he shall
      chaste[n their sons ...]

If the words וכן למגרש in line 17 refer to a man who divorces his
wife, we may argue that the author of the Damascus Document did
not exclude the possibility of divorce.

Admittedly, the assumption that these words indeed relate to a
man who divorces his wife is problematic, since the severe damage
of the manuscript at this point makes the context unclear. However,
Qimron, in his recent edition of the Damascus Document,[21] based
on a new and improved reading of the manuscript, suggests restor-
ing the text as follows:

---

[19] See Baumgarten, DJD 18.175 (and parallels on 132 and 154).
[20] See, for example, J. A. Fitzmyer, "Divorce among First Century Palestinian
Jews," *Eretz Israel* 14 (1978) *103-*110, and the bibliography listed there.
[21] See: E. Qimron, "The Text of CDC," *The Damascus Document Reconsidered* (ed.
M. Broshi; Jerusalem: Israel Exploration Society, Shrine of the Book, Israel
Museum, 1992) 35.

16   וכן לכל לוק]ח אשה[

17   וה]ן   [   ] [   ] עצה וכן למגרש והוא יי]סר את בניהם[

16   And so whoever takes a wife
17   And h[e] [   ] council, and to the one who divorces and he shall
     chaste[n their sons ...]

This restoration seems to be corroborated by a recently published
fragment from Cave 4, which reads:[22]

4   וכן לכל לוק]ח אשה[

5   הואה בעצה וכן]למגרש[

6   והנ]וא[ן ייסר את בניהם]ובנותיהם[

7   בר]וח ענ[נוה ובא]ה[בת חסד[

8   אל]טור להנ]ם[באף ועבנ]רה[

4   And so whoever takes a wife
5   is in the council, and also to the one who divorces
6   And he shall chastise their sons and their daughters
7   [in a spi]rit of humility and loving kindness
8   He shall not told a grudge to them, with anger and ire.

This fragment shows that Qimron's restoration is undoubtedly correct
and indicates that line 16 refers to a man who marries a wife. It is
therefore to be concluded, that the words וכן למגרש in line 17 indeed
refer to a man who divorces.[23] This, in turn, makes clear that the
Damascus Document does not prohibit divorce as such. Moreover, as
Brin recently argued, some new texts from Qumran seem, in fact, to
encourage divorce in certain circumstances.[24] All these facts indicate that
divorce was not forbidden by the Qumran community.[25]

Moreover, as Vermes emphasized, one should not ignore the context and scriptural proof-texts the author adduces in favor of his
claim. These verses are best understood with the assumption of the
author accusing his opponents of polygamy, not of second mar-

---

[22] The fragment is 4Q266 frg. 9, 3, published by Baumgarten, DJD 18.70.

[23] See too Brin, "Divorce at Qumran," 238-39.

[24] See Brin, "Divorce at Qumran," 232-38.

[25] My colleague, Aharon Shemesh, who drew my attention to the above-mentioned fragment of the Damascus Document (4Q271), argues that while the
Damascus Document does not prohibit divorce, nevertheless it does prohibit second
marriage while the first spouse is still alive. He emphasizes the fact that while this
fragment relates to the marriage of a virgin and the marriage of a widow (אלמנה), it
fails to mentions the possibility of the marriage of a divorcee (גרושה). This fact, he
argues, indicates that the text did not recognize the legitimacy of marriage after divorce. See his "4Q271.3: A Key to Sectarian Matrimonial Law," *JJS* 49 (1998)
246. The term אלמנה, however, does not necessarily mean "widow"; rather it
means, as is the case in mishnahic Hebrew, "a woman previously married," i.e., a
widow or a divorcee. See, for example: m. Ket. 1:1-2; 5:1-2. This broad meaning,

riage.[26] Furthermore, had the author's intent been to prohibit marriage to a second wife while the first is still alive, one would expect him to cite Lev. 18:18 explicitly ואשה אל אחתה לא תקח לצרר לגלות ערותה עליה בחייה, as it is the best biblical text to bring in support of such a view. The fact that he did not utilize this verse indicates that remarriage (after divorce) was not the issue under discussion.[27] Taking all these factors into consideration, it seems to me that the first accusation should be understood as a reference to polygamy. Its association with a negative reference to marrying one's niece, an association also at the base of m. Yev. 1:1-4, indicates that our text refers to actual social practice among Palestinian Jews of the Second Temple era.

---

which refers both to a divorcee and to a widow, is applied by rabbinic sources, especially in contrast to בתולה ("virgin"), which bears the meaning of a woman who is still unmarried (or one who is soon to enter marriage), as is the case here.

[26] See Vermes, "Sectarian Matrimonial Halakhah," 200; Knibb, *Qumran Community*, 43. It should be noted, however, that Vermes' claim regarding the evidence that the author adduces from David, that "the only matrimonial offense for which David is excused here is polygamy," though a plausible understanding, is not stated explicitly in the text itself. Those who would insist on interpreting our text as prohibiting marriage to a second woman while the first is still alive could argue that the allusion to David refers to his marriage with two living sisters. Cf. t. Soṭ. 11:18 (ed. Lieberman, 224) (= b. San. 19b): "Rabbi Yose's disciples asked him: How is it that David married his wife's sister? He told them: he married her [only] after Merav's death" (שאלו תלמידיו את ר' יוסה: היאך נשא דוד אחות אשתו? אמ' להן: לאחר מיתת מרב נשאה). Rabbi Yose's disciples surely assumed that David's marriage to Michal took place while Merav was alive, and such an assumption, one may argue, explains the allusion to David in our text also, if we insist on understanding its accusation as referring to second marriage while the first wife is still alive. Moreover, they may argue, this could serve as a solution to the difficulty of why the author spoke only of David and not of other biblical figures who married more than one wife. However, the reason for the author's allusion to David is probably rooted in the view that David's deeds are normative. See M. Kister, "Plucking of Grain on the Sabbath and the Jewish-Christian Debate," *Jerusalem Studies in Jewish Thought* 3.3 (1983-84) 353-54. See also C. A. Evans, "David in the Dead Sea Scrolls," *The Scrolls and the Scripture. Qumran Fifty Years After* (ed. S. E. Porter and C. A. Evans; JSPSup 26; Sheffield: JSOT, 1997) 187-88.

[27] To this one may add another consideration. Baumgarten, in his "Qumran-Essene Restraints on Marriage," 14, has already noted that "one of the questions which should have been posed but has not ... is how such restrictions would have been reconciled by the Qumran exegetes with Pentateuchal law which explicitly condones both polygamy and divorce." Deut. 21:15, for example, speaks explicitly of a man who has two wives. How would the author of the Damascus Document have reconciled his view with this verse? I assume he would argue that the verse does not refer to a man who has two wives simultaneously but rather to a man who married a second wife after the first marriage had ended in either divorce or her death, which is legitimate.

SCRIPTURAL INTERPRETATIONS IN THE DAMASCUS DOCUMENT AND THEIR PARALLELS IN RABBINIC MIDRASH

Aharon Shemesh

Bar-Ilan University

1. *Introduction*

For some years now, scholars have been disputing the question of whether, and to what extent, the sectarian literature from Qumran contains halakhic midrash.[1] This dispute, however, is marred by a methodological problem: it is concerned not so much with the interpretation of sectarian literature as with the definition of "halakhic midrash." On the one hand, it is generally agreed that the legal passages in the Qumran writings are intimately bound up with the sectarians' interpretation of the biblical text; on the other, it is also clear that the writers of that literature can hardly be credited with explicit use of the same hermeneutic rules and techniques as the authors of rabbinic halakhic midrash. Scholarship has therefore concentrated on assessing similarities and differences between these two bodies of literature, and each scholar's decision as to the presence (or lack) of halakhic midrash at Qumran depends ultimately on that

---

* I am indebted to my friend Adiel Schremer, whose comments helped me to clarify some of the details in the first part of this paper. I also owe thanks to Daniel Schwartz, Moshe Halbertal, Cana Werman, Israel Knohl and Hayyim Shapira, who read a draft version of the paper and offered useful and important remarks.
The translation of the Damascus Document cited in this paper is from J. M. Baumgarten and D. R. Schwartz, "Damascus Document," *The Dead Sea Scrolls. Hebrew, Aramaic and Greek Texts with English Translation* (ed. J. H. Charlesworth; Tübingen: Mohr-Siebeck/Louisville: John Knox, 1995), with slight changes; translations of the Babylonian Talmud are based on the Soncino edition.
[1] Prominent among scholars who frequently ascribed classical techniques of halakhic midrash to sectarian writings are Y. Yadin, in his commentary to the *Temple Scroll*, and L. Schiffman in various publications. For a detailed list of scholars who hold that the sectarians consistently used halakhic midrash, see S. D. Fraade "Looking for Legal Midrash at Qumran," *Biblical Perspectives: Early Use and Interpretation of the Bible in Light of the Dead Sea Scrolls. Proceedings of the First International Symposium of the Orion Center, 12-14 May 1996* (ed. M. E. Stone and E. G. Chazon; STDJ 28; Leiden: Brill, 1998) n. 7. See also: E. Slomovic, "Toward an Understanding of the Exegesis in the Dead Sea Scrolls," *RevQ* 7 (1969) 3-15. Among the dissenting scholars is M. J. Bernstein, "Midrash Halakhah at Qumran?," *Gesher* 7 (1979) 145-66.

scholar's definition of halakhic midrash and the degree to which that definition is applicable to the texts of sectarian literature.

Two scholars have recently returned to the subject, making an important contribution to the debate by diverting it from the question of interpretive methods to an examination of literary genre. Steven Fraade and Menachem Kister[2] have, independently, redirected attention to the contrast between the sectarian pesher literature and the legal texts at Qumran: the pesharim, typically, are continuous commentaries to the Bible, verse by verse, citing the relevant verses (fully or in part), while the legal passages lack this feature. There is a similar difference between sectarian legal commentaries and rabbinic halakhic midrash. The latter is a "commentary" in the sense that it offers a continuous interpretation of a whole textual unit. Contrary to the usual style of halakhic midrash, which always begins by quoting the relevant verse and goes on to explain how that verse is a proof-text for a certain law, such quotations are extremely rare in Qumran literature.

Fraade and Kister have suggested different explanations. While Kister attributes the phenomenon to the gradual transition from the biblical to the post-biblical period, Fraade argues for an ideological reason. In Kister's view, commentaries on biblical verses began to develop as the world of the Bible gradually receded into the past; the creation of a commentary obliges the commentator to position himself outside the world of the text being interpreted. First to evolve were the pesharim, which did not expound the biblical text itself but endeavored to show that various prophecies were being fulfilled in the present. The next stage was the development of commentaries on prophetic texts and biblical poetry, while exegesis on biblical prose, including, in particular, the legal sections of the Torah, did not arrive until the rabbinic period.

Fraade, however, suggests that the lack of "halakhic midrash" at Qumran was deliberate; even where it is obvious that the sectarian law was derived by interpreting the Bible, the writers consistently refrain from presenting it as such, concealing from the reader the techniques by which they inferred the law from the scriptures and the fact that the law was the result of intellectual, that is, human inquiry into the verses of the Bible. The motive was ideological, rooted in the sectarian conception that the ultimate authority for the new laws, that is, the laws that they called "hidden," was divine revelation.[3] This contrasted with

---

[2] S. D. Fraade, "Looking for Legal Midrash," 59-79; M. Kister, "A Common Heritage: Biblical Interpretation at Qumran and Its Implications," *Biblical Perspectives*, 101–9.

[3] See A. Shemesh and C. Werman, "Hidden Things and Their Revelation,"

the rabbinic approach which cultivated the idea of an Oral Law and stressed the power of hermeneutics as a tool for its development.

Fraade and Kister are certainly right in their description of the phenomenon. The same feature, however, may be found in rabbinic literature. Besides halakhic midrash, rabbinic literature also includes the Mishnah. Generally speaking, one might say that the legal literature from Qumran and, in particular, the legal sections of the Damascus Document, with their abstract style, resemble the Mishnah more than halakhic midrash. I have shown elsewhere that some *mishnayot*, though certainly in the classical style of the Mishnah, are best interpreted only if one assumes that they are reworked versions of halakhic midrash in the style of the Mishnah.[4] In other words, such passages are simply halakhic midrashim that omit the verse(s) from which the law in question has been derived.[5] Hence, the two elements proposed as a characterization of midrash—quotation of verses and continuity of exposition—are not necessarily interdependent. One can find continuous commentaries on one or more verses of the Bible which do not actually quote those texts. It is in that direction that this article hopes to contribute to the discussion of halakhic midrash in Qumran literature. Through two examples, I will show that once the biblical backdrop for the law is uncovered, the legal texts in question actually constitute continuous exegesis of single textual units. Comparison of these laws with rabbinic midrashim on the same verses may throw light on the interpretation of these laws and their position in the whole corpus.

a. First example

CD 6:21-7:1

לאהוב איש את אחיהו כמהו
ולהחזיק ביד עני ואביון וגר
ולדרוש איש את שלום אחיהו
<u>ולא ימעל איש בשאר בשרו להזיר מן הזונות כמשפט</u>
להוכיח איש את אחיהו כמצוה ולא לנטור מיום ליום.

RevQ 18/71 (1998) 409-27. Our thesis in that paper is that the sectarians were also aware of the crucial contribution of human-intellectual examination of the biblical text to the final consolidation of halakhah.

[4] See my article, "Exile of Involuntary Manslayers to a City of Refuge," *Maḥanayim* 13 (1995) 200-10 (Hebrew), and my Ph.D. dissertation, "Punishment by Flogging in Tannaitic Sources" (Bar-Ilan University, 1994) 176-91 (Hebrew).

[5] It is not my contention that such passages of the Mishnah are based on an actual existing text, only that underlying them is the exegesis of a continuous textual unit of the Bible.

... to love each man his brother as himself,
to support the poor, destitute and proselyte,
and to seek each man the peace of his brother.
*And let no man trespass with regard to his near kin; (rather, let him) stay away
     from unchastity in accordance with the precept;*
let each man rebuke his brother in accordance with the ordinance
     and not keep a grudge from one day to the next.

CD 8:4-8

מאשר לא סרו מדרך בוגדים
ויתגוללו בדרכי זונות ובהון רשעה
ונקום ונטור איש לאחיו
ושנוא איש את רעהו
ויתעלמו איש בשאר בשרו ויגשו לזמה
ויתגברו להון ולבצע ויעשו איש הישר בעיניו.

... because they did not depart from the way of traitors,
but rather wallowed in the ways of prostitutes and wicked wealth
avenging and bearing grudges each man against his brother, and each
     hating his brother;
and each ignored the relation of his flesh. And they drew near (one to
     another) for incest
and they strove mightily for wealth and profit and each man did what
     was right in his own eyes.

These two passages are clearly seen to be antithetical: according to
the first passage, the things that a person joining the community undertakes to do and not to do are precisely the opposite of the sins of
the wicked, as recounted in the second passage. The initiate undertakes to love his brother as himself, while the wicked hate their
brothers; the former undertakes to support the poor, the destitute
and the proselyte, while the traitor wallows in ill-gained wealth and
strives for riches, doing what is right in his or her own eyes. The
same applies to the duty to rebuke one's fellow and to refrain from
revenge, in contrast to the wicked who seek revenge and bear
grudges. But we are particularly interested here in the underlined
words: What are the sins committed by the wicked with "near kin"
שאר בשר that the initiates avoid? It has been pointed out that the
word שאר occurs elsewhere in the Damascus Document.[6] In 5:7-11
the author condemns his opponents for marrying

---

[6] L. Ginzberg, *An Unknown Jewish Sect* (New York: JTS, 1976) 32-33; D. R.
Schwartz, "Damascus Document," *The Dead Sea Scrolls* (ed. J. H. Charlesworth), 29,
n. 80.

each one his brother's daughter or sister's daughter. But Moses said, "To your mother's sister you may not draw near, for she is your mother's *near relation* (שאר)." Now the precept of incest is written from the point of view of males, but the same (law) applies to women, so if a brother's daughter uncovers the nakedness of a brother of her father, she is a (forbidden) *close relationship* (שאר).

Hence it seems plausible that the "prostitution" mentioned in these passages also refers specifically to marriage with one's niece. Accordingly, the meaning of the expression "each ignored the relation of his flesh, and they drew near (one to another) for incest" would be that the traitors were committing incest, ignoring the restriction on marriage with one's close kin. The faithful of the community, however, undertook not to "trespass" with regard to their close kin, i.e., not to marry a niece, who is included in the category of forbidden unions, and so to avoid the grave sin of incest.

The conjecture that these carnal sins refer to the sectarian prohibition of marrying one's niece may be further corroborated. One must realize that the text is essentially a midrash. Louis Ginzberg[7] first suggested that the expression "each ignored the relation of his flesh" (ויתעלמו איש בשאר בשרו) might be associated with Isa. 58:7: "It is to share your bread with the hungry, and to take the wretched poor into your home; when you see the naked, to clothe him, and not to ignore your own kin" (ומבשרך לא תתעלם). The directive "to love each man his brother as himself, to support the poor, destitute and proselyte" is presumably a development of the first part of the verse, "to share your bread with the hungry and to take the wretched poor into your home." The obligation to reprove transgressors, cited in our text, is also associated with the same verse, as another expression of the injunction not to ignore one's kin, by reproving him or her as required. Thus, the entire text CD 6:21-7:1 is an exposition of the verse from Isaiah. Moreover, if one examines the whole of the relevant prophecy of Isaiah, the association of the laudable actions with the teachings of the sect and the deplorable ones with the rebels who "did not depart from the way of traitors" (CD 8:4-8) becomes quite plausible. The prophet first describes the misdeeds of Israel who, while observing the ritual of the fast, do not at the same time perform the appropriate deeds of charity and justice: "Is such the fast I desire, a day for men to starve their bodies? Is it bowing the head like a bulrush and lying in sackcloth and

---

[7] Ginzberg, *Unknown Jewish Sect*, n. 6; see also C. Rabin, *The Zadokite Documents* (Oxford: Clarendon, 1958) 26, 33.

ashes? Do you call that a fast, a day when the Lord is favorable?"
(Isa. 58:5). In the subsequent verses the prophet goes on to outline
the proper path to be taken. Thus, the members of the sect are fulfilling the prophet's demands, while their opponents persist in their
evil ways.

In light of these conclusions, it is instructive to consider the following *baraita*:

> Our Rabbis taught: [...] Concerning him who loves his neighbors,
> who befriends his relatives, marries his sister's daughter, and lends a
> *sela* to a poor man in the hour of need, Scripture says, Then shalt
> thou call, and the Lord will answer; then shalt thou cry and He will
> say, "Here I am" (b. Yeb. 62b).

This *baraita* is simply a rabbinic midrash on the same verse of Isaiah,
as is evident if one realizes that the cited verse, "Then when you
call..." (Isa. 58:9), occurs in the same passage, two verses after the
verse, "It is to share your bread...." Whoever observes the demands
listed in the *baraita* will be granted a divine response to his or her
prayer, having fulfilled the conditions listed by the prophet in the
previous verses: a person who lends a poor man a *sela* in time of
need is thereby obeying the injunction to "share your bread with the
hungry"; people who love their neighbors and bring their relatives
near are thereby fulfilling the command not to ignore their own kin.
Noteworthy, however, is the occurrence in the *baraita* of one who
"marries his sister's daughter." Why was this detail included in the
list? To my mind, this is proof that the carnal sins mentioned in the
Damascus Document should indeed be associated with the sectarian
prohibition of marrying one's niece. The Sages were presumably
aware that the members of the sect interpreted the verse in this way,
and for that very reason offered an alternative exposition with the
opposite conclusion, in keeping with rabbinic halakhah: "Not to ignore your own kin—this refers to one who marries his sister's
daughter."[8]

The relationship between sectarian law and rabbinic halakhah is
indicated elsewhere as well. The author of the Damascus Document
uses a rather unusual expression in 8:7: ויגשו לזמה "and they drew
near to incest." The word זמה, meaning depravity of some kind, occurs twice in the Torah, in connection with the prohibition against
marrying a woman and her daughter (זמה היא Lev. 18:17) and in the

---

[8] On the rabbinic recommendation to marry one's niece, see A. Schremer,
"Kinship Terminology and Endogamous Marriage in the Mishnaic and Talmudic
Periods," *Zion* 60 (1995) 13-21 (Hebrew); for a bibliography of previous research,
see nn. 34 and 41.

prohibition, "Do not degrade your daughter and make her a harlot, lest the land fall into harlotry and the land be filled with זמה" (Lev. 19:29). We read in the Tosefta, "A man shall not take a wife until his sister's daughter grows up, or until he finds a good match, as Scripture says, 'lest the land be filled with זמה'" (t. Qid. 1:4, ed. Lieberman, 276). According to the Tosefta, marriage to an unsuitable woman is considered זמה, while marriage to one's niece is an example of a good match. Here, too, the Rabbis interpreted the term זמה in direct antithesis to the sectarian view: whereas Qumranic law considered marriage with one's niece an act of depravity זמה, rabbinic halakhah praised such a match.

b. *Second example*

One of the most interesting pieces of information to emerge from the newly published fragments of the Damascus Document from Cave 4 concerns the original order of the laws in the work. Two different fragments have now provided evidence that column 9 of the Damascus Document from the Cairo Genizah is the direct continuation of column 16.[9] Armed with this information, one can now better understand the sequence of laws in this part of the work and possibly also determine the content of the last part of column 16. The reconstructed Genizah fragment and the Cave 4 fragments are as follows:[10]

CD 16:13-21

על משפט הנדבות. אל ידור איש למזבח מאום אנוס וגם
הנכ]הנים אל יקחו מאת ישראל   [ואל] יקדש איש את מאכל
פיןהו לאן[ל כי הוא אשר אמר יאיש את רעיהו יצדו חרם·   ואל
ואם מ]שדה אחזתו   ס   ויקדש איש מכל
ונעגש   ו]י]קדש לן גם המשפט ה
הנודרן את חמן]שית   כסף ערכו
ד אחר ה   ולשופ]טים לשפוט צדק
אם אנוס הוא]ע]ד אשר יוסר ושלם האונס אם לו דבר אמת עלם רעהו עד אשר
ואשר אמר   מב כמוה. כי לא הקים את]דברו לדבר אמתן.

[9] J. M. Baumgarten, *Qumran Cave 4.XIII. The Damascus Document (4Q266-273)* (DJD 18; Oxford: Clarendon, 1996) 2; see previously J. T. Milik, *Ten Years of Discovery in the Wilderness of Judea* (tr. J. Strugnell; London: SCM, 1959) 151–52.
[10] 4Q266, frg. 8 ii (DJD 18.65); 4Q270, frg. 6 iii (156-58); 4Q271, frg. 4 ii (178-79). Hebrew text completed in brackets relates to passages not documented in any of the texts.

Concerning the law of donations: Let no man vow to the altar anything violently acquired, nor / shall the priests take it from an
Israelite. Let no man sanctify the food / of his mouth unto God, for
this is what he said: "They trip one another with proscription." Let /
no man sanctify [   ] And if he should sanctify any land that he
holds to / [   ] the law   / And the one who vowed
shall pay a penalty of one fifth its assessed value. /... to the judges to
judge righteously [   ] after [   ] / if it is illegally be-
gotten until he is chastised and the oppressor makes restitution, if he
did not speak the truth with his neighbor until / [   ]
like it. For he did not keep his [word to speak the truth]. And concerning that which he said

CD 9:1-8

כל אדם אשר יחרים אדם מאדם בחוקי הגוים להמית הוא
ואשר אמר לא תקום ולא תטור את בני עמך וכל איש מבאי
הברית אשר יביא על רעהו דבר אשר לא בהוכח לפני עדים
והביאו בחרון אפו או ספר לזקניו להבזותו נוקם הוא ונוטר
ואין כתוב כי אם נוקם הוא לצריו ונוטר הוא לאויביו
אם החריש לו מיום ליום ובחרון אפו בו דבר בו בדבר מות
ענה בו יען אשר לא הקים את מצות אל אשר אמר לו הוכח
תוכיח את רעיך ולא תשא עליו חטא.

Any man who destroys a man among men by the statutes of the
Gentiles is to be put to death. / And as to that which he said, "You
shall not take vengeance nor keep a grudge against the sons of your
people," anyone of those who enter / the covenant who brings a
charge against his neighbor without reproof before witnesses, / but
brings it in his burning wrath or tells it to his elders to put him to
shame, is taking vengeance and bearing a grudge. / It is written only,
"He takes vengeance against his adversaries and keeps a grudge
against his enemies."/ If he was silent from day to day and in his
burning wrath charged him with a capital offense, / his iniquity is
upon him, for he did not fulfill the ordinance of God which says to
him, "You shall surely / reprove your neighbor so that you do not
bear sin because of him."

2. *Structure of the passage and its delimitation*

I must first justify my delimitation of the above passage. Schiffman[11]
has suggested that the entire fragment from the top of column 9 to
10:10 should be seen as a single unit, and has also offered an explanation for the sequence of laws that it sets out. Now, however, we
know that column 9 is the continuation of column 16, and this sug-

[11] L. H. Schiffman, *Law, Custom and Messianism in the Dead Sea Sect* (Jerusalem: Merkaz Zalman Shazar le-toldot Yisrael, 1993) 27-28 (Hebrew).

gestion is no longer tenable. As we shall show presently, the law at the top of column 9, "Any man who destroys a man among men...," is the direct sequel to the unit that begins with the heading, "Concerning the law of donations" (16:13). To my mind, it is no longer questionable that the primary, basic subdivision of the unit of laws in this part of the work is defined by the headings, "Concerning the X" (16:10, 16:13, 9:8, 10:10, 10:14), although various other matters may be raised within the sub-units so defined. Hence the unit beginning with the words "Concerning the law of donations" goes on until 9:8, where a new sub-unit, "Concerning oaths," begins.

The heading "Concerning the law of donations" is followed by four laws: "Let no man vow...," "Let no man sanctify the food of his mouth...," "Let no man sanctify...," "And if he should sanctify any land that he holds...." Although the precise import of these laws is not always clear, their main thrust is to curtail needless vows and voluntary offerings by laying down firm limits. The second law, "Let no man sanctify the food of his mouth unto God," is accompanied by a proof-text, "They trip one another with proscription" (Mic. 7:2).[12] Line 18 prescribes a monetary sanction to be imposed upon a person who consecrates something improperly (probably in violation of the preceding law). Lines 19-21 present an injunction to the judges "to judge righteously." In view of the phrase "and the oppressor makes restitution" in line 20, the text is presumably referring to judgment in connection with the first law, which commands, "Let no man vow to the altar anything violently acquired," and goes on to impose punishment upon whoever consecrates someone else's property.[13] Column 9 opens with the law, "Any man who destroys a man among men by the statutes of the Gentiles is to be put to death," and the last part of the text sets out the laws of reproof and the injunctions against revenge and bearing a grudge.

a. *Discussion: part I*

The key to understanding the structure of the whole passage is, I believe, the law "Any man who destroys [יחרים] a man among men by the statutes of the Gentiles is to be put to death." It is my contention that by examining this law we can explain the sequence of law preceding it and the subsequent appending of the laws of rebuke.

Despite the fact that lines 18-21 separate this law from the four

---

[12] Note the variant reading of the verse as compared with the MT איש את אחיהו / רעהו יצצו חרם.

[13] See Rabin, *Zadokite Documents*, 77, n. 13:2.

laws at the beginning of the section, it is essentially another item in
the same series and should be read as a continuity. The fact that the
proof-text attached to the second law, Mic. 7:2, contains the word
חרם "ban, proscription" links this law (9:9), which is also concerned
with חרם aimed at a person, to the first four laws. The actual meaning of this law has been debated by numerous scholars,[14] and we
shall return to that point later. At this stage, suffice it to say that the
most plausible interpretation is prescription of the death penalty for
a person who delivers someone to his death by Gentile authorities.[15]
As Baumgarten has shown, this corresponds exactly to Targum
Jonathan to Mic. 7:2, which reads "They deliver one another to be
put to death." [16]

This raises the possibility that the verse is not intended as a proof-
text for the law, "Let no man sanctify the food of his mouth," but
rather as a general source for the entire series of laws, "Concerning
the laws of donations." All the laws in the series are aimed at cur-
tailing the prevalent practice of oaths and dedication; the author
cites Micah in order to highlight the negative aspect of dedication,
that it is a two-edged sword capable of causing more damage than
benefit. This negative aspect is represented by the use of the verb
יצד: dedication may destroy both persons involved.[17]

Accordingly, I believe that the whole unit is based on the laws of
dedication in Lev. 27:28-29: "But of all that anyone owns, be it man
or beast or land of his holding, nothing that he has dedicated [איש
יחרים] to the Lord may be sold or redeemed; every dedicated thing

---

[14] See the list of translations and interpretations in J. D. M. Duncan, "'Behuqey
Hagoyim' Damascus Document IX,i Again," *RevQ* 11 (1983) 409, n. 1.
[15] J. M. Baumgarten and D. R. Schwartz, "Damascus Document," 43, n. 139.
[16] J. M. Baumgarten, "Qumran and the Halakhah in the Aramaic Targumim,"
Proceedings of the World Congress of Jewish Studies: Bible Studies and Ancient Near East
(Jerusalem: World Union of Jewish Studies, 1988) 45-60.
[17] Fraade, "Looking for Legal Midrash," 71-74, offers a similar suggestion in regard to another proof-text in the Damascus Document. In cols. 10ff., a series of
Sabbath laws begins: "Concerning the Sa[bba]th, to guard it according to its precept. Let no man do work on the sixth day from the time that the sphere of the sun
is distant from the gate by its fullness, for that is what he said: 'Guard the Sabbath
day to make it holy.'" According to Fraade, the author of CD, citing the verse from
Deut. 5:12, is not suggesting a proof-text for the specific law prohibiting work shortly before sundown on Friday. His intention is merely to stress one's duty to observe
the Sabbath laws meticulously. Thus, the verse is actually the basis for the whole series of Sabbath laws, although syntactic considerations give the impression that it is
quoted to support the first law: "for this is what he said." A further element of similarity between these two groupings of laws is the fact that both end in citation of a
verse. The last law in the series of laws of oaths, "Any man who dedicates a
man...," is a paraphrase of Lev. 27:29, while the series of laws "On the Sabbath"
ends with the words "For thus it is written, "Apart from your Sabbaths," which is a
variant of Lev. 23:38.

[כל חרם] is totally consecrated to the Lord. No human being who has been dedicated can be ransomed: he shall be put to death."[18] The laws of dedication are extremely harsh, compared with the laws of valuation that precede them in the Bible: dedication is irreversible, in the sense that "nothing that he has dedicated... may be sold or redeemed" and, worst of all, a dedicated person must be put to death. This distinction is clearly expressed in the wording of the biblical text, which begins the passage with the word אך "but," in contrast to the previous directives concerning valuation and consecration.

I shall begin with the last law. This is evidently an interpretive paraphrase of Lev. 27:29, "No human being who has been dedicated can be ransomed: he shall be put to death." Regardless of the original meaning of the verse,[19] it is clear that the Qumran sectarians, like the later Sages, could not accept the literal meaning of the text, that the Torah could permit one person to dedicate another and cause the latter's death. The Sages, therefore, explained the verse as an admonition that, if a person had already been condemned to death by legal procedure, it was forbidden to accept a ransom in order to save that person's life.[20] The solution adopted by the author of the Damascus Document was to shift the death penalty to the person who dedicates his fellow human being to destruction: "Any man who destroys a man among men by the statutes of the Gentiles is to be put to death." Accordingly, I believe that the first laws in our passage derive from a midrashic exegesis of Lev. 27:28. Support for this hypothesis comes from a comparison with rabbinic exegesis of the verse.

In the m. Arakhin 8:5, we read: "If a man dedicated his son or his daughter, his Hebrew male or female slave, or the field which he has bought, they are not deemed [validly] dedicated, for a man may not dedicate what is not his." This provision undoubtedly derives from

---

[18] The heading of these laws is indeed "On the laws of donations" and not "on the laws of dedication," but the continuation indicates that the author made no distinction between the different modes of consecration, as he uses all the terms נדר, הקדש and חרם.

[19] See S. A. Loewenstamm, "Proscription," *Encyclopaedia Biblica* 3 (1958) col. 291 (Hebrew).

[20] "R. Ishmael son of R. Johanan b. Beroka said: 'Since we find that those to be put to death by the hand of heaven can offer a monetary expiation and thereby obtain atonement, as it is said: *If there be laid on him ransom*, I might have thought that the same applied to those who are to be put to death by the hand of man; therefore are we taught: *No human being who has been dedicated can be ransomed*'" (b. Arakhin 6b). See also Sifra, Be-Hukkotai 12:7 (ed. A. H. Weiss, 115a) and the commentary of R. Abraham b. David ad loc.

the wording of Lev. 27:28: "But of all *that anyone owns*...," from which
one may infer, in typical rabbinic style, "Of all that he owns—but
not what he does not own." This is equivalent to the first law in our
text: "Let no man vow to the altar anything violently acquired." A
further series of interpretations of the same verse occurs in Sifra:

> "Anything that a person dedicates to the Lord, of all that he owns"—
> and not all that he owns. "Of man"—including his Canaanite male
> and female slave; or should the word "man" be understood as includ-
> ing his Hebrew male and female slave as well?—[that is not the case,]
> as Scripture teaches us: "of man," and not "every man." "Of
> beast"—and not every beast. "Of land of his holding"—and not all
> the land of his holding. May we infer that if a person dedicated them
> all, they would be dedicated?—[that is not the case,] as Scripture
> teaches us: "but." Said R. Eleazar b. Azariah: "Since a person is not
> allowed to dedicate [all] his property to God, how much more so is it
> true that a person must have mercy upon his property?!" (Sifra, Be-
> Hukkotai 12; ed. A. H. Weiss, 114d).

The midrash begins with a general homily, inferring from the letter
mem in the words מכל אשר לו (= "*of* all that he owns") that a person is
forbidden to dedicate his entire property. The rest of the text effectively repeats the same idea, reaching the same conclusion with regard to each item in the verse (man, beast and land).

The structure of this exposition closely resembles the series of laws
in the Damascus Document. The first law, "Let no man vow to the
altar anything violently acquired," is immediately followed by three
further injunctions, like the number of interpretations in Sifra: "Let
no man sanctify the food of his mouth... Let no man sanctify [   ]...
And if he should sanctify any land that he holds." It seems probable,
therefore, that these three laws should also be associated with the
three words in Lev. 27:29 on which the inferences are based, man,
beast and land. The third law does, in fact, deal explicitly with "land
of holding."

A final comment is in order concerning the meaning of the law,
"Let no man sanctify the food of his mouth." Following Rabin,[21] this
injunction has been explained with reference to the rebuke of Micah, "for this is what he said: 'They trip one another with proscription'." The import of the law, on this basis, is an admonishment not
to consecrate food in such a way as to prevent others benefiting
from it. However, this interpretation involves a difficulty: the

[21] *Zadokite Documents*, 77.
[22] See M. Benovitz, "The Prohibitive Vow in Second Temple and Tannaitic
Literature: Origin and Meaning," *Tarbiz* 64 (1995) 219-21, esp. n. 65 (Hebrew).

pronominal suffix in פיהו "his mouth" must be understood as referring not to the person sanctifying the food but to his or her fellow,
an explanation at variance with the plain meaning of the sentence.[22]
In light of our previous suggestion that the verse is cited not as a
proof-text for this specific law, and the similarity between our text
and the passage from Sifra, one can now retain the plain meaning,
understanding the text as directing one not to consecrate food in
such a way as to have nothing to eat, along the lines of R. Eleazar b.
Azariah's injunction, "a person must have mercy upon his property."

b. *Discussion: part II*

The last part of the passage is concerned, as we have seen, with
one's duty to rebuke one's fellow and not to bear grudges. The content of this law, so central to sectarian literature,[23] has been discussed at length in the scholarly literature, and this particular occurrence has been compared with other occurrences in the literature; I
have no intention of making any further contribution on that count.
My interest here lies in the special place of the law in the Damascus
Document.

The key may be found, rather surprisingly, in the Temple Scroll.
In col. 64 (ll. 6–8) of the scroll we read:

כי יהיה איש רכיל בעמו ומשלים את עמו לגוי נכר ועושה רעה בעמו
ותליתמה אותו על העץ וימת

> If a man is traitor against his people and gives them up to a foreign
> nation, so doing evil to his people, you are to hang him on a tree until
> dead.[24]

This passage of the Temple Scroll is essentially a combination of two
biblical verses: "Do not go about as a talebearer (רכיל) among your
countrymen" (Lev. 19:16) and "If a man is guilty of a capital offense,
and is put to death, and you impale him on a stake..." (Deut. 21:22).
Yadin, and most other scholars, agree that the text refers to a person
who endangers his people by slandering them to the Gentiles.
Moreover, the above translation follows Yadin in interpreting the
passage in a military context, explaining the talebearer (רכיל) as a

[23] See A. Shemesh, "Rebuke, Warning and the Obligation to Testify—in the
Judean Desert Writings and Rabbinic Halakha," *Tarbiz* 66 (1997) 149-68 (Hebrew).
[24] M. O. Wise, M. G. Abegg and E. Cook, *The Dead Sea Scrolls. A New Translation*
(San Francisco: Harper San Francisco, 1996) 490.

AHARON SHEMESH

traitor conveying information to the enemy.[25] Although this particular law deals with the case of a person betraying the community as a whole, it is a plausible assumption that the prohibition לא תלך רכיל was understood as applying to whom who denounces an individual Jew to foreign authorities as well.[26] In other words, the law "Do not go about as a talebearer" is essentially equivalent to that enunciated in the Damascus Document: "Any man who destroys [i.e., dedicates to destruction] a man among men by the statutes of the Gentiles is to be put to death."[27] Thus the sectarian law prescribing the death penalty for a person betraying his fellow to death at Gentile hands is based on the interpretation of two verses: "No human being who has been dedicated can be ransomed: he shall be put to death" (Lev. 27:29) and "Do not go about as a talebearer..." (Lev. 19:16).

In Leviticus, the verse concerning the talebearer is immediately followed by the injunctions to rebuke one's fellow man and to avoid revenge and bearing grudges: "You shall not hate your kinsfolk in your heart. Reprove your kinsman but incur no guilt because of him. You shall not take vengeance or bear a grudge against your countrymen. Love your fellow as yourself: I am the Lord" (19:17-18). It seems quite clear that this particular ordering of the laws in CD 9:2-8 is due to the dual source of the law of the talebearer: Lev. 19:16 and 27:29. Although the text in the Damascus Document was a paraphrase on the law of dedication, "No human being who has been dedicated...," the fact that the law was also associated with "Do not go about as a talebearer" caused the expositions on the subsequent verses to be included in the same passage.

3. *Summary and conclusions*

The two examples discussed in this paper demonstrate that that the Damascus Document contains textual units whose structure is based upon biblical verses, although the latter are not explicitly cited. In their derivation from an interpretation of an entire thematic discus-

---

[25] Y. Yadin, *The Temple Scroll* (Jerusalem: Israel Exploration Society, 1977) 1.286; 2.203.

[26] The reading of this verse in a legal sense rather than as a moral commandment is probably due to the second half of the verse, "Do not stand upon the blood of your fellow" (Lev. 19:16b), which points to the possibility that tale-bearing might result with death.

[27] Schwartz, "Damascus Document," 43, n. 139. On חרמין in the sense of tax collectors, hence חרם = delivering a person up to government officials, see S. Lieberman (in cooperation with Y. Kutscher), "*Haragin, Haramin* and *Taggarin*" *Leshonenu* 27 (1963) 34-39 (Hebrew).

sion in the Torah these passages resemble rabbinic midrash halakhah, despite the fact that their abstract formulation resembles the style of the Mishnah.

The analysis of these examples points to other possible implications regarding the character and structure of sectarian halakhic literature (and I stress halakhic literature rather than the halakhah itself). According to the analysis of CD 16:13 / 9:8 proposed in this paper, the final halakhot in this unit (the obligation to rebuke and the prohibition against taking revenge and bearing a grudge) appear at this point in the document because of the preceding halakhah, "And any man who destroys a man among men by the statutes of the Gentiles is to be put to death." The reason lies in the dual source of this law, Lev. 19:16 and 27:29. If this analysis proves correct, we must contemplate its significance in the larger context of the redaction of CD. Is this an intentional move reflecting the editor's policy of weaving various halakhot into one overall legal web? Perhaps this is no more than an editorial "accident," and the laws of rebuke do not really belong to the framework of the "the laws of donations" but were dragged over by association, due to the double scriptural source of the halakhah of giving a Jew up to foreign authority (9:1). If the latter is correct, we may conclude that the author (or editor) of CD had before him, either in textual form or committed to memory, legal portions ordered according to their scriptural source. In this respect too, then, the development of Qumranic halakhic literature resembles the development of rabbinic literature as it is commonly assumed among scholars. The midrashic form of halakhot adjacent to their biblical source preceded the mishnaic form of abstract halakhot organized by subject matter.

TOWARDS PHYSICAL RECONSTRUCTIONS
OF THE QUMRAN DAMASCUS DOCUMENT SCROLLS

HARTMUT STEGEMANN

Göttingen University, Germany

1. *The textual evidence*

Ten copies of the so-called Damascus Document are identified among the manuscripts from the Qumran caves, 4QD[a-h] (4Q266-273),[1] 5QD (5Q12),[2] and 6QD (6Q15).[3] All of them are very fragmentary. Furthermore, it is impossible to reconstruct totally at least one of the original scrolls without basic support by some external evidence.

Fortunately, such external evidence for the reconstruction of the Damascus Document scrolls from the Qumran caves is provided by the nine folios with eighteen pages from two or three different medieval codices, published by S. Schechter as *Fragments of a Zadokite Work* (1910) and today usually called "The Cairo Damascus Document" (CD).[4] The text of the Qumran fragments basically agrees with the text of CD except for a few minor variants.[5] Most often the variant is a different word or one word more, here or there. In a few cases, one or even two lines of CD are missing in the Qumran fragments, or a Qumran text may be half a line longer than the CD evidence. But the Qumran evidence itself is also sometimes different in this respect if we have two or more copies of the same passage. Nevertheless, basically all copies of this work—whether from Qumran or known by CD—had the same text, except CD 19:1-33 (version B) which, as is well-known, differs greatly from CD 7:5-8:21 (version A); in this case the Qumran evidence fits rather closely CD's version A.[6]

---

[1] Edited by J. M. Baumgarten, *Qumran Cave 4.XIII. The Damascus Document (4Q266-273)* (DJD 18; Oxford: Clarendon, 1996).

[2] Edited by J. T. Milik, in *Les "petites grottes" de Qumrân* (DJDJ 3; Oxford: Clarendon, 1962) 181 and pl. xxxviii.

[3] Edited by M. Baillet in DJDJ 3.128-31 and pl. xxvi.

[4] Folios 1-4 (= A₁) have 21 lines on each page, folios 5-8 (= A₂) 23 lines; therefore, they may represent two different codices. This article refers to the text of CD as prepared by Elisha Qimron in M. Broshi, ed., *The Damascus Document Reconsidered* (Jerusalem: Israel Exploration Society, Shrine of the Book, Israel Museum, 1992) 9-49.

[5] Baumgarten, DJD 18.6f.

[6] Baumgarten, DJD 18.6.

Only with the help of CD could the fragments of 4QD[a-f], 5QD and 6QD be identified as belonging to the same work. The remains of 4QD[g] and 4QD[h] textually overlap with some portions of 4QD[a], 4QD[b], and 4QD[d], which did not survive from the medieval CD codices. They were identified as D-manuscripts only with the help of 4QD[a,b,d].

5QD is just one fragment which corresponds textually to CD 9:7-10. No one can know, independent of other evidence, anything about the appearance of the original scroll.

6QD frgs. 1-4 correspond textually to CD 4:19-21, 5:13-14, 5:18-6:2, and 6:20-7:1. Those fragments are the remains of two subsequent columns of this scroll with 25-26 lines each, while frg. 5 was identified by J. T. Milik and J. M. Baumgarten as corresponding textually to the far distant evidence of 4QD[e] frg. 2 ii 14-19,[7] which is not represented by CD. Also this evidence is too scanty to reconstruct the scroll 6QD in a reliable fashion.

Therefore, we are left solely with the 4QD evidence to reconstruct physically the original structure of the entire Damascus Document.

2. The scroll 4QD[a]

Only one D-manuscript exists whose opening columns, as well as its final columns, have survived, i.e., 4QD[a]. At the same time, no other D-scroll has so many fragments still available. Therefore, 4QD[a] is the principal manuscript for every attempt at physical reconstructions of the D-scrolls.[8]

The start towards an idea of the original disposition of the scroll 4QD[a] is an amalgam of a *textual* reconstruction with the criteria of a *physical* reconstruction: as far as the text of the fragments of 4QD[a] corresponds to the textual evidence of CD, the fragments should be arranged according to these correspondences. At the beginning and at the end of the scroll, this evidence can be supplemented with the help of some fragments of 4QD[b-e]. In this way, the *ten opening* and *ten final columns* of the original scroll can be reconstructed. The remaining problem is the original *middle section* of the scroll 4QD[a], where no CD evidence is available: How many columns were there? How

---

[7] Baumgarten, DJD 18.144-46.
[8] My undertaking the physical reconstruction of scrolls 4QD[a-h] has been extensively supported by Dr. Annette Steudel (since 1991) and by Alexander Maurer (since 1994) at the University of Göttingen.

should the surviving fragments of 4QD[a] and the textually corresponding evidence of 4QD[b-h] be arranged in this section? Only insofar as answers to these questions become available can we know about the original textual structure of the original middle section of 4QD[a] and the overall compositional structure of the Damascus Document.

Another fundamental starting point for the physical reconstruction of 4QD[a] is some distinctive damage, which was caused in different ways to the still-unopened scroll in its cave.

In the final sheets of the manuscript there is a gap from the top of the columns down to line 8. In frg. 11, this kind of gap is reduced to a rectangular hole ranging five times from line 2 to line 4. This hole was eaten into the scroll by some helpful little beast which had entered from the top of the closed scroll—note the extensions of the first and second rectangular hole to the top—and hollowed out through several layers without penetrating to the innermost layers of the scroll.[9] The distances between these holes clearly increase from left to right, starting with 3.10 cm. and expanding to 3.35–3.60–3.85 cm. The real distances may differ by half a millimeter as the hole must not have been straight to the axis of the scroll but, perhaps, in a slanting direction. Nevertheless, this evidence demonstrates (a) that when the scroll was damaged this way it was still rolled up with the beginning of the manuscript on the outside and its end inside, and (b) that the distances between these holes increased from left to right, a little more than 2 mm. from turn to turn in this scroll.[10]

On the other hand, the fragments of the opening columns of this scroll clearly show again corresponding patterns of damage. Furthermore, all measurements at the beginning of the scroll are dependent upon the width of the text of CD 1:1-21 filled into the gap of 4QD[a] frg. 2 i 6-25. These reconstructions result in a width of 4QD[a] col. ii of about 12.5 cm., while the distances between corre-

---

[9] Baumgarten, DJD 18, pls. xii-xiv. Similar evidence is found in the 11QPs[a] scroll, where another little beast entered the scroll from its shaft in the middle and left the scroll towards the bottom in cols. xv-xiv; see J. A. Sanders, ed., *The Psalms Scroll of Qumran Cave 11 (11QPs[a])* (DJDJ 4; Oxford: Clarendon, 1965) pls. x-xvii. These holes are 11 to 12 cm. from the top of the scroll. Their distance increases from 2.5 cm. at the end of the scroll to 12.5 cm. in cols. xv-xiv.

[10] A problem for distance measurements or calculations based on this kind of physical evidence is the fact that the thickness of the leather of the scroll may differ from sheet to sheet. The result is that those distances from turn to turn of the scroll are sometimes a little shorter, sometimes a little longer, than at one specific place, where one can measure them exactly.

sponding patterns of damage may still range from at least 13 cm. to about 15 cm. at most. Finally, the measurement of the *true* distances between corresponding patterns of damage in this part of the scroll remains dependent on the physical reconstruction of the *entire* scroll, especially its original middle section.

3. *The opening columns i-ix of 4QD*[a]

As noted above, a physical reconstruction of the ten opening columns of 4QD[a] is possible only with textual help from CD 1-8 and 19-20. The presentation of the evidence by J. M. Baumgarten in his edition proves to be basically correct except for two findings:

1. Like almost all other columns, cols. iii and iv should have had 25 lines each, not only 24 lines.[11] Col. iv was probably followed by a sewing seam, and in this scroll the columns before sewings are often smaller than the others.[12] This fact was neglected by the textual arrangements in the edition.

2. At the top of col. x, frg. 4b, lines 1-2, clearly correspond textually to CD 20:33-34, followed by a word of line 3 which goes beyond the evidence of CD. The shape of this fragment resembles rather closely the shape of the left edge of frg. 3 iv(a) with lines 1-4 of its column. Therefore, frg. 4b 1-3 should be labeled as col. x 1-3, not lines 7-9 as in the edition.[13]

As correctly noted in the edition, the parallel text of CD 1:1ff starts in 4QD[a] at the end of col. ii, line 6 (frg. 2 ii 6). The additional text of lines 1-5, as well as the text of col. i, lines 20-25, is also attested by 4QD[b] frg. 1 1-8 and/or by 4QD[c] frg. 1 1-8 which, at the same time, bridge the gap between cols. i and ii of 4QD[a] and add some words to its textual evidence.[14]

4QD[a] frgs. 1 a-b evidently represent the opening column of the whole manuscript with a broad margin of about 4 cm., which still includes the reinforcing tab of the scroll. How frgs. c-f might be included in this column will be discussed at the end of this article. In every case, the next column (frg. 2 i) starts with a sewing. Therefore, 4QD[a] is one of the very few Qumran manuscripts where the open-

---

[11] See Baumgarten, DJD 18.36-40 and the note on p. 24: "Number of lines per column: 24-25." One line of text should be added to the bottom part of frg. 2 ii, while the column of frg. 2 iii was still narrower.
[12] In 4QD[a] the narrowest column is frg. 9 iii (only about 6 cm.). Unfortunately, the original sewing at its left edge is now lost.
[13] Baumgarten, DJD 18.45-47 and pls. iv-v.
[14] Baumgarten, DJD 18.31-34. Unfortunately, the text of 4QD[c] frg. 1, line 1, is missing in the presentation of 4QD[a] frg. 1, line 25, on p. 32.

ing sheet of the scroll had just one column. Other examples of this kind are 4QH[a] and 4QH[e].[15]

In 4QD[a], only cols. i-iii contain fragments of the manuscript which still combine the top parts of the original columns with their bottom parts. Already in these columns a cut between the upper and lower parts of the columns is visible—the best evidence is col. iii between lines 13 and 14 (frg. 2 ii 13f)—caused by the fastening string of the scroll.[16] Of cols. iv-x, except col. ix, a pile of fragments from the top parts of those columns still survived, mainly representing the text of their lines 1-6; only in col. vi, lines 1-13 remain. From the bottom parts of those columns, a pile of fragments of cols. iv and vi-vii survived, and all of the fragments represent some text of the original lines 17-25. Lines 14-16 are missing completely in cols. iv-x.[17] From col. vii to col. x, textual evidence is missing after lines 1-6.

The text corresponding to CD 1-8 and 19-20 once ended in 4QD[a] at the top of col. x, line 3.

Those fragments of 4QD[b-f] which come from the opening columns of the work as comprised by 4QD[a] i 1-x 3, or by CD 1-8 and 19-20, are[18]:

4QD[b] (4Q267) frgs. 1-3, which may represent cols. i, vii, and xi of its scroll, while the corresponding text of CD 1-8 and 19-20 may have ended about the middle of its col. xii. The surviving fragments seem to belong to a pile from the middle to the bottom of their original columns.

4QD[c] (4Q268) frg. 1, the text of which corresponds to 4QD[a] i 25-ii 14. According to my calculations there may have been only 22 lines in the opening col. i of this scroll, not 24 lines as suggested in the edition.[19] The shape of this large fragment is characteristic for the opening layers of a decayed, originally rather large, scroll.[20]

4QD[d] (4Q269) frgs. 1-6 represent a pile of fragments from the original top lines of their columns.

---

[15] To be published by E. Schuller in a forthcoming DJD volume.

[16] This kind of physical evidence was first noticed by Stephen Pfann. Its observation is often extremely helpful for the reconstruction of the opening columns, or even sheets, of the original scrolls. See below, n. 47.

[17] This damage was clearly caused by the string; see n. 16 above.

[18] For complete details, see Baumgarten, DJD 18.95-173 and pls. xviii-xxxvii.

[19] Baumgarten, DJD 18.115 and 119.

[20] The bulk of this scroll disappeared from Cave 4 except for the small frgs. 2 and 3. Regarding the fate of the scrolls once hidden in Cave 4, see H. Stegemann, *The Library of Qumran. On the Essenes, Qumran, John the Baptist and Jesus* (Grand Rapids: Eerdmans, 1998) 61-64 and 74f. No one knows whether the bulk of scroll 4QD[c] was (a) taken from Cave 4 by its medieval visitor and now lost, (b) destroyed by him, all other fragments meanwhile blown by the wind down to Wadi Qumran, or (c) discovered by Bedouins in 1952 but never reached the museums.

4QD^e (4Q270) frgs. 1 i-ii: the very poor remains of the opening part of this scroll may come from the top lines of two consecutive columns with a sewing at the left edge, perhaps cols. iii-iv of the original scroll.

4QD^f (4Q271): only one small fragment with text corresponding to CD 5:18-20 is identified within the opening part of the scroll. This fragment comes from the bottom of its column.

4. *The final ten columns of 4QD^a*

The final ten columns of 4QD^a include frgs. 8 i, ii, iii; 9 i, ii, iii; 10 i, ii, and 11. Those fragments are obviously numbered this way as they represent the remains of four different sheets of this scroll, even if frgs. 10 ii and 11 are still physically connected.[21]

The text of frgs. 8 i - 10 i corresponds to CD 9-16. Frg. 8 ii 1-8 corresponds to the text of CD 16:17-23, while frg. 8 ii 8-10 continues with the text of CD 9:1-2. This is the same kind of evidence we encounter in 4QD^e frg. 6 ii. Therefore, there is no longer any doubt that the original sequence of pages in CD was 15-16, followed by 9-14.

4QD^a frgs. 10 i-ii and 11 clearly have preserved the upper margin of the scroll. The same evidence is correctly attributed by the editor to frg. 9 i, ii, iii, even if this becomes certain only by comparing the shapes of those fragments to the shapes of frgs. 10 i-ii and 11. In contrast, after the ten lines of frgs. 8 ii, iii, the edition suggests a bottom margin,[22] which should include the evidence of the ten lines of frg. 8 i, as both columns are still physically joined. But there is no need to postulate a bottom margin in those columns. At least a textual reconstruction of the final columns is possible which starts with frg. 8 i 1 (= CD 15:10), in the *second* line of the ninth column, before the end of the scroll, while the parallel text to CD 15:1-10 (about the middle of that line) was in the final eleven lines of the column (now lost) preceding it in 4QD^a.[23]

In the physical reconstruction of the ten opening and ten final columns of 4QD^a, the sheet represented by frgs. 10 i-ii is the only one with two columns, while all other sheets have three columns, ex-

---

[21] See Baumgarten, DJD 18, pls. xiii and xiv.

[22] Baumgarten, DJD 18.65f.

[23] I.e., only the final nine columns of this scroll are at present documented by some material evidence, while a tenth column before is only *postulated* to have once included a text corresponding to CD 15:1-10 in its lines 15-25.

cept the opening sheet (frg. 1) and the concluding sheet (frg. 11), which both had only one column.

There is no need here to discuss in detail further aspects of the physical reconstruction of the ten final columns of 4QDᵃ, as Baumgarten's edition is basically correct in this respect. Only the corresponding evidence of 4QDᵇ⁻ᶠ should additionally be listed[24]:

4QDᵇ (4Q267) has several—sometimes composite—fragments with text corresponding to CD 9-14 + the original end of the work, which are labeled in the edition as frgs. 9 i-iv. No top or bottom margin is preserved, but the shapes of those fragments demonstrate that they formed a pile in the scroll in the middle parts of their columns down to the bottom parts. Frg. 9 i comes from the left edge of its column; the next column is lost. Frgs. 9 ii-v represent an original sheet of the scroll with four columns, sewings being attested both at the right edge of frg. 9 ii and at the edge of left frg. 9 v, with an extremely broad margin of about 3.5 cm. before the sewing. No fragments are attributed to the next two columns, frg. 9 vi belonging to the *third* column after frg. 9 v. This means that the six columns of frg. 9 i-vi cover the space of nine columns of the original scroll (only the final column of the scroll is missing afterwards); the text of 4QDᵇ frg. 9 vi 1-5 corresponds to the text of 4QDᶜ frg. 7 i 11-13.

4QDᵈ (4Q269) has four—only in the case of frg. 11 i-ii composite—fragments, which represent the six final columns of this scroll. Frg. 10 was textually not identified in the edition. Nevertheless, the text of frg. 10 i 5-7 corresponds to CD 13:5-7, the text of frg. 10 ii 1-12 to CD 13:16-14:7.[25] Frg. 11 i 1-9, with text corresponding to CD 14:18-22, has no "top margin,"[26] but comes from lines 7-15 or 8-16 of the next column. Afterwards, one column is missing, while frg. 11 ii 1-3 represents the beginnings of lines 1-3 of the next column. The ends of lines 2 and 5 of this column are preserved on an additional frg. 15; the ends of several lines of the final column of this scroll are on an additional frg. 16. 4QDᵈ frgs. 15 and 16 were not included in the Baumgarten edition. They were found only after the publication of this edition, on inventory plate no. 75 of the Rockefeller Museum together with other still unidentified fragments.[27] 4QDᵈ is now the

---

[24] For complete details, see Baumgarten, DJD 18.105-83, pls. xx-xxxix.

[25] H. Stegemann, "More Identified Fragments of 4QDᵈ (4Q269)," *RevQ* 18 (1997-98) 497-509, esp. 498-501. See also 269. 4QDamascus Documentᵈ frgs. 10, 11, 15, 16 (DJD 36; Oxford: Clarendon, forthcoming).

[26] This "top margin" is postulated in Baumgarten, DJD 18.134. Instead, there may have been a further *vacat* in the line above.

[27] Stegemann, "More Identified Fragments," 502-8, with a photograph of the additional frgs. 15 and 16 on 509, pl. i.

third D-manuscript after 4QD^a and 4QD^e, the final column of which is still attested.[28]

4QD^e (4Q270) originally had twenty-one lines in each column, but almost the same amount of text in each column as 4QD^a with its twenty-five lines, as the smaller script of 4QD^e occupies less space than the hand of 4QD^a. What is labeled in the edition as frgs. 6 i-v and 7 i-ii are the remains of the nine final columns of this scroll, three columns now missing between frgs. 6 v and 7 i. Diverging from the arrangement of those fragments in the edition, I prefer to transfer the small fragment with the ends of the lines, frg. 6 i 20-21 (= CD 15:4-5) and the beginnings of the lines on frg. 6 ii 20-21 (= CD 16:7-8) from the bottom part of the scroll to the top of the following columns, i.e., now frg. 6 ii 5-6 and 6 iii 5-6, while the two pieces of frg. 6 ii 17-19 should become frg. 6 iii 1-3. This way the three pieces of now frg. 6 ii 5-10 move down in their column to become frg. 6 ii 9-14. The results are: (a) there is no longer an independent column represented by frg. 6 i and (b) the corresponding text of CD 15:1 now starts close to the beginning of 4QD^e 6 ii 2. Another outcome is that there are only nine columns from "frg. 6 i" to the end of the scroll, not ten columns as in the edition. The material evidence for this part of 4QD^e is that only frg. 7 i represents the remains of all twenty-one lines of the original column. Frg. 7 ii provides the very end of the scroll. From the columns before frg. 7 i-ii, a pile of smaller fragments survived with the top lines of frg. 6 ii, two fragments of the middle part of frg. 6 ii, large fragments from the middle part down to the bottom of frgs. 6 iii-v and, perhaps, two small fragments from about lines 14-16 of the original columns frg. 6 vi and frg. 6 viii, without any remains of the original column frg. 6 vii.

4QD^f (4Q271) had also, like 4QD^e, twenty-one lines in each column. There are two composite fragments with text corresponding to CD 15-16 and 9-14 or to the ten final columns of 4QD^a. The very poor remains of frg. 4 i overlap with some evidence in CD 15:2-10, while the text parallel to CD 15:1 may have started not far from the beginning in the line frg. 4 i 5. Frg. 4 ii 1-17 corresponds to CD 15:20-16:18, the final lines 18-21 of this column being lost. Left of frg. 4 i-ii, two columns are completely lost. The next column 5 i has a clear top margin as well as a clear bottom margin and twenty-one lines between, with text corresponding to CD 11:4-12:6. Of the column represented by frg. 5 ii, only the beginnings of lines 2-5, 9 and

---

[28] See the final columns of 4QD^a and 4QD^e in Baumgarten, DJD 18, pls. xiv and xxxv.

20-21 survived with a few letters corresponding to the text of CD 12:8-11, 12:16, and 13:5-6. Left of frg. 5 i-ii, four columns are lost up to the end of the scroll without any surviving fragments.

5. *The middle section of 4QD^a*

At the right edge of the final nine columns of 4QD^a a turn of the scroll occupied a space of about 8.4 cm. At the left edge of the ten opening columns of 4QD^a this distance was between about 11 cm. and 13 cm. There should have been about 170 cm. of the scroll, or about twelve columns, between these two parts of the scroll, their original text not being preserved by CD 1-8 + 19-20 or 15-16 + 9-14.

The available evidence for the physical reconstruction of this original middle section of 4QD^a are its frgs. 4(c-d); 5 i-ii; 6 i-iv and 7 i-iii, which altogether may represent up to nine additional columns, and most of the still unidentified frgs. 12-75 of this scroll.

The additional evidence from the other D-scrolls is as follows:

4QD^b (4Q267) frgs. 4, 5 i-iii, 6, 7, and 8, and most of the unidentified frgs. 10-18.
4QD^c (4Q268) frg. 2 and, perhaps, frg. 3.
4QD^d (4Q269) frgs. 7, 8 i-ii, and 9, and the unidentified frgs. 12-14.
4QD^e (4Q270) frgs. 2 i-ii, 3 i-iii, 4, and 5, and the unidentified frgs. 8-12.
4QD^f (4Q271) frgs. 2 and 3.
4QD^g (4Q272) frg. 1 i-ii, and the unidentified frgs. 2 and 3.
4QD^h (4Q273) frgs. 1, 2, 3, 4 i-ii, 5, and 6, and the unidentified frgs. 7-9.
6QD (6Q15) frg. 5.

The start towards a physical reconstruction of the middle part of scroll 4QD^a is rather easy and already convincingly done by J. M. Baumgarten.[29] Frgs. 5 i-ii (a-b) and 6 i-ii (except the minor frgs. a-e) represent the top and middle parts of four subsequent columns with a sewing between frgs. 5 ii and 6 i. This sequence is well attested (a) by the shapes of those fragments, which were caused by some damage to the scroll, and (b) by the papyrus 4QD^h: the evidence of its— not composite!—frg. 4 i-ii corresponds textually to 4QD^a frgs. 5 ii and 6 i.[30] Furthermore, 4QD^g frg. 1 i-ii overlaps with 4QD^a frg. 6 i-

---

[29] Baumgarten, DJD 18.47-57 and pls. vi-vii.
[30] Baumgarten, DJD 18.49-54 and 195-97. Cf. pl. xli.

ii,[31] and the two distant frgs. 5 ii-iii of 4QD[b] textually correspond to
4QD[a] frg. 5 i-ii.[32] Finally, 4QD[d] frg. 7, 10-13 textually overlaps with
4QD[a] frg. 6 i 1-4.[33] On the other hand, there is no textual overlap of
4QD[a] frgs 5 i-ii and 6 i-ii—or further evidence from the related fragments of 4QD[b], 4QD[g], and 4QD[h]—with any evidence of the other
D-manuscripts, especially also no overlap with 4QD[e] and 4QD[f].

If one tries to establish the proper placement of the four columns
of 4QD[a] frgs. 5 i-ii and 6 i-ii in the original scroll, there are two
basic problems:

1. The shapes of the two frgs. 5 i and 5 ii are very similar,[34] but
the true distance between them is unknown. No parallel text bridges
the gap at the left edge of the first fragment. There are a few letters
from the ends of five lines, most of which were tentatively combined
with the other text of frg. 5 i in the edition.[35] But this gap could have
been wider. Therefore, one cannot know how far frgs. 5 i and ii
would have been from one another in the scroll.

2. On the surface of 4QD[a] frg. 5 ii, there is a clear impression of
the sewing, which is well preserved at the right edge of frg. 6 i, visible from line 2 in front of the word פצל down to line 14 in front of
the word וזה.[36] But one cannot measure precisely the true distance
between that sewing and its impression on the surface of frg. 5 ii, as
the left half of this column is lost. Even if the text at the ends of lines
1-2 can be partially completed with the help of 4QD[b] frg. 5 iii 3-5,[37]
there are still several opportunities for guess work. Furthermore, no
one can know how wide the left margin of this column would have
been[38] or how far this margin may have been used by the scribe to
fill in some letters. All these problems together leave a range of up to
3 cm., more or less, for speculation, which basically prevents the use
of this evidence as a starting point for exact measurements.

In the huge mass of the above-listed fragments which contain evidence for the original middle section of the Damascus Document,
there is only one opportunity to find the true distance for one turn of
a scroll, namely, the large piece 4QD[a] frg. 6 i with a sewing at its

---

[31] Baumgarten, DJD 18.52-56 and 188-91.
[32] Baumgarten, DJD 18.47-51 and 101-2.
[33] Baumgarten, DJD 18.52-53 and 129-30.
[34] Baumgarten, DJD 18, pl. vi. The left edges, especially, of both larger fragments have the same kind of shape.
[35] Baumgarten, DJD 18.47f.
[36] Baumgarten, DJD 18, pl. vi.
[37] Baumgarten, DJD 18.49-51.
[38] The only evidence of the left margins of columns before sewings in 4QD[a] are
frg. 8 iii on pl. x (2 cm.) and frg. 10 ii on pl. xiii (1.2 cm.?).

right edge.[39] The preserved length of this fragment is up to 15 cm. Because the scroll 4QD[a] was rolled with the beginning of the text outside and the end inside, there should be an impression of the sewing on the back of this fragment at a distance greater than 8.4 cm., but less than 13 cm.[40] The exact measurement of this distance would allow one to place that fragment in the original scroll.

Unfortunately, 4QD[a] frg. 6 i had disappeared from the Rockefeller Museum in Jerusalem already in the summer of 1990, when Prof. Baumgarten started his work there on the original 4QD manuscripts.[41] At the same time he entrusted me with the physical reconstruction of those scrolls,[42] but I could not finish this task without the original of that missing fragment. After we discussed this problem with Dr. Magen Broshi, former curator of the Shrine of the Book, on the occasion of the Third International Symposium of the Orion Center in Jerusalem, 4-8 February, 1998, Magen Broshi succeeded in finding this fragment in the Israel Museum and bringing it back to the Rockefeller Museum. There I studied it in summer, 1998, and I found the impression of the sewing on its reverse side, just 11.0 cm. distant from the sewing itself.[43]

The first result of this measurement is that the distance between the sewing at the right edge of 4QD[a] frg. 6 i and the impression of

---

[39] Baumgarten, DJD 18, pl. vii.

[40] For these calculations, see above p. 185.

[41] Personal communication from Prof. J. M. Baumgarten, 1991.

[42] In July, 1990, in Jerusalem, Prof. J. M. Baumgarten graciously gave me photocopies of all plates of 4QD[a-h] and of the transcriptions of their texts by J. T. Milik. I used those materials in strict confidence, i.e., I never quoted them or revealed their contents to anyone except Dr. Annette Steudel and Alexander Maurer (cf. n. 8 above) with special permission from Prof. Baumgarten. Only now, after the official publication of the 4QD evidence in DJD 18, 1996, I begin to quote also from the manuscripts of Milik; see below 194-96, notes 74-77.

[43] This example may demonstrate the importance of the impressions of sewings for the physical reconstruction of scrolls. Unfortunately, the reverse sides of the scrolls or fragments are very rarely published as they are usually blank. Therefore, only examination of the originals allows one to check this physical evidence. The best example of impressions on the inscribed *surface* of scrolls is the Temple Scroll; see Y. Yadin, *Megillat ha-Miqdaš* (Jerusalem: Israel Exploration Society, 1977) vol. 3 (Hebrew) = Y. Yadin, *The Temple Scroll* (Jerusalem: Israel Exploration Society, Shrine of the Book, 1983) pls. 33-82. The distance between the sewings and their impressions to their right ranges from 3.2 cm. (col. 66) to 13.8 cm (col. 18). Often humidity crept into the scroll along the sewings and destroyed the layers of the scroll vertically, before and after the sewings, e.g., pl. 33 (col. 18), pl. 40 (col. 25), and pl. 47 (col. 32). The discovery of such specific damage on the back or on the surface of fragments often helps to determine their original distance from sewings, even if those sewings are now lost or were never published, because "unwritten evidence" was not thought worthy preservation. Much unwritten evidence from the Qumran caves is now lost.

the sewing on the surface of frg. 5 ii[44] must have been about 11.2 cm. This result helps to establish the width of the gap to the left of frg. 5 ii independent of 4QD^b frg. 5 iii. Furthermore, the distance between corresponding shapes of damage in 4QD^a frgs. 5 i and 5 ii should now be about 11.3 cm., i.e., 1.8 cm. more than on pl. vi of Baumgarten's edition, where this distance is only 9.5 cm. This means that the gap between the right piece of frg. 5 i and the ends of several lines on the left piece was 1.8 cm. broader than calculated by the editor.[45]

The second result is that (a) the four columns of 4QD^a frg. 5 i-ii and frg. 6 i-ii should follow rather closely the ten opening columns of this scroll and that (b) in col. i of 4QD^a one turn of the scroll occupied about 14 cm., not much more or less.

The final conclusions require further calculations and measurements. At present I make the following suggestions:

1. The four columns represented by 4QD^a frgs. 5 i-ii and 6 i-ii were cols. xii-xv of the original scroll.

2. Frg. 6 iii 1-10, which overlaps textually with 4QD^b frg. 6 and with 4QD^c frg. 3 ii, may be the top part of the original col. xvi. The sewing at its left edge marks the end of the sixth sheet of this scroll. This sheet had three columns like all the previous sheets, with the exception of the opening sheet which had only one column.

3. The shape of frg. 6 iv 19 is rather similar to the shape of frg. 6 iii.[46] Therefore, it may represent the top of the next column, col. xvii. But its final position in this scroll is still dependent on the results of the complete physical reconstruction of 4QD^a.

In the physical reconstruction of the original scroll 4QD^a, there is no surviving evidence from the bottom parts of its columns except in cols. i-iii and vi-vii. The top parts of the columns have survived, more or less, in cols. i-iii, v-vi, viii, x, xii-xvii and in all nine final columns except the fourth. Physical evidence from the original middle parts of the columns, i.e., around lines 9-16, is preserved only in cols. i-iii, xii-xvii, from the top down to line 16 at most (frg. 6 i), and in the six final columns, from the top down to line 20 in the final column (frg. 11).[47]

---

[44] See n. 36 above.

[45] 4QD^a frg. 5 i 9-18 in Baumgarten, DJD 18.47-49.

[46] Baumgarten, DJD 18, pl. viii. Cf. also the similar shape of the top part of frg. 6 ii on pl. vii.

[47] Stephen Pfann states in this edition, "Damage due to the pressure of the tied thong can be traced the entire length of the scroll"; see Baumgarten, DJD 18.25. But it is difficult to find the impression of the thong in the middle part of the scroll or still in the final columns, which were too far from the beginning of the scroll.

Most of the still dislocated fragments of 4QD^a may come from the original top and middle parts of several columns of the middle part of the scroll, and less probably from their original bottom sections, but it is impossible to place them only physically. Therefore, the remaining evidence of the scrolls 4QD^{b,d,e,f}, together with the physical reconstructions of those scrolls, must help to place them, particularly the evidence of 4QD^e. Most of the still dislocated fragments of 4QD^a may belong to its cols. x-xi or to the five columns between 4QD^a col. xvii (frg. 6 iv) and the final nine columns apart from the bottom part of the preceding column, where the text parallel to CD 15:1ff. may have started at about line 15.[48]

6. *The middle section of 4QD^e*

There are five larger composite fragments of 4QD^e which must belong to the original middle section of this scroll, according to their numbering in the edition: frgs. 2 i-ii, 3 ii, 3 iii, 4, and 5. The additional frg. 3 i is a special case, which will be discussed below.

All these fragments evidently come from a pile.[49] Frgs. 2 i-ii and 4 have text from the tops of their columns down to the bottom lines. Frgs. 2 i-ii, 3 ii, 3 iii, and 5 also have preserved the bottom margins of their columns. Unfortunately, no fragment of the other D-scrolls overlaps with frg. 2 i-ii, while frg. 4 may have one word in common with the still unplaced frg. 12 of 4QD^a. On the other hand, the smaller frgs. 3 ii, 3 iii and 5 overlap textually with several fragments of other D-manuscripts, which complete their modest evidence to almost full columns. The only clear textual overlap of all these fragments with the already placed 4QD^a evidence is frg. 3 ii = 4QD^a frg. 6 iii,[50] which was (still hypothetically) col. xvi of the original scroll.

A special case in several respects is 4QD^e frg. 3 i. In my opinion, the two pieces of this fragment are wrongly put together in the edition, the left piece being better placed immediately at the right edge of the right piece.[51] The second line on this fragment is a dry-line without any script.[52] The third line was written with red ink, which

---

[48] According to Pfann, "Minimum number of columns in scroll: 31"; see Baumgarten, DJD 18.24. This may well have been the true original number: 9 sheets with 3 columns, 1 sheet with 2 columns, plus 2 sheets with 1 column each.

[49] Baumgarten, DJD 18, pls. xxvii-xxxi.

[50] For complete details, see Baumgarten, DJD 18.142-55.

[51] Cf. Baumgarten, DJD 18.147 and pl. xxviii.

[52] The photograph in DJD 18 does not show this dry-line but it is quite clear on the original.

is not visible on the photograph in the edition. To my eyes, the preserved text seems to be something like] ° אַרְצֹוּת [קוּת]הֹ[. In every
case, this red rubric belongs to the heading for some laws on agriculture in the following section, as we have them in frg. 3 ii. This is
the reason why the editor placed frg. 3 i in front of frg. 3 ii. A further problem is that the fifth line of this fragment is not followed by
a bottom margin, as noted in the edition,[53] but again by an unwritten dry-line.[54] Therefore, line 3 may represent the heading of the
subsequent section, while lines 4-5 are the remains of an introductory passage, followed by the corpus of those laws after a *vacat* in line 6
or after a full *vacat* line. Perhaps frg. 3 i belongs to the same column
as frg. 3 ii, a little above its lines 12-21. But the true position of frg.
3 i in this scroll is still dependent on further considerations.

The main problem of the exact placement of all these fragments
in the original scroll is the position of frg. 2 i-ii with its "catalogue of
transgressors" or "of transgressions,"[55] followed by a sapiential
rubric in frg. 2 ii 19ff which resembles other rubrics of this kind
(4QD[a] i 5ff., CD 1:1ff., 2:2ff., and 2:14ff.). This *textual* evidence is behind the idea of the editor to place 4QD[e] frg. 2 i-ii at the end of the
"Admonitions" CD 1-8 + 19-20, hypothetically even identifying a
few letter traces at the ends of the lines of frg. 2 i 1-3 with words of
CD 20:32-33.[56]

In this case, the text corresponding to 4QD[e] frg. 2 i-ii must have
been in 4QD[a] in cols. x-xi, immediately followed by the evidence of
col. xii (= frg. 5 i). This placement is favoured also by two further
considerations:

1. The shape of the bottom part of frg. 2 i-ii is very similar to the
shape of frg. 3 ii, which overlaps textually with 4QD[a] frg. 6 iii (= col.
xvi of that scroll), while the bottom parts of 4QD[e] frgs. 3 iii and 5
are less similar to it, i.e., those fragments should be placed *left* of frg.
3 ii in 4QD[e].[57]

2. If frg. 2 i-ii had been in the scroll together with frgs. 3 iii, 4 and
5, to the *left* of frg. 3 ii, one would need at least eight columns for
them as, in this case, the textual overlaps with the other 4QD-
manuscripts and the transition to the final columns would require at

---

[53] Baumgarten, DJD 18.147.
[54] Again the photograph does not show this dry-line but on the original it is evident.
[55] This section is called "Catalogue of Transgressors" in DJD 18.3 and "catalogue of transgressions" in DJD 18.143.
[56] Baumgarten, DJD 18.142.
[57] See the shapes of those fragments in Baumgarten, DJD 18, pls. xxvii-xxxi.

least three more columns without surviving 4QD^e evidence.[58] Even if the columns, which are represented by frgs. 4 and 5, were relatively small, this would be too much text for the approximately five columns of text after frg. 6 iii (= col. 16) in 4QD^a.

The present state towards my physical reconstruction of the original middle section of scroll 4QD^e is the following:

1 The middle section of this scroll started with the two columns of frg. 2 i-ii, which continue the text of CD 20.
2 Afterwards there were three columns without surviving 4QD^e evidence, followed by
3 the two columns of frgs. 3 ii-iii with frg. 3 i perhaps on top of frg. 3 ii,
4 subsequently at least one missing column, followed by
5 a column represented by frg. 5,
6 subsequently again at least one missing column, followed by
7 a column represented by frg. 4, perhaps immediately followed by
8 the final columns starting with the text corresponding to CD 15:1 ff.

But this preliminary arrangement may still be modified in the future.[59]

7. The first column of 4QD^a

For the first time 4QD^a provides us, together with 4QD^b frg. 1 and 4QD^c frg. 1, with the original opening of the Damascus Document,[60] which was not preserved by CD. But the textual evidence of this opening column is rather poor, and the edition leaves us with two basic problems:

---

[58] Those three "empty" columns would be (a) the column left of frg. 3 ii, (b) a column between frgs. 5 and 4 to its left, and (c) a column between frg. 2 ii and the evidence of frgs. 6 i-ii (= CD 15-16).

[59] At the Third International Symposium of the Orion Center, 1998, I still discussed possibilities for the placement of 4QD^e frg. 2 i-ii other than at the end of the "Admonitions" overlapping with CD 20, mainly because of the shape of frg. 2 i-ii which resembles, in several respects, the shape of frg. 7 i; see DJD 18, pls. xxvii and xxxiv. At the same time, only these two fragments of 4QD^e have text from the top to the bottom of the scroll, including bottom margins. Frgs. 6 i-6 v come from two sheets with 4 + 3 = 7 columns, which have a kind of leather different from the sheets before and after them and, therefore, were damaged in different ways. Therefore, I favoured a placement of 4QD^e frg. 2 i-ii as close as possible to the *final* columns of this scroll. After I was able to measure the impression of the sewing on the back of 4QD^a frg. 6 i in summer 1998 (see above, 187), I dismissed all other possibilities for placing 4QD^e frg. 2 i-ii; instead I now agree to their placing in the edition by Prof. Baumgarten at the very *beginning* of the original middle section of the Damascus Document. Consequently, the corresponding text in 4QD^a was in its cols. x-xi.

[60] Baumgarten, DJD 18.31-34 and pl. i.

1. How wide was the gap between the distant fragments a and b?

2. Is the combination of the additional frgs. c-f correct, and do they really belong to lines 9-14 of this column?[61]

Already the present, still preliminary, state of the physical reconstruction of this scroll allows us to solve these problems at least partially.

1. The measurement of the impression of the sewing at the right edge of frg. 6 i on the back of that fragment resulted in a distance of 11.0 cm.[62] The distance between this sewing and the very beginning of the scroll was consequently about 185 cm. Therefore, in col. i, one turn of the scroll occupied 14 cm. or a little less, and the length of the lines in the top part of col. i was 10.5 cm., not only 9.5 cm. as suggested by the photograph in the edition, i.e., one must add 1 cm. to the gap between frgs. a and b on pl. i in the edition.

2. In the edition there is no hint at all as to why Milik once combined frgs. c-f and why he attributed them to col. i. The easiest explanation is that all of them stuck somewhere to the back of frg. 2 i-ii, and as the text of those additional fragments does not exist in CD 1:1-3:6, Milik may have allotted them to the new text of col. i.

But there are still more problems. On the one hand, I doubt that the join of frg. c to frg. e is correct: the distance between the two top lines of frg. c is considerably smaller than the distance between the two bottom lines of frg. e,[63] and the resulting combined text לדבר דר אל נב] is at least rather strange, if not impossible. Also the distant join of frg. f to frg. e seems to be optional. Frgs. c and f may have been close to frgs. d and e on the back of frg. 2 i-ii, but not exactly in the position which is suggested in the edition.

Otherwise, the join of frg. d with frg. e is convincing.[64] Moreover, the shape of this combination resembles very closely the shape of the left bottom edge of the upper part of frg. 2 ii 9-14, as well as the shape of the left part of the remnants of lines 10-14 in frg. 2 i, just one turn of the scroll before.[65] Frgs. d + e should be the next evidence of this pile, one turn of the scroll to the right, the right edge of frg. d being about 17 mm. distant from the right margin of col. i. Last but not least, the bottom of frg. e was clearly cut by the outer string of the scroll, like the upper part of frg. 2 ii within line 14; this

[61] Baumgarten states, "The placement of these four fragments, combined by Milik, is uncertain. They may belong to the lacuna between lines 9-14 of the first column"; Baumgarten, DJD 18.34.
[62] See above, 187.
[63] Baumgarten, DJD 18, pl. i.
[64] See the letters bridging frgs. d and e in line 3.
[65] Baumgarten, DJD 18, pl. ii.

very specific evidence[66] confirms that the five lines of frgs. d + e are to be identified with lines 9-13 of 4QD[a] col. i,[67] as Milik did, probably when he found frgs. d + e on the back of frg. 2 i.

The hand of the scribe of 4QD[a] varies greatly (see, e.g., frg. 5 i [a-b] compared to frg. 5 i [c-d]).[68] In col. i, there were usually about 45 scribal units (i.e., letters or spaces between words) in each line, with a few more letters in the opening lines as the scribe began to write relatively narrowly in line 1 and more broadly already in lines 2-4.[69]

The original text of 1QD[a] col. 1 1-13 may have been similar to the following version, which includes some supplementation[70]:

(50)	[זה מדרש התורה האחרון לכול בֹֹן]ֹנֹי אור להנֹזֹר מדרכֹנֹי חושך]	1
(46)	[ולהתהלך תמים על פי התורה]עֹד תום יֹמועד פקודה בקֹץֹ	2
(48)	[הרשעה כי בחרון אפו ישמ]ֹיד אל אתכול מעשיה להבי כלֹ[ה]	3
(48)	בתֹ[נֹ]בל ואין שרית ופליֹטֹה]למֹסיני נבול וכלה יעשהֹן לכולֹ[	4
(46)	רשעֹהֹ[ן ועתה בנים שמעֹ]ו לי ואודיעה לכם בֹמֹ[עֹשֹי אל]	5
(45)	הנורֹאֹ[י]ֹם ונבורותֹ[ן פלאו]ֹספררה לכֹ[ם ולוֹא נסתרה עוד]	6
(44)	מאנושֹ[ן חכמת שֹ[מֹים אשר חי כֹ[וֹ]ֹחֹלֹ] אוהבה ואבינה אתכם]	7
(45)	בעמקֹתֹ[ן כול רזֹ]ֹי הקֹוֹדֹ[ש אשר היו נסתרים מקדם כי אל]	8
	חתם [את לֹ[ו]ֹחות הנֹבֹרית	9
	[אשר]ֹצֹוֹה ביד מושֹ[ה]	10
(45)	[על התבֹ]ֹלֹ הֹו היוֹם [אשר יפקד אל את הארץ והצדיקים]	11
	[יספרו בֹשֹ[ן]ֹמֹחה את מעֹ[שֹי אל הנדולים	12
	[ ]ֹ יֹדֹ אל נבֹ[ן	13

Comments on the readings and supplements

Line 1   The opening of the work may have included its title, which was repeated at the end, as in the Book of Jubilees. This title should have been מדרש התורה האחרון; see 4QD[e] frg. 7 ii 15 and 4QD[a] frg. 11 20f.[71] The concluding words in *Jub.* 50:13 are "Here the words regarding the divisions of times are completed,"[72] which

---

[66] See above, 181, with note 16 and 188 with note 47.

[67] The distances between the lines may differ from sheet to sheet in a scroll. 4QD[a] col. i belongs to the *first* sheet of the scroll, while cols. ii-iii are on the *second* sheet. The cut caused by the string is in col. i at the bottom of line 13, while it runs through the top of line 14 in frg. 2 ii, at exactly the same distance from the original top of the scroll.

[68] Baumgarten, DJD 18, pl. vi.

[69] See the evidence on frg. 1b, DJD 18, pl. i.

[70] The numbers at the ends of the lines refer to the scribal units in each of these lines.

[71] See also the discussion of the textual evidence in the final lines of 4QD[a] and 4QD[e] by Stegemann, "More Identified Fragments," 507f.

[72] J. C. VanderKam, ed., *The Book of Jubilees* (CSCO 510; Louvain: Peeters, 1989)

are formally rather close to the final rubric of D. The prologue of
the Book of Jubilees reads[73]:

> These are the words regarding the divisions of the times of the law
> and of the testimony ... as he related (them) to Moses on Mt. Sinai
> when he went up to receive the stone tablets—the law and the com-
> mandments—on the Lord's orders as he had told him that he should
> come up to the summit of the mountain.

This prologue is quoted here in some length as 4QD[a] i 9f seems to
refer to it. The beginning of the prologue with "These are the
words" (= אלה הדברים) may have been imitated by the author of D
starting with זה; cf. the beginnings of many *sections* in this work with
(ו)זה (see the concordances), also 1QS 5:1 and 1QSa 1:6.
Baumgarten preferred to start 4QD[a] i 1 with [פרוש המשפטים למשכיל
לב]נّי אור.

At the end of line 1, I prefer to add חושך as a negative counterpart to ב]נّי אור, even if this terminology is not attested elsewhere
in D. The edition supplies מדר[כי רשעה]. Otherwise, עולה, רשעים,
נדה, or זנות could also be discussed here.

Line 2   The suggestion for the text in the first half of this line refers
to the terminology of CD 2:15, 7:7, 19:4, 4QD[a] frg. 5 i 19 and
similar findings; cf. also 1QS 1:8, 2:2, 3:9f.

The edition notes correctly, "The supralinear *he* belongs with
פקודה; for the phraseology cf. 1QS IV 19." The intended reading
was מועד הפקודה.

At the end of the line the edition suggests ב.[רוח עולה]. I prefer to
read here בקץ as suggested by J. T. Milik in his earlier draft of
this column.[74]

Line 3   As the suffix of מעשיה needs a feminine noun in the preceding text, now missing, the editor supplied עולה at the end of the
line before. I prefer to supply הרשעה at the beginning of line 3.
For קץ הרשעה, cf. CD 6:10, 14; 12:23; 15:6; 4QD[d] frg. 8 ii 5 =
4QD[f] frg. 2 12.

The phraseology to fill the gap by בחרון אפו is taken from CD
9:4, 6 and 10:9.

Erroneously, the edition offers ד[שמי]י instead of ד[שמ]י.

אתכול may have been written here as a *single* word, as we find
sometimes in 1QS, e.g., 2:1, 4; 5:18; 9:13; cf. also 1QSa 1:4, 23.

1, 255 (Ethiopic text); idem, ed., *The Book of Jubilees* (CSCO 511; Louvain: Peeters,
1989) 1, 327 (English translation).
[73] According to J. C. VanderKam, CSCO 511.1.
[74] Cf. note 42 above.

Line 4 בת]בל was suggested here already by Milik in his earlier draft[75] (cf. also ישמיד מתבל, 1QS 5:19). The edition supplies instead בת]ועי רוח at the beginning of this line.

The phrase ואין שרית ופליטה is taken from CD 2:6f. Cf. 1QS 6:14. Instead of [לכול], the edition has [לפועלי] at the end of this line.

Line 5 The edition fills in only ועתה שמעו [לי with a long *vacat* before. But in other openings in D of this kind, usually people are named: see כל יודעי צדק CD 1:1; כל באי ברית CD 2:2; בנים CD 2:14; or again כל יודעי צדק 4QD^e frg. 2 ii 19. I prefer the short word בנים here, which may refer to כול ב]נֵּי אור in line 1, with a smaller *vacat* in front of it.

The letter after לכם was certainly a ב, not a מ, followed by a letter trace which fits better with the top of a מ than with the top of a ה. Therefore, I suggest here בֹמ]עשי אל] / הנורא]ים, cf. כול מעשיך, הנוראים 1QH^a 5:31 (Sukenik: 13:14), instead of the edition's supplements מֹח]שבות אל] / הנורא]ות, which also have no terminological equivalent elsewhere.

Line 6 ספררה was corrected to אספררה in the manuscript but the corrector missed deleting one of the *reshes*. The intended reading was אספרה.

Lines 6-7 After לכ]ם the edition supplies אשר [סתרו] / מאנוש [מספר מֹמ]י. I prefer the above suggestions. "Wisdom of heaven" may well be what was revealed to Moses in the Book of Jubilees, or to Enoch in his writings.

Line 7 The edition does not offer any supplements for the end of this line. In relation to חכמה, as suggested in the first gap of this line, also אוהבה seems to me better than עושיה or שומרה. Instead of אבינה, אשכילה may also be discussed but the root שׂכל is very rarely used in the D-manuscripts.

Line 8 To read here הקֹ]דֹש [° was already suggested by Milik in his earlier draft.[76] The edition reads only]הֹקֹ [. The further supplements of this line are dependent on the suggestion of ה]ברית ל]וֹחות in the next line.

הקודש should be regarded here as a designation of the sanctuary above—God's temple in the heavens—the idea of which underlies, e.g., the Songs of the Sabbath Sacrifice, which at the same time depicts some of the "mysteries" of this sanctuary. Other "mysteries of the heavens" are clearly behind the D-manuscripts, such as those revealed to Enoch in his Astronomical Book (the true calendar) or in his Book of the Watchers (e.g., cosmology or

---

[75] Cf. note 42 above; Milik's note is with a question mark.
[76] Cf. note 42 above; this time, Milik's note is without a question mark.

the consequences of the transgressions of the fallen angels; see CD
2:17-21). In every case, כול רז ֿ[ן] הֿקֿ[ֹוֿדֿש] may not refer to any special revelation to the Teacher of Righteousness or to members of
the *Yaḥad*, but solely to knowledge about the heavens from traditional literary sources.

Line 9 The top line of the additional frg. d is read רוב סל[ֿי]ֿחוֿת ה] in
the edition.[77] The new context may favour instead [את ל[ֿוֿחוֿת
ה]בֿרית after חתם at the beginning of this line, the subject of which
should be God. For לוחות הברית, see Deut. 9:9, 11, 15; cf. also
4QMidrEschat x 12 (= 4Q177 1-4 12). The sense may be that the
preexistent Law (= the Pentateuch) was totally "hidden" before
God revealed it to Moses. For another time when the Law again
was "hidden" (this time it was concealed in the ark and therefore
could not be studied by David until the ark reached Jerusalem [2
Sam. 6]), see CD 5:2-5. Perhaps the sense behind 4QDᵃ i 7-11 is
polemical: whatever God once revealed to Enoch, Noah or other
ancestors was not yet the Law, which only *later* constituted God's
everlasting covenant with the people of Israel and which was revealed exclusively to Moses (cf. especially the evidence of line 10).

Line 10 The same text is suggested by the edition, where only כאשר
is supplied instead of אשר. For the terminology, cf. 1QS 1:3 and
8:15.

Line 11 The edition reads here]ל°°ֿהֿאֿדֿם[, but this is rather doubtful. The photo of the additional fragments on pl. i shows a clear
top of a ל on frg. d and, after a *vacat* of about two or three letters,
the word הו, which is written this way instead of הוא; cf. also in
4QDᵃ frg. 11 9, where God is praised as הו הכול, "(You are) he
(who represents) everything."

At the beginning of the line, [על התב]לֿ is a free guess relating
to the context, but cf. also the beginning of line 4 above. In lines
1-11 (beginning), "all the world" is viewed, but from line 11 (third
word) onwards, especially "the land."

The traces of היום are evident and lead to some supplementation of the text as above, cf. CD 8:2f = 19:15 and, furthermore,
CD 5:15f and 7:9 = 19:6. Instead of את הארץ, עוון רשעים or some
other terminology is also possible. Regarding the end of the line,
see commentary on line 12.

Line 12 In the given context, there is scarcely any possibility other
than to restore the word ending with מֿחה[to the noun ש]מֿחה,

---

[77] Unfortunately, Milik's transcriptions of the additional fragments c-f and his
notes on them were not included in the materials I received from Prof. Baumgarten
in 1990 and they are still unknown to me.

even if it is not attested elsewhere in the D-manuscripts. For further supplementation, cf. 1QM 14:4 and 17:7. For the restoration of והצדיקים at the end of line 11, cf. 4QD^f frg. 5 i 14 = CD 11:21, but ויודעי צדק or some other term of this kind would also be possible. Also, instead of יספרו at the beginning of line 12, some other verb like יברכו, יהללו, יתרוממו or ירננו. of this kind is debatable. For מעשי אל, cf. the restoration in line 5 above; for the additional הנדולים, cf. 1QH^a 15:35f. and 18:13 (Sukenik: 7:32f. and 10:11).

Line 13   The letter at the beginning of this line may have been א, ד, ה, ו, ז, ח, י, ר or ת.

It is very difficult to complete the further letters of this line in a reasonable fashion. Was there something of splendour (ה[דר), or a flock (ע[דר), or someone whose name ended with דר[, sent to the Babylonian king נב[וכדנאצר (cf. 4QD^a frg. 2 i 11 = CD 1:6) or to some kind of נביאים like צדק נב[יאי?

Finally, one may search for suitable places for 4QD^a frg. 1c (or its two parts) and frg. 1f in the environs of frgs. 1d and e: at least they may not belong to col. i, lines 19-21, where God is praised in the second person singular, but to some lines before. Unfortunately, I cannot find a suitable place for them solely on the grounds of their poor physical evidence.

8. *The combined edition of all D-manuscripts*

To complete the physical reconstructions of the scrolls 4QD^a-h and to find the original place of at least some of the still dislocated fragments of 4QD^a requires further examination of the originals at the Rockefeller Museum in Jerusalem. Only afterwards (about the year 2002) can the combined edition of all D-manuscripts be published. This edition is in preparation since 1990 but could not be finished mainly because of the missing original of 4QD^a frg. 6 i.[78] Without the evidence from the back of this fragment, any physical reconstruction of this scroll would have been too theoretical a base for an edition. At the same time, neither CD nor any other QD scroll can establish the original literary structure and the sequence of contents in the long middle section of the Damascus Document.

The basic text of this future edition is the original scroll 4QD^a. Its text is arranged in this edition according to the columns and lines of the physical reconstruction of this manuscript. The text of all other D-manuscripts, including CD, is filled in. All variants of the different manuscripts are noted and discussed.

[78] See above, 187.

Col. XV (frg. 6ii)   Col. XIV (frg. 6i)

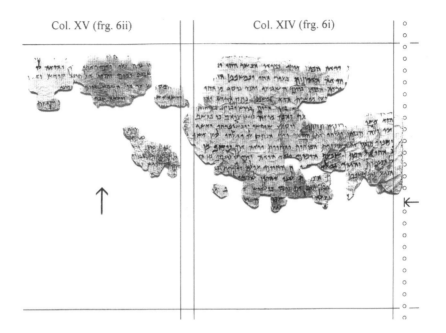

Col. XVII (frg. 6iv)   Col. XVI (frg. 6iii)

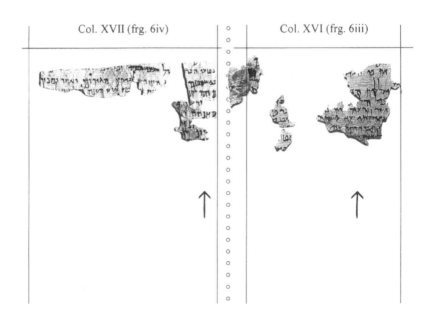

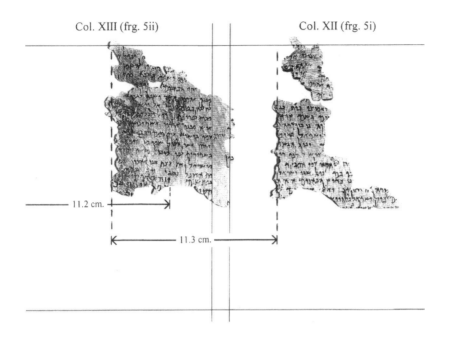

Col. XIII (frg. 5ii)   Col. XII (frg. 5i)

11.2 cm.

11.3 cm.

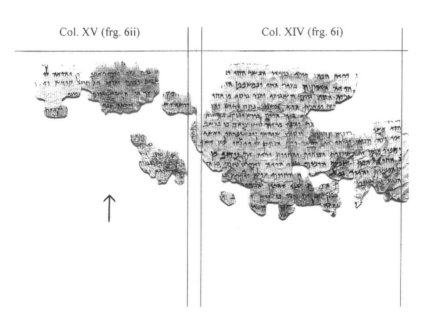

Col. XV (frg. 6ii)   Col. XIV (frg. 6i)

This edition will also have a concordance to the full D evidence, but every word is quoted only once, even if it is attested in several manuscripts. All other occurrences of this word are noted with their actual context in footnotes, which include references to variant readings or problems of textual restoration. This method of recording the textual evidence will make it easier to know how often a word is attested in the original D-text. Even if this edition is published very late, it should become a reliable guide for future students of the very important Damascus Document, which was the final halakhic orientation of the Essenes for all pious Jewish people within the borders of "the land of Israel,"[79] to survive God's imminent final judgement and to participate in eternal life on earth a few decades in the future.[80]

---

[79] See the rather frequent use of הארץ in the special sense of the "Holy Land" or the "Land of Israel" in the D-manuscripts and elsewhere in the Qumran corpus; K. G. Kuhn, *Konkordanz zu den Qumrantexten* (Göttingen: Vandenhoeck & Ruprecht, 1960) 22f. and Baumgarten, DJD 18.205.

[80] The Damascus Document was composed during the period between the death of the Teacher of Righteousness in the past and the future extermination of the wicked in the final judgement, which should take place "about forty years" after the Teacher's death; see CD 20:13-15. Cf. Stegemann, *The Library of Qumran*, 116-18, 123-25, 128f. and 132f. The date of the composition of the Damascus Document was about 100 BCE.

CD XI:17: APART FROM YOUR SABBATHS

CANA WERMAN

Ben-Gurion University

A Midrash in CD and in the Words of the Sages

In the Damascus Document (CD) 11:17, we find the following law: "Let no man bring on the altar on the Sabbath any offering except the burnt offering of the Sabbath for thus it is written 'apart from your Sabbaths'." Although the biblical quotation given here is not precise, it is clear that the author of CD refers to the verses from Lev. 23:37-39:

> These are the appointed times of the Lord, which you are to proclaim as proclamations of holiness, to bring near fire offerings to the Lord, a burnt offering, and a meal offering, a peace offering, and pour offerings, everything upon its day—*apart from the Sabbaths of the Lord*, and apart from your gifts and apart from all your vows, and apart from all your freewill offerings, that you give to the Lord. However, on the fifteenth day of the seventh month, when you have gathered in the fruit of the land, you are to celebrate a feast to the Lord seven days: on the first day shall be a sabbath and on the eighth day shall be a sabbath.

The quoted verses are found in the middle of a section that deals with the festival of Succoth. According to Israel Knohl[1] these verses in Leviticus 23 were intended as an epilogue to the chapter on holidays. The Holiness School, which wanted to include the populist themes associated with Succoth, added a supplementary section in which the requirements of the four species and sitting in Booths were appended. Thus, we find a summary in the middle of a section. This difficulty undoubtedly troubled readers in the time of the Second Temple.

Two possible interpretations of the key phrase "apart from the Sabbaths of the Lord" suggest themselves. The phrase lends itself either to the sacrifices required on the Sabbath, or to the Sabbath itself.[2] The first interpretation is related to the material found in the

---

[1] I. Knohl, *The Sanctuary of Silence: The Priestly Torah and the Holiness School* (Minneapolis: Fortress, 1995) 37-38.

[2] See Targum Ps.-Jon., "apart from the *days* of the Sabbath of the Lord." The Septuagint translates this phrase *verbatim*, making it impossible to determine how they understood the verse.

rest of the verse, where the gifts, vows and freewill offerings are also paired with the word מלבד (apart from): "and apart from your gifts and apart from all your vows, and apart from all your freewill offerings...." The second interpretation would also appear to be reasonable since the quoted phrase does not mention the word "sacrifice," but only the Sabbath, a specific time. On the other hand, if the time description (i.e., the Sabbath) is the intended meaning of the verse, where is the preposition -ב (on)?

The interpretation given to the "Sabbaths of the Lord" will determine the meaning of מלבד. If the sacrifices of Sabbath are intended, then מלבד appears to indicate that in addition to the sacrifices listed in the previous verse (burnt offering, meal offering, peace offering and pour offerings), one should also offer the Sabbath sacrifice.[3] If, however, a time is intended, then מלבד indicates "apart from" the Sabbath: all these sacrifices are to be offered but not on the Sabbath.[4]

The author of CD chooses the second interpretation. He declares that one must not offer the festival sacrifices, including the sacrifices of the intermediary festival days on the Sabbath (note that a Holy Day [*yom tov* יום טוב] never falls on Sabbath according to the Qumran calendar; thus all his references are to the intermediary festival days). According to the Damascus Document the quoted verses are not a summary but are intended to pronounce a new law: all the festival sacrifices mentioned in chapter 23—burnt offering, meal offering, peace offering, and drink offerings—are daily requirements during the festivals, but not on the festival Sabbath. It is reasonable to conclude therefore, that according to CD, the Sabbath is not counted as part of the seven or eight days of the festival; if the Sabbath were to be added to the count of festival, the number of days in which festival sacrifices are offered would be reduced by one.[5]

The prohibition of bringing festival sacrifices on the Sabbath is clearly at odds with the Pharisaic approach. According to the Pharisees, the required sacrifices for the festival and the intermediary festival days are also offered on the Sabbath that falls during the festivals. Thus we find in a midrash on this verse: "Where do we learn that the Musaf sacrifices [additional sacrifices for the Sabbath]

---

[3] This is the common meaning of the word in the Pentateuch: מלבד means "in addition to." See Knohl, *Sanctuary of Silence*, 56-58.

[4] For מלבד with this meaning, see Gen. 46:26.

[5] This is also Yadin's opinion. See: Y. Yadin, *The Temple Scroll* (Jerusalem: Israel Exploration Society, 1983), 1.130-31.

are to be offered [first] with the sacrifices intended for the holiday? We learn from the phrase 'apart from the Sabbaths of the Lord'" (Sifra Emor 102:2).

Despite the halakhic dispute, an interpretation of the phrase, "apart from the Sabbaths of the Lord," similar to that found in CD, may be found in the laws of the School of Hillel. The parallel is not explicit and it is necessary to clarify the reasoning used by the School of Hillel to highlight the similarities.

The following midrash summarizes the points of dispute between the two major Pharisaic schools:

> The School of Shammai say one might think that a man can celebrate (יחוג, meaning to bring the festive peace offering [חגיגה] and the burnt offering [ראיה]) to the Temple[6] on *yom tov* (itself) but we learn *however* (אך), that one celebrates (in this sense) on the intermediary festival days but not on *yom tov* itself. The School of Hillel say one might think that a man can celebrate (in that sense) on the Sabbath, but we learn *however* (אך), you celebrate on *yom tov* and not on the Sabbath (Sifra Emor 102:3).

The dispute refers to the festive peace offering (חגיגה) and the burnt offering (ראיה) that the pilgrims are expected to bring on the festivals. These sacrifices differ from those previously discussed: they are sacrifices offered by individuals and not the congregational sacrifices spoken of earlier. According to the School of Hillel, one may make these sacrifices on *yom tov* itself but not when *yom tov* falls on the Sabbath of the festival; according to the School of Shammai, one may not make these sacrifices on *yom tov* but only on the intermediary festival days. The word "however" (אך), follows the verses quoted above:

> These are the appointed times of the Lord, which you are to proclaim as proclamations of holiness, to bring near fire offerings to the Lord, a burnt offering, and a meal offering, a peace offering, and pour offerings, everything upon its day: apart from the Sabbaths of the Lord, and apart from your gifts and apart from all your vows, and apart from all your freewill offerings, that you give to the Lord. However (אך), on the fifteenth day of the seventh month, when you have gathered in the fruit of the land, you are to celebrate a feast to the Lord seven days: on the first day shall be a sabbath, and on the eighth day shall be a sabbath (Lev. 23:37-39).

How do both schools derive the law of the festive peace offering (חגיגה) and the burnt offering (ראיה) from the verses in question? We

---

[6] Further elucidation is given below.

have seen that both the School of Hillel and the School of Shammai
refer to the word אך.

The School of Hillel regard both the festive peace offering (חגיגה)
and the burnt offering (ראיה) as forbidden on the first day of a holiday that falls on the Sabbath but obligatory on the first day of a holiday which does not fall on the Sabbath. "However on the
fifteenth"—the festive peace offering (חגיגה) and the burnt offering
(ראיה) are permitted on the fifteenth, on *yom tov*, but not on the
Sabbath. It appears that the discordant element is to be identified in
the previous verse: "apart from the Sabbaths of the Lord."
Consequently, the festive peace offering and the burnt offering are
forbidden on the Sabbath but permitted on *yom tov*.

If this reading is correct, these verses were not interpreted by the
School of Hillel as summaries of the laws previously listed but as
new laws concerning the burnt offering (ראיה) and the peace offering
(חגיגה). According to the School of Hillel, the words "to bring near
fire offerings to the Lord, a burnt offering, a meal offering, a peace
offering, and pour offerings" refer to the festive peace offering and
the burnt offering that are to be brought by the pilgrims, not on the
Sabbath of the Lord, but rather on the fifteenth day of the month,
the first day of the festival. The Sabbath, as well as the fifteenth day
of the month, is an expression of time. Thus, it resembles the
midrashic interpretation found in the Damascus Document.

The School of Shammai understand the word אך as forbidding
the burnt offering and peace offering on the *yom tov*. "However on
the fifteenth"—the burnt and peace offerings are forbidden on *yom
tov* and only permitted on the intermediary festival days. The opinion stated by the School of Shammai that the burnt and peace offerings are not to be brought on *yom tov* itself is derived from the end of
the verse: אך "however, on the fifteenth day of the seventh
month...you are to celebrate a feast to the Lord seven days": *but* "on
the first day shall be a sabbath and on the eighth day shall be a sabbath" *and you may not bring sacrifices thereon.* From the interpretation
given by the School of Shammai to verse 39 ("However, on the fifteenth...") it can be concluded that this School read verses 37-38 *verbatim*, as a conclusion, contrary to the interpretations found in CD
and in the words of the School of Hillel.

The Dispute between the Schools of Shammai and Hillel

A dispute similar to that found in the Sifra between the Schools of Hillel and Shammai may be found in t. Ḥag. 2:8, 10-13. [7] Here, too, the matter is not obvious; I will cite the Tosefta fully and discuss it.

1 They never differed except about the laying on of hands (2:8).

2 In what sort of laying on of hands did they differ? The School of Shammai says, "They do not lay on hands on the festival day and so too peace offerings. He who offers his festal offering through them (החוגג בהם) lays hands on them on the eve of the *yom tov*."

And the School of Hillel says, "They bring peace offerings and burnt offerings and lay hands on them."

3 Said the School of Hillel, "What about a time at which you are not permitted to work, even to prepare food, for an ordinary person, but you are permitted to sacrifice to the Most High? Certainly, at a time when you are permitted to prepare food for an ordinary person, should you not also be permitted to sacrifice to the Most High?"

4 The School of Shammai replied to them, "Sacrifices brought in fulfillment of vows and as thank-offerings will settle the matter. For you are permitted to prepare (food) for an ordinary person on *yom tov*, but you are not permitted to sacrifice these, as offerings on *yom tov*, to the Most High."

5 The School of Hillel answered: "No. If you have stated the rule concerning sacrifices brought in fulfillment of vows and as thank-offerings, which are not subject to a fixed time for their offerings, will you state the same rule concerning the festal-offering (חגיגה), the time of which is fixed?"

6 The School of Shammai then replied, "Also in the case of the festal offering (חגיגה), there are occasions at which its

---

[7] For the literary aspect of this source, see J. Fraenkel, "Hermeneutic Problems in the Study of the Aggadic Narrative," *Tarbiz* 47 (1977-78) 146-49 (Hebrew). For the legal ramifications of this source, see C. Shapira and M. Fisch, "Disputes of the Schools," *Shenaton ha-Mishpat ha-Ivri* (in press; Hebrew). A brief summary of the interpretations throughout the generations can be found in S. Lieberman, *Tosefta ki-Peshutah* (New York: JTS, 1962) 5.1300 (Hebrew). I was aided in my translation of the Tosefta by the work of J. Neusner, *The Tosefta: Moed, Translated from the Hebrew* (New York: Ktav, 1981).

time is not fixed. For he who did not bring a festal-offering on the first *yom tov* of the festival may bring a festal-offering on any other day of the festival, including on the last *yom tov* of the festival..." (2.10).

7 Once Hillel the Elder laid on hands on a burnt-offering in the courtyard, and the disciples of Shammai combined forces against him. He said to them, "Go and see it, for it is female, and I must prepare it for sacrifices of peace-offerings." He put them off with a bunch of words, and they went their way. And the power of the School of Shammai immediately became strong, and they wanted to decide the law permanently in accord with their opinion.

Now Baba b. Buta, one of the disciples of the School of Shammai, was there, but he acknowledged that the law is in accord with the opinions of the School of Hillel in every last detail. He went and brought the whole Qedar-flock and set them up in the courtyard and announced, "Whoever is required to bring burnt-offerings and peace-offerings—let him come and take a beast and lay on hands." So everybody came along and took a beast and offered up burnt-offerings, having laid on hands. On that very day the law was confirmed in accordance with the opinion of the School of Hillel, and not a single person challenged it (2.11).

8 Another disciple of the disciples of the School of Hillel laid hands on a burnt-offering. One of the disciples of Shammai found him out. He said to him, "What is this laying on of hands?" He replied to him, "What is this shutting up?"
And he shut him up by rebuking him (2.12).

Careful analysis reveals that there are inconsistencies in the sections dealing with the dispute between the Schools of Hillel and Shammai. The first section proclaims that there was no dispute other than that of the laying on of hands. But we find in the section immediately following that there was an additional dispute, i.e., whether we are to bring a burnt offering (ראיה) on *yom tov* or not. According to the School of Shammai, the burnt offering is not made on the first day of the festival, on *yom tov*, since only the peace offering is mentioned (in addition to the requirement to lay hands on the sacrifice only on the eve of the festival). According to the School of Hillel, both peace offerings and burnt offerings are to be brought on *yom tov*, and there is to be laying on of hands.

Section 7 is inconsistent with section 1. According to section 7, Hillel lays hands on the burnt offering in the courtyard. The students of the School of Shammai attack him for this and he convinces them that the sacrifice is a peace offering and not a burnt offering. The dispute is therefore not really about the laying on of hands, but rather about whether one may bring a burnt offering or only peace offerings on *yom tov*. Later, in the same section, Baba b. Buta brings "the whole Qedar-flock," in order that all the people might offer burnt offerings and peace offerings. The narrator points out that "everybody came along and took a beast and offered up burnt-offerings, having laid on hands." It appears that in addition to the earlier dispute over whether one might offer a burnt offering on *yom tov*, another dispute has been appended: the matter of laying on of hands. This addition comes to dominate the discussion and obscures the original dispute.

Only one subsequent section is congruent with section 1, and that is section 8. There we find the dispute centered on whether one may lay hands on the burnt offering or not. But the awkwardness of the dispute between the disciples of the two schools is obvious: "He said to him, 'What is this laying on of hands?' He replied to him, 'What is this shutting up?' *And he shut him up by rebuking him.*"

Furthermore, a careful reading reveals that the basic dispute in the Tosefta is about whether one may bring burnt offerings and peace offerings on *yom tov*, or whether both are forbidden. We shall examine sections 3 to 6, which is a unit containing the dispute between the Schools of Hillel and Shammai on this matter.

First, I shall clarify the term חגיגה that appears in sections 5 and 6. Elsewhere in Tosefta Ḥagiga (1:4, ed. Lieberman, 377), we find that both the burnt offering and the peace offering can be called חגיגה. Since we find references in Tosefta Ḥagiga 2 to both burnt offerings and peace offerings, it is difficult to assume that the term חגיגה is intended to stand for burnt offerings, and not the sacrifice that normally is associated with that name, the peace offering. The term חגיגה refers therefore either to both classes of sacrifice or specifically to the limited meaning of חגיגה, peace offering. We must reject the possibility that we are dealing only with peace offerings, since this assumption leads to the conclusion that the Tosefta suddenly jumps from a description of a dispute on the nature of ראיה in section 2, to the dispute on the nature of חגיגה in sections 3-6. We come to the conclusion that the term חגיגה refers to both sacrifices. Thus we find a continuation between the sections; in section 2 we find a dispute dealing with ראיה and in sections 3-6, the dispute centers on both sacrifices, the ראיה and חגיגה.

In fact, the subject matter of the dispute in sections 3-6 indicates that two kinds of sacrifices are under discussion. I shall now demonstrate this point. The dispute begins with the words of the School of Hillel:

> What about a time at which you are not permitted to work, even to prepare food, for an ordinary person,[8] but you are permitted to sacrifice to the Most High? Certainly, at a time when you are permitted to prepare food for an ordinary person, should you not also be permitted to sacrifice to the Most High?

Here we learn a *qal ve-ḥomer* (*a minori ad majus*) which can be interpreted in two ways: 1) since the burnt offering of the Sabbath is brought on a day when cooking is prohibited, *qal ve-ḥomer* that a burnt offering should be brought on a day when cooking is permitted. According to this interpretation, the dispute is only concerning burnt offerings. 2) Since the Sabbath offering is brought on a day when cooking is prohibited because it is the day's requirement, *qal ve-ḥomer* that both burnt and peace offerings are permitted on a day when cooking is permitted, since they are the day's requirement. According to the second interpretation, the dispute is concerning both burnt offerings and peace offerings.

The second interpretation is closer to the response of the School of Shammai, in which there is explicit reference to both kinds of sacrifice, to burnt offerings and peace offerings:

> The School of Shammai replied to them, "Sacrifices brought in fulfillment of vows and as thank-offerings will prove the matter. For you are permitted to prepare (food) for an ordinary person on *yom tov*, but you are not permitted to sacrifice these, as offerings on *yom tov*, to the Most High" (section 4).

The School of Shammai are aided by thankofferings and vows in order to reject the view of the School of Hillel. Thankofferings and vows, that can be both burnt offerings and peace offerings, are not brought on *yom tov*, even though cooking is permitted. Just as these voluntary offerings are not brought on *yom tov*, despite cooking being

---

[8] *Verbatim*: "It is permitted to prepare for the layman." This expression may be interpreted in two different ways: (a) one may cook (thus, one may cook on the holiday); (b) one may bring a peace offering on the holiday. If we accept the second interpretation, the section will mean that the School of Hillel attacks the School of Shammai for permitting peace offerings and forbidding burnt offerings. In that case, we may reject the claim that the School of Shammai also forbids peace offerings. The second interpretation is, however, not possible in view of the fact that in the fourth section, the School of Hillel claims that vow offerings and gift offerings are forbidden on the days when "it is permitted to prepare for the layman." Vow offerings and gift offerings also have the function of peace offerings and burnt offerings, and thus the phrase "it is permitted to prepare" must be understood as permission to cook on the holiday.

permitted, burnt offerings and peace offerings are not brought on *yom tov*, even though cooking is permitted.

We can therefore conclude that this Tosefta is composed of several layers. The oldest layer is characterized by the assumption that the School of Shammai do not permit the festive peace offering (חגיגה) and the burnt offering (ראיה) on *yom tov*; the School of Hillel require them. This layer is represented by sections 3 to 6.[9]

The second layer in the Tosefta presents the view that the dispute refers only to the burnt offering (ראיה) and not to the festive peace offering (חגיגה). Here both Schools agree that the festive peace offering is required. This appears not as a dispute but as a story. Hillel brings a burnt offering. When members of the School of Shammai oppose him because of this deed, he convinces them that he is not bringing a burnt offering but a peace offering. Baba b. Buta brought the whole Qedar-flock so that the pilgrims might bring burnt offerings and peace offerings; but the narrator tells us that the pilgrims offered burnt offerings, while peace offerings are not mentioned.

The third layer clouds the deep-seated dispute and asserts that the dispute is only about the laying on of hands. Section 8, as I have indicated, belongs to this layer. The opening of the Tosefta (section 1) is also part of this layer: "They never differed except about the laying on of hands." In addition, sections 2 and 7 are fashioned with the intent of showing that the laying on of hands is the central issue. This becomes apparent when section 2 is compared with the mishnaic source, where the dispute about the burnt offering is explicitly stated: "The School of Shammai say 'one may bring peace offerings but not lay hands on them but no burnt offerings may be offered' and the School of Hillel say 'one may bring peace offerings and burnt offerings and lay hands on them'" (m. Ḥag. 2:2-3).

The Tosefta limits the dispute to a marginal matter. As Shapira and Fisch have shown,[10] unlike the Mishnah, in this chapter the Tosefta views disputes negatively. This probably explains why the Tosefta makes an effort to conceal the principal dispute over whether the burnt offering (ראיה) and the festive peace offering (חגיגה) are obligatory or not.

It is important to note that in the dispute in sections 3-6, the School of Shammai apparently do not view the burnt offering and the peace offering as required by *yom tov*, and thus forbid them on *yom tov*.

Elsewhere in t. Ḥagiga, the assumption is that the School of

---

[9] This analysis justifies our determination that the dispute in Sifra concerns *both* ראיה and חגיגה.
[10] See note 7, above.

Shammai consider the festive offering to be obligatory on *yom tov*. Thus, in 1:4 (ed. Lieberman, 377):

> Concerning what did they differ? Concerning the festal-offering on Yom Tov. For the School of Shammai say, "Let him bring the whole from unconsecrated funds." And the School of Hillel say, "Let that which one brings in fulfilment of his obligation derive [to be sure] from unconsecrated funds. But what if he wanted to add tithe-funds, he may do so [to buy a better animal]."

The School of Shammai are more restrictive with respect to the festal-offering more than the School of Hillel, and do not allow it to be brought from moneys of the second tithe, since both are obligatory in their own right.

However, several lines earlier in the Tosefta, there is uncertainty as to the nature of ראיה and חגיגה.

> What is the definition of a ראיה? These are the burnt offerings which are brought for [designated as] the appearance offering. What is the definition of a חגיגה? These are the peace offerings which are brought for [designated as] the festal-offering (1:4, ed. Lieberman, 377).

Lieberman points out that these definitions are intended to negate the idea found in Sifre Deuteronomy that ראיה is charity and the obligatory peace offering is not חגיגה but rather the שמחה sacrifice.[11] This *baraita* deliberately ignores the older layer in which the School of Shammai does not require the burnt and peace offerings, and therefore attributes an extreme view to the School of Shammai.

If according to the School of Shammai peace offerings and burnt offerings are voluntary rather than obligatory sacrifices, the concepts, burnt offering (ראיה) and festive peace offering (חגיגה), might well be terms invented by the School of Hillel. We shall attempt to show when this terminology was introduced.

It is worthwhile pointing out that these terms, used by the School of Hillel, are not found in Second Temple literature, Qumran literature, the Pseudepigrapha or even in Josephus. Pseudo-Jonathan translates "And they shall not appear before the Lord empty" (Deut. 6:16) as "you must not appear before the Lord your God empty of *mitzvot*." Only later was the verse from Deuteronomy (or its parallel in Exodus) interpreted as requiring the festive peace offering (חגיגה) and the burnt offering (ראיה) to be brought to the Temple.[12]

---

[11] Lieberman, *Tosefta ki-Peshuta*, 5.1278-79.
[12] See *Mekhilta d'Rabbi Simon b. Jochai* (ed. J. N. Epstein and E. Z. Melamed; Jerusalem: Sumptibus Mekize Nirdamim, 1955) 218.

In Ben Sira, we find, "appear not before the Lord empty handed, for all that you offer is in fulfillment of a precept" (35:6-7). As Kister has pointed out, this is an interpretive paraphrase of the same verse in Deuteronomy.[13]

In a midrash from Mechilta de R. Ishmael, we find this same verse related to the giving of charity and not to sacrifices: "'And they shall not appear before the Lord empty'—with peace offerings. You say with peace offerings; perhaps with money?" (333). Another midrash interprets the verse as indicating that two requirements fall on the pilgrim who comes to the Temple on a holiday: "'And they shall not appear before the Lord empty' [Deut. 6:16] of charity. And the Sages gave a quantity. The School of Shammai say the רֹאיה [in the sense of charity], two pieces of silver and שמחה [a peace offering], one silver coin. And the School of Hillel say the רֹאיה, one piece of silver and שמחה, two" (Sifre Deut. 196). Lieberman explains this midrash as follows[14]: on the three annual pilgrimages the pilgrim is commanded to fulfill two obligations, charity and the שמחה sacrifice. The midrash makes no reference to either the festive peace offering (חגיגה) or the burnt offering (רֹאיה).

It appears from the above that (1) there is no evidence for burnt offerings (רֹאיה) and festive peace offerings (חגיגה) during the time of the Temple; (2) in the earliest layers of Tannaitic literature we find no reference to either חגיגה or רֹאיה as required for the pilgrim ascending to Jerusalem to celebrate the festival; (3) the dispute between the School of Shammai and the School of Hillel represents a basic difference in outlook. It is therefore likely that the view of the School of Shammai represents the halakhah as practiced during Second Temple times.

This conclusion is important for understanding the halakhic disputes and the different halakhic approaches at the time of the Second Temple. It is generally held that during the period of the Second Temple there were disputes both between the Pharisees and the Sadducees and among the Pharisees themselves, that is between the Schools of Hillel and Shammai. While extra-Tannaitic sources confirm disputes between the Sadducees and the Pharisees, there is no such confirmation of disputes among the Pharisees. One cannot rule out the possibility that only the School of Shammai represented the Pharisaic view.[15]

---

[13] M. Kister, "Notes on the Book of Ben Sira," *Leshonenu* 47 (1983) 128-29, n. 8.

[14] Lieberman, *Tosefta Kifshuta* 5.1278-79.

[15] The proposal that the School of Shammai is the only Pharisaic school in the Second Temple period is not completely untenable if we recall that the School of

It is important to note that the law promulgated by the School of Hillel is an expression of the tendency of the Pharisees to involve all the people in the Service of the Lord. The School of Hillel requires everyone, without exception, to bring sacrifices on their pilgrimages to the Temple. The involvement of the general population was viewed with horror by the Sadducees, who resented any impingement on their Temple prerogatives.[16] If the author of the Damascus Document had encountered a view similar to that of the School of Hillel, I am sure he would have presented a strongly negative response.

Hillel derives its legitimacy from Hillel himself and from his descendants, led by Rabban Gamliel. Scholars have, however, noted that the dynasty of Gamliel is not really connected to Hillel (see J. Neusner, *The Rabbinic Traditions about the Pharisees before 70* [Leiden: E. J. Brill, 1971] 1.375), and in most cases where we find laws in the name of his dynasty, they could easily be attributed to the School of Shammai. See S. Safrai, *In the Time of Temple and Mishna: Studies in Jewish History* (Jerusalem: Magnes, 1994) 2.390-400.

[16] See I. Knohl, "Participation of the People in the Temple Worship—Second Temple Sectarian Conflict and the Biblical Tradition," *Tarbiz* 60 (1991) 139-46.

INDICES

INDEX OF ANCIENT SOURCES

Micah
7:2   169, 170

Psalms
105:15   81
116:12   66

Proverbs
15:8   34

Daniel
2   37
7   37
11–12   12
12   38

APOCRYPHA

Ben Sira
35:6–7   211

1 Maccabees
1:62–63   99
2:36   23

2 Maccabees
5:27   99
14:3   98
14:7   98

NEW TESTAMENT

Mark
1:7   99

Romans
4   11
11   11
11:26   11
14:1–5   10
14:10   10
14:14   10
15:1   10

1 Corinthians
7:1–16   10
7:17–20 10
7:25–31 10
7:32–35 7
11:25   10

Galatians
4:10   11
5:12   11

1 Timothy
3:2   149

PSEUDEPIGRAPHA

1 Enoch   195

Jubilees   4, 195
7:35–37   78, 142
50:8   19, 22
50:13   193

DEAD SEA SCROLLS

CD
1–8   180, 181, 185, 195
1:1   80, 190
1:1–21   179
1:1–3:6 192
1:4   31
1:4–5   31
1:5   34
1:6   31, 65, 197
1:7   32, 59
1:8–11   9

1:10   55
1:14   59
1:14–18 105
1:16   6
1:20   64
2:2   80, 86, 190, 195
2:2–13   31
2:6   195
2:9   59
2:12–13 81
2:14   80, 190, 195

7:8	89
7:8–21	88
7:9	88, 89
7:9–10	89
7:10	89
7:10–12	89
7:12	89
7:13	88
7:13–14	89
7:14–15	89
7:15	89
7:15–16	89, 91
7:16–17	89
7:17	89
7:17–18	89
7:18–21	89, 90
8:5–9	39
8:12–16	92
8:14	92
8:15	196
9:4–6	39
9:7	92
9:9–11	37
9:13	194
20:14–15	36
20:27–28	36

1Q28a (1QSª) 71
1:1	40
1:4	194
1:6	194
1:7	65
1:23	194
2:4–9	76

1Q33(1QM)
2–9	40
5:6	65
5:9	65
5:14	65
7:4–6	76
14 40	
14:4	197
15–19	40
17:7	197

1Qhª (1QHodayotª)
5:31	195
15:35	197
18:13	197

4Q158 (BibPar=4QRPª) 135

4Q159 (Ordinancesª) 25
| 1 ii 2–5 | 78 |

4Q174 (Flor=4QMidrEschatª?)
| 1:3–5 | 76 |

4Q177 (Catenaª=4QMidrEschatᵇ?)
| 1–4 12 | 196 |

4Q251 (Halakha A) 144
1 4	21
12	124
17	138
17 1	135, 138
17 2–3	140

4Q256 (Sᵇ, olim Sᵈ) 88

4Q258 (Sᵈ, olim Sᵇ) 88

4Q264 (Sʲ)
| 1 ii 8 | 23 |

4Q264a (Halakha B, olim Sᶻ) 23

4Q265 (Misc. Rules, olim Serekh Damascus) 71, 87
| 6 | 23 |
| 6 4 | 22 |

4Q266 (Dª, olim Dᵇ) 88, 97, 177, 178, 179, 189
1 a–b 5	80
1 1	5
2 i 5–6	12
2 i 6–25	179
2 i 11	197
2 i 12–15	9
2 i 19–20	6
2 ii	179
2 ii 9–14	192
2 ii 13	181
2 ii 21	66
2 ii 21–23	9
2 ii 79	142
3 i 4–6	6
3 ii 12	9
3 ii 25	9
3 iii 2–3	7
3 iii 6	6
3 iv 4	7
3 iv 6	5
4 c–d	185
4 ii 6	180
4 x 1–2	180
5 i	186, 188, 199
5 i–ii	185, 186
5 i 9–18	188
5 i 19	194
5 ii	75, 185, 186, 188, 199
5 ii 1–3	76
5 ii 1–16	74
5 ii 4–5	97

9	185
10 i 5–7	183
10 ii 1–12	183
11 i–ii	183
11 i 1–9	183
11 ii 1–3	183
12–14	185
15	183
16	183
4Q270 (Dᵉ)	88, 177, 178, 179, 182, 186, 189
2 i–ii	18, 185, 189, 190, 191
2 i 1–3	190
2 i 9–ii 17	81
2 i 9–ii 21	80
2 i 10	140
2 ii 6	82, 142
2 ii 7–8	82
2 ii 12	82
2 ii 13	81
2 ii 14	81
2 ii 14–19	178
2 ii 15	82, 143
2 ii 16	140
2 ii 17–18	80
2 ii 19	195
3 i 78, 190	
3 i–iii	185
3 ii	78, 188, 189, 190
3 ii–iii	191
3 ii 19–21	143
3 ii 20–21	141
3 iii	189, 190
3 iii 13–15	78
4	185, 189, 190
4 14	65
5	185, 189, 190
6 i	184
6 i–v	184
6 i 20–21	184
6 ii	182
6 ii 2	184
6 ii 5–6	184
6 ii 5–10	184
6 ii 9–14	184
6 ii 20–21	184
6 iii	66, 167
6 iii 1–3	184
6 iii 5–6	184
6 iv 17	65
6 vi	184
6 vii	184
6 viii	184
7 i	184
7 i–ii	184
7 i 1–2	89
7 i 1–11	88

7 i 3–4	89
7 i 4	89
7 i 5	89
7 i 5–6	89, 91
7 i 6–7	89
7 i 7–8	89
7 i 8–10	89, 90
7 i 11–13	183
7 ii	184
7 ii 15	193
8–12	185
4Q271 (Dᶠ, olim Dᵉ)	177, 178, 179, 182, 186, 189
2	185
2 1–5	78
2 8–10	141
2 10–13	139
2 12	194
3 185	
3 12 12–13	19
4 i 184	
4 i–ii	184
4 i 5	184
4 ii	167
4 ii 1–17	184
5 i	184
5 i 14	197
5 i 17–18	139
5 i 18	64, 140
5 i 18–19	140
5 ii	184
9 3	159
10–15	157–58
4Q272 (Dᵍ)	177, 179, 186
1 i–ii	77, 185
2	185
3	185
4Q273 (papDʰ)	97, 177, 179, 186
1	185
2	97, 185
2 1–2	74
3	97, 185
4 i–ii	185
4 i 5–11	74
4 ii	77
5	185
6	185
7–9	185
4Q274 (Tohorot A)	
2 i	24
3 ii	47
4Q275 (Communal Ceremony, olim Tohorot Bᵃ) 87	

INDEX OF MODERN AUTHORS

STUDIES ON THE TEXTS
OF THE DESERT OF JUDAH

1. Wernberg Møller, P. *The Manual of Discipline*. Translated and Annotated, with an Introduction. 1957. ISBN 90 04 02195 7
2. Ploeg, J. van der. *Le rouleau de la guerre*. Traduit et annoté, avec une introduction. 1959. ISBN 90 04 02196 5
3. Mansoor, M. *The Thanksgiving Hymns*. Translated and Annotated with an Introduction. 1961. ISBN 90 04 02197 3
5. Koffmahn, E. *Die Doppelurkunden aus der Wüste Juda*. Recht und Praxis der jüdischen Papyri des 1. und 2. Jahrhunderts n. Chr. samt Übertragung der Texte und Deutscher Übersetzung. 1968. ISBN 90 04 03148 0
6. Kutscher, E.Y. *The Language and linguistic Background of the Isaiah Scroll (1 QIsaᵃ)*. Transl. from the first (1959) Hebrew ed. With an obituary by H.B. Rosén. 1974. ISBN 90 04 04019 6
6a. Kutscher, E.Y. *The Language and Linguistic Background of the Isaiah Scroll (1 QIsaᵃ)*. Indices and Corrections by E. Qimron. Introduction by S. Morag. 1979. ISBN 90 04 05974 1
7. Jongeling, B. *A Classified Bibliography of the Finds in the Desert of Judah, 1958-1969.* 1971. ISBN 90 04 02200 7
8. Merrill, E.H. *Qumran and Predestination*. A Theological Study of the Thanksgiving Hymns. 1975. ISBN 90 04 042652
9. García Martínez, F. *Qumran and Apocalyptic*. Studies on the Aramaic Texts from Qumran. 1992. ISBN 90 04 09586 1
10. Dimant, D. & U. Rappaport (eds.). *The Dead Sea Scrolls*. Forty Years of Research. 1992. ISBN 90 04 09679 5
11. Trebolle Barrera, J. & L. Vegas Montaner (eds.). *The Madrid Qumran Congress*. Proceedings of the International Congress on the Dead Sea Scrolls, Madrid 18-21 March 1991. 2 vols. 1993. ISBN 90 04 09771 6 *set*
12. Nitzan, B. *Qumran Prayer and Religious Poetry* 1994. ISBN 90 04 09658 2
13. Steudel, A. *Der Midrasch zur Eschatologie aus der Qumrangemeinde (4QMidrEschatᵃ·ᵇ)*. Materielle Rekonstruktion, Textbestand, Gattung und traditionsgeschichtliche Einordnung des durch 4Q174 („Florilegium") und 4Q177 („Catena A") repräsentierten Werkes aus den Qumranfunden. 1994. ISBN 90 04 09763 5
14. Swanson, D.D. *The Temple Scroll and the Bible*. The Methodology of 11QT. 1995. ISBN 90 04 09849 6
15. Brooke, G.J. (ed.). *New Qumran Texts and Studies*. Proceedings of the First Meeting of the International Organization for Qumran Studies, Paris 1992. With F. García Martínez. 1994. ISBN 90 04 10093 8
16. Dimant, D. & L.H. Schiffman. *Time to Prepare the Way in the Wilderness*. Papers on the Qumran Scrolls by Fellows of the Institute for Advanced Studies of the Hebrew University, Jerusalem, 1989-1990. 1995. ISBN 90 04 10225 6
17. Flint, P.W. *The Dead Sea Psalms Scrolls and the Book of Psalms*. 1997. ISBN 90 04 10341 4
18. Lange, A. *Weisheit und Prädestination*. Weisheitliche Urordnung und Prädestination in den Textfunden von Qumran. 1995. ISBN 90 04 10432 1
19. García Martínez, F. & D.W. Parry. *A Bibliography of the Finds in the Desert of Judah 1970-95*. Arranged by Author with Citation and Subject Indexes. 1996. ISBN 90 04 10588 3

20. Parry, D.W. & S.D. Ricks (eds.). *Current Research and Technological Developments on the Dead Sea Scrolls.* Conference on the Texts from the Judean Desert, Jerusalem, 30 April 1995. 1996. ISBN 90 04 10662 6

21. Metso, S. *The Textual Development of the Qumran Community Rule.* 1997. ISBN 90 04 10683 9

22. Herbert, E.D. *Reconstructing Biblical Dead Sea Scrolls.* A New Method applied to the Reconstruction of 4QSam^a. 1997. ISBN 90 04 10684 7

23. Bernstein, M., F. García Martínez & J. Kampen (eds.). *Legal texts and Legal Issues.* Proceedings of the Second Meeting of the International Organization for Qumran Studies, Cambridge 1995. Published in honour of Joseph M. Baumgarten. 1997. ISBN 90 04 10829 7

25. Lefkovits, J.K. *The Copper Scroll – 3Q15: A Reevaluation.* A new Reading, Translation, and Commentary. ISBN 90 04 10685 5

26. Muraoka, T. & J.F. Elwolde (eds.). *The Hebrew of the Dead Sea Scrolls & Ben Sira.* Proceedings of a Symposium held at Leiden University, 11-14 December 1995. 1997. ISBN 90 04 10820 3

27. Falk, D.K. *Daily, Sabbath, and Festival Prayers in the Dead Sea Scrolls.* 1998. ISBN 90 04 10817 3

28. Stone, M.E. & E.G. Chazon (eds.). *Biblical Perspectives: Early Use and Interpretation of the Bible in Light of the Dead Sea Scrolls.* Proceedings of the First International Symposium of the Orion Center for the Study of the Dead Sea Scrolls and Associated Literature, 12-14 May, 1996. 1998. ISBN 90 04 10939 0

29. Hempel, C. *The Laws of the Damascus Document.* Sources, Tradition and Redaction. 1998. ISBN 90 04 11150 6

30. Parry, D.W. & E. Ulrich (eds.) *The Provo International Conference on the Dead Sea Scrolls.* Technological Innovations, New Texts, and Reformulated Issues. 1998. ISBN 90 04 11155 7

31. Chazon, E.G. & M. Stone (eds.) *Pseudepigraphic Perspectives.* The Apocrypha and Pseudepigrapha in Light of the Dead Sea Scrolls. Proceedings of the International Symposium of the Orion Center for the Study of the Dead Sea Scrolls and Associated Literature, 12-14 January, 1997. 1998. ISBN 90 04 11164 6

32. Parry, D.W. & E. Qimron (eds.) *The Great Isaiah Scroll (1QIsa^a).* A New Edition. 1998. ISBN 90 04 11277 4

33. Muraoka, T. & Elwolde, J.F. (eds.) *Sirach, Scrolls, and Sages.* Proceedings of a Second International Symposium on the Hebrew of the Dead Sea Scrolls, Ben Sira, and the Mishnah, held at Leiden University, 15-17 December 1997. 1999. ISBN 90 04 11553 6

34. Baumgarten, J.M. & E.G. Chazon & A. Punnick (eds.) *The Damascus Document: A Centennial of Discovery.* Proceedings of the Third International Symposium of the Orion Center for the Study of the Dead Sea Scrolls and Associated Literature, 4-8 February, 1998. 1999. ISBN 90 04 11462 9